Proceeding of the 19th International Congress on Logistics and Supply Chain Management Systems

Ming Li · Cheng Ren · Shenle Pan ·
George Q. Huang
Editors

Proceeding of the 19th International Congress on Logistics and Supply Chain Management Systems

AI-Empowered Logistics and Supply Chain

Springer

Editors
Ming Li
Department of Industrial and Systems Engineering
Hong Kong Polytechnic University
Hong Kong, China

Cheng Ren
Department of Industrial and Systems Engineering
Hong Kong Polytechnic University
Hong Kong, China

Shenle Pan
Centre for Management Science
PSL University, Mines Paris
Paris, France

George Q. Huang
Department of Industrial and Systems Engineering
Hong Kong Polytechnic University
Hong Kong, China

ISBN 978-981-95-7699-9 ISBN 978-981-95-7700-2 (eBook)
https://doi.org/10.1007/978-981-95-7700-2

This Springer imprint is published by the registered company Springer Nature Singapore Pte Ltd.
The registered company address is: 152 Beach Road, #21-01/04 Gateway East, Singapore 189721, Singapore

Preface

The 19th International Congress on Logistics and Supply Chain Management Systems (ICLS 2025) was held from 7 to 9 July 2025 at The Hong Kong Polytechnic University in Hong Kong, China. The congress was hosted by the Department of Industrial & Systems Engineering (ISE) and the Research Institute of Advanced Manufacturing (RIAM) of The Hong Kong Polytechnic University.

ICLS 2025 provided an international forum for researchers, practitioners, and industry stakeholders to present and discuss novel advances and applications in logistics and supply chain management systems, with an emphasis on *AI-empowered logistics and supply chain technologies*. The program included plenary speeches, panel sessions, tutorials, workshops, interactive sessions, and invited/special sessions, fostering interdisciplinary exchange and collaboration across academia and industry.

All papers included in these proceedings underwent a rigorous peer-review process to ensure high scientific quality and relevance. The contributions collected herein reflect a broad range of research achievements and innovative practices in the field. They offer valuable insights into both theoretical development and practical implementation in logistics and supply chain systems.

We extend our sincere gratitude to all authors for their excellent contributions, the reviewers for their constructive evaluations, and the organizing committee and volunteers for their dedicated efforts in making ICLS 2025 a successful event. We also thank Springer for their continued support in publishing these proceedings.

Contents

Research and Application of Cold Chain Logistics in Agricultural Products Supply Chain

Chenyi Wei[1], Jingyun Liu[1(✉)], Bingke Zhu[1], and Tongyu Zhang[2]

[1] College of Urban Rail Transit and Logistics, Beijing Union University, Beijing, China
ljy@buu.edu.cn

[2] School of Economics and Management, Beijing Jiaotong University, Beijing, China

Abstract. With the increasing complexity of agricultural supply chain, cold chain logistics has attracted much attention as a critical link to ensure the quality and safety of agricultural products. This paper focuses on the research and application of cold chain logistics in agricultural supply chains, and discusses its key role in improving supply chain efficiency and guaranteeing the quality and safety. The paper reviews the current state of cold chain logistics in transportation and storage processes, identifying challenges such as insufficient technological adoption, underdeveloped information management systems, uneven distribution of cold chain resources, and limited research on low-temperature grain storage technologies. To address these issues, the study proposes strategies such as optimizing cold chain management systems, innovating with artificial intelligence technologies, and standardizing cold chain logistics protocols. The study recommends enhancing cold chain infrastructure, optimizing resource allocation, promoting multi-technology integration, refining standardization frameworks, and prioritizing professional talent development to advance the transition of agricultural supply chains toward greater efficiency, low-carbon practices, and intelligent operations. This research provides theoretical insights and practical guidance for optimizing and innovating cold chain logistics in agricultural supply chains.

Keywords: Agricultural supply chain · Cold chain logistics · Application status · Optimization and innovation

1 Introduction

With the development of global logistics and transport of agricultural products, the complexity and importance of the supply chain of agricultural products have gradually received more attention. As an important daily consumable and a strategic national and international material, the supply chain of agricultural products covers production, processing, transport, storage and marketing. In view of the perishable, transportable and seasonal characteristics of agricultural products, storage and long-distance transport in their supply chain are crucial to ensure the safety and quality of agricultural products. In the transport process, temperature control is a key factor affecting the quality and safety of agricultural products, especially when crossing the cold and temperate zones, tropical and

M. Li et al. (Eds.): ICLS 2025, *Proceeding of the 19th International Congress on Logistics and Supply Chain Management Systems*, pp. 1–17, 2026.
https://doi.org/10.1007/978-981-95-7700-2_2

subtropical regions, rapid changes in storage conditions or external climatic conditions can lead to sharp fluctuations in the temperature and humidity gradient. Therefore, cold chain logistics has become an indispensable part of the supply chain as a method to ensure that agricultural products are at the right temperature environment throughout the supply chain. In recent years, with the rapid development of artificial intelligence technology, AI has been increasingly used in the logistics and supply chain industry. Through complex data analysis and prediction algorithms, AI is able to optimize all aspects of cold chain logistics, improve supply chain efficiency, reduce transport costs, and strengthen temperature and humidity management and regulation, promoting the development of agricultural supply chain and cold chain logistics in the direction of intelligence.

This paper examines the development of cold chain logistics technology within the agricultural supply chain, providing a comprehensive summary of its current application and highlighting existing challenges. Through an analysis of cold chain logistics technology, the paper aims to offer a theoretical foundation for enhancing the efficiency of the agricultural supply chain, optimizing logistics processes, ensuring quality and safety, and promoting the advancement of modern, intelligent, and sustainable agricultural logistics.

2 Overview of the Agricultural Supply Chain and Cold Chain Logistics

The rapid development of digital technology, the Internet has promoted the deep integration of the traditional agricultural supply chain and artificial intelligence technology. On the basis of maintaining the original supply chain model of high-quality agricultural products, new agricultural product logistics models supported by cold chain logistics and AI technology are emerging. Traditional agricultural product logistics is gradually transforming to intelligence and digitalization, which has become the development trend of the industry.

2.1 Overview of the Agricultural Supply Chain and Cold Chain Logistics Development

The supply chain of agricultural products coordinates the conversion of interests among suppliers of agricultural production materials, producers of agricultural products, distributors and consumers by controlling the logistics, capital flow and information flow of agricultural products in the process of circulation. This process is centred on the production and operation of agricultural products, and forms a value-added network system through the systematic integration of nodes such as production bodies, logistics service providers, distribution channels and terminal markets. The supply chain of fresh agricultural products usually consists of four layers: the production layer, the intermediate layer, the sales layer and the user layer, covering the whole process from production to sales [1], as shown in Fig. 1. Its essence lies in the use of supply chain synergy theory to achieve the value of the whole process of agricultural products from the origin to the table, which has the characteristics of extremely high timeliness, high cost loss rate, strict safety standards, and the influence of market supply and demand factors.

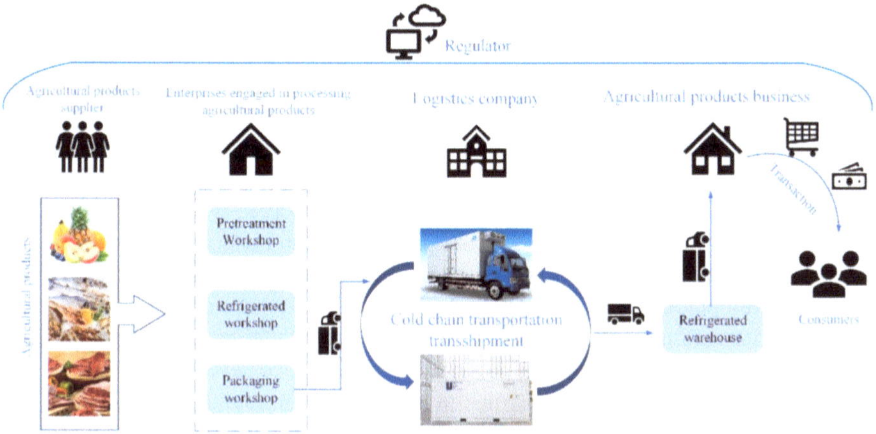

Fig. 1. Agricultural Products Cold Chain Logistics Process.

China has a clear plan for cold chain logistics, aimed at building a modern cold chain logistics system by 2035. As carbon emissions and environmental pollution are prevalent in the traditional logistics industry, the development of green logistics has become a key aspect of the sustainable global logistics industry, as well as the low-carbon and recycling-based development of the logistics system. Cold chain logistics requires strict temperature control and minimal energy loss. Meanwhile, there are challenges such as carbon emissions from transportation and high distribution costs throughout the process. Green logistics advocates for the logistics industry to collectively improve environmental awareness, optimize management systems, and apply innovative artificial intelligence technologies, which can effectively reduce environmental pollution and promote the intelligent, high-quality development of cold chain logistics. According to data from the China Federation of Logistics & Purchasing (CFLP), the total annual demand for cold chain logistics is expected to be 365 million tonnes in 2024, representing a year-on-year growth of 4.3%. The total revenue of cold chain logistics is expected to reach 536.1 billion yuan in 2024, representing a year-on-year growth of 3.7%.

From the perspective of global cold chain logistics development, the cold chain logistics infrastructure in certain developed countries and regions remains at the forefront of the global market. North America, led by the United States and Canada, continues to hold the largest share of the global cold chain market. According to a report by Mordor Intelligence, the market size of the North American food cold chain logistics sector is projected to reach USD 81.24 billion in 2024, with an estimated growth to USD 112.29 billion by 2029, as illustrated in Fig. 2. This represents a Compound Average Growth Rate (CAGR) of over 6.94% during the forecast period (2024–2029). The rapid growth in cold chain logistics demand in North America can be attributed to changing dietary habits, increasing obesity and disease rates among the population, and shifting consumer preferences for food. Additionally, the rapid expansion of e-commerce has significantly contributed to the rise in cold chain logistics demand. The UK cold chain logistics industry is characterized by a large scale and abundant cold chain resources, particularly its substantial reserve of cold storage facilities, which accounts for approximately 40% of the total cold storage capacity in Europe. The UK cold chain sector is highly competitive and concentrated, and it is anticipated that this concentration will continue to increase in the future. Although Japan faces challenges due to the agricultural conditions of its smallholder economy, the country has developed a comprehensive cold chain logistics system, supported by its high level of industrialization and urbanization. Japan's cold chain logistics technologies, market development, and the sophistication of its intelligent equipment systems are among the most advanced globally [2].

Compared to China's cold chain logistics, the cold chain and supply chain logistics systems in developed countries, such as the United States and Japan, are more advanced and their development is relatively mature. These countries have also established well-developed circulation systems for cold chain logistics, some aspects of which could serve as valuable references for China's cold chain logistics development [3]. Despite the rapid growth of cold chain logistics in China, the per capita cold chain logistics resources remain lower than those in developed countries like the United States and Japan [4].

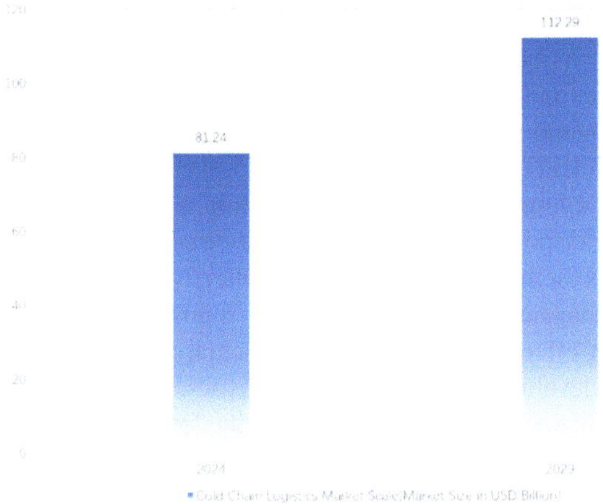

Fig. 2. North America Food Cold Chain Logistics Market (Market Size in USD Billion).

2.2 Current Status of Development of Cold Chain Logistics Standard System

The primary focus of the entire cold chain logistics process for agricultural products is the control of temperature and humidity, with key components being cold chain transportation and low-temperature storage. Temperature control equipment is the core infrastructure that ensures agricultural products are properly transported and stored. Common types of temperature control equipment include low-temperature cold storage, refrigerated trucks, and refrigerated containers. These systems are designed to regulate temperature in real time, preventing temperature fluctuations caused by external factors, which could otherwise damage products due to excessive heat or cold. As the technical capabilities of cold chain logistics in China continue to advance and urban cold chain infrastructure gradually improves, ensuring the safety, quality, and temperature control of cold chain logistics has become a critical issue for both the Chinese government and society. When establishing temperature bands for cold chain logistics, the main consideration is to ensure the bands are contiguous, allowing for both current and future cold chain items to be accommodated within appropriate temperature ranges. Additionally, in line with international standards, code names are used instead of specific names to avoid confusion or inconsistencies in terminology. The specific temperature band divisions and settings are provided in Table 1 [5].

The Hong Kong Special Administrative Region (HKSAR) and Macao differ from Mainland China in the development of cold chain logistics standards due to variations in regional systems, laws, and regulations. Taking Guangdong Province as a representative example of Mainland China's standards, an analysis of the cold chain logistics standards in Guangdong, Hong Kong, and Macao within the Greater Bay Area reveals several commonalities in technical content. Guangdong follows China's unified standardization framework and primarily adopts national standards. Hong Kong, on the other hand, focuses on cold chain standards related to food safety, addressing practical needs. Macao, meanwhile, develops its own specifications, taking into account local requirements and referencing the standards of both Guangdong and Hong Kong [6].

Table 1. Cold Chain Logistics Temperature Zone Classification.

Classification	Subdivided Categories	Temperature Zone
Cold	C1	10 °C < $C_1 \leq$ 25 °C
	C_2	0 °C < $C_2 \leq$ 10 °C
Frozen	F1	-18 °C <$F_1 \leq$ 0 °C
	F2	-30 °C < $F_2 \leq$ -18 °C
	F3	-55 °C < $F_3 \leq$ -30 °C
	F4	$F_4 \leq$ -55 °C

The International Organization for Standardization (ISO), with the American National Standards Institute (ANSI) serving as its secretariat, has developed a series of standards relevant to cold chain logistics. For instance, ISO 23412:2020 establishes indirect temperature control requirements for cold chain logistics services involving temperature-sensitive goods, including foodstuffs, during land transport [7]. This standard emphasizes real-time temperature monitoring, dynamic management, and risk assessment throughout transportation to ensure the quality and safety of cold chain goods. A key distinction between this standard and Chinese standards is its emphasis on dynamic management, rather than the use of fixed temperature intervals. The temperature range is determined based on the specific needs of the goods, allowing for greater flexibility. Additionally, the standard prioritizes the stability of temperature during intermediate transshipment, making it particularly applicable to cross-border or complex supply chain scenarios.

In 2018, Japan's Ministry of Land, Infrastructure, Transport and Tourism (MLIT), in collaboration with the transport authorities of the Association of Southeast Asian Nations (ASEAN), launched the Japan-ASEAN Cold Chain Logistics Initiative, aimed at enhancing local business capacity by promoting high-standard logistics services. Subsequently, the Japan Specification Association (JSA) and the Japan Industrial Standards Council (JISC) developed the JSA-S standard and the JIS standard, respectively, to advance cold chain logistics within Japan. The JIS standards include various regulations for refrigerated transport equipment, and ISO 23412:2020 serves as the international counterpart to JSA-S-01004:2020. Additionally, JSA-S1004:2020, titled Cold Chain Logistics Services - Requirements for Low-Temperature Storage and Low Temperature Transport Services, developed by JSA, is based on this initiative and outlines the technical requirements to be included in contracts between logistics companies and shippers [8]. JSA certifies cold chain logistics companies that meet these standards, helping logistics providers, food manufacturers, and distribution companies across ASEAN and beyond to enhance the quality of their cold chain logistics operations.

The United States has established a series of regulatory frameworks related to cold chain logistics, with key legislation including the Food Safety Modernization Act (FSMA) [9]. This act provides a comprehensive food safety regulatory system, encompassing transport regulations for agricultural products and the management of cold chain logistics. A critical component of the FSMA is the Sanitary Transportation of Human and Animal Food rule, which outlines specific provisions regarding temperature control and sanitation measures for cold chain logistics.

The European Union (EU) has established stringent requirements for cold chain logistics, which not only mandate high accuracy for temperature monitoring equipment but also require frequent validation. In 2013, the EU issued the Directive on Refrigeration Equipment and Cold Chain Logistics, providing comprehensive specifications and regulations for cold chain logistics. These include detailed provisions on temperature control, hygiene, and safety measures, and require companies to implement timely and transparent regulatory practices to ensure food safety and quality. Additionally, the Hazard Analysis and Critical Control Point (HACCP) system, adopted by EU member states, is designed for cold chain logistics enterprises, which must enforce strict control and supervision of temperature and humidity.

3 Technologies and Applications of Cold Chain Logistics in the Agricultural Supply Chain

3.1 Temperature Monitoring and Control Technology for Cold Chain Logistics

Cold chain logistics for agricultural products is a systematic operation designed to maintain the quality of transported goods and minimize losses by continuously preserving a low-temperature environment throughout various stages, including product processing, storage, transportation, and consumption [10]. Based on the type of products being transported, agricultural cold chain logistics can be broadly categorized into several types, including the cold chains for fruits and vegetables, dairy products, frozen foods, seafood and aquatic products, and meat products, among others.

Cold chain logistics places high demands on efficient refrigeration, energy consumption reduction, and environmental pollution control. Traditional cold chain logistics equipment often relies on refrigeration technologies that result in increased energy consumption, higher transportation costs, and elevated greenhouse gas emissions. In the cold chain logistics of fresh produce, some researchers have explored emerging phase change cold storage technologies, which can extend the shelf life of agricultural products, maintain a uniform temperature throughout transportation, and enable the selection of appropriate refrigeration materials based on varying external conditions. For example, water, organic composite phase change materials, or inorganic composite phase change materials can be used when transport conditions are above zero degrees Celsius, while eutectic water salts or inorganic composite phase change materials are more suitable when temperatures fall below zero degrees Celsius [11]. In the agricultural supply chain, maintaining product quality and temperature control is especially crucial in seafood and aquatic cold chain logistics. Studies have demonstrated that phase change materials with adjustable phase change temperatures, high cold storage capacities, flexible applications, and low costs can meet the temperature requirements of different aquatic products. Additionally, their flexibility can help mitigate the risks associated with supply chain disruptions [12].

Fruit and vegetable products are often subjected to forced-air precooling before transport in cold chain logistics, with forced-air precooling being one of the most widely used methods. Several studies have examined the precooling rate of fruits and vegetables within packaging boxes, finding that the opening rate of the box significantly impacts both the cooling rate and the deviation in precooling temperature. These studies indicate that, while meeting design requirements, a smaller box opening area is more effective [13]. Low-temperature storage of cereal grains plays a crucial role in the cold chain logistics of the agricultural supply chain. Effectively reducing the temperature of cereal grains and minimizing moisture loss are key objectives. One study explored the use of "chilled aeration" technology to cool stored wheat, bringing it to a safe temperature. This approach addresses temperature issues during the wheat's entry and exit from warehouses in high-temperature summer conditions, while also reducing the impact of pests on the stored wheat [14].

Refrigerated trucks play a crucial role in the agricultural supply chain by providing the necessary temperature environment for fresh agricultural products through their refrigeration systems, thereby extending shelf life and reducing cost losses caused by temperature fluctuations. Cold chain transportation of fruits, vegetables, and other agricultural products primarily relies on road transport. To effectively maintain the quality of these products during transit and expand the scope of cold chain logistics, many experts and scholars have conducted extensive research on refrigerated transport vehicles. This research has focused on areas such as improving the sustainability of refrigeration systems, enhancing heat preservation effectiveness, optimizing airflow distribution within the vehicle compartment, and upgrading vehicle facilities. For instance, some researchers have developed a solar-assisted power supply refrigeration system for mechanically cooled refrigerated trucks. This system stores energy generated by solar cells in an accumulator, which serves as the system's energy storage. A three-order dynamic model of this system is shown in Fig. 3. [15]. The findings indicate that enhancing equipment in refrigerated trucks can significantly improve the quality of cold chain transportation for fruits and vegetables. Another study revealed that when natural losses in the fruit and vegetable supply chain exceed 24%, the use of ultrasonic humidifiers can reduce these losses by more than 20% [16].

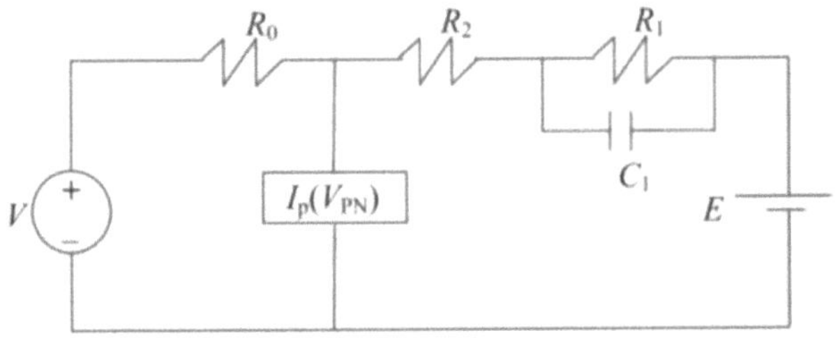

Fig. 3. Three Order Dynamic Model of Accumulator.

3.2 Data and Informational Intelligence Technology

With the application of technologies such as the Internet of Things (IoT), blockchain, big data, and artificial intelligence (AI), the cold chain logistics industry is steadily advancing toward digitization and intelligence. However, challenges such as the insufficient efficiency of existing cold chain logistics systems and low data availability must be addressed through the research and application of intelligent technologies. By 2025, technologies primarily based on artificial intelligence are expected to drive the intelligent development of cold chain logistics within the agricultural supply chain. Digital technologies will be more widely and deeply integrated into all aspects of cold chain logistics.

Researchers have proposed a blockchain-based integration platform for cold chain logistics in fresh agricultural products. This platform utilizes sensors and IoT technology to monitor temperature fluctuations in real-time during the cold chain logistics process. The temperature control data is recorded on the blockchain, ensuring that it remains open, transparent, and tamper-proof. By analyzing this data, the temperature control strategy can be optimized, thereby improving the efficiency of cold chain logistics [10]. When combined with advanced technologies such as big data analytics and the Internet of Things, blockchain technology can not only bring significant improvements and added value to the logistics supply chain system [17], but also promote the sustainable development and green transformation of the agricultural supply chain [18]. Currently, some agricultural product logistics information management systems face challenges, including insufficient data sharing, low transparency, and over-reliance on traditional databases and information systems, which hinder the overall coordination of the supply chain. For example, in the case of the cold chain logistics information platform for Gannan navel oranges, the distributed ledger function enabled by blockchain technology allows all participants to access and verify logistics data, thereby enhancing the efficiency of agricultural product logistics and improving data transparency [19].

Supply chain traceability technology ensures that agricultural products have verifiable data throughout the cold chain logistics process, enabling the assessment of their safety and quality [20]. Traditional traceability technologies rely on manual data entry, which can lead to issues such as the vulnerability of the enterprise's own database and third-party data security management. These challenges may result in data being tampered with or leaked during the delivery process. In contrast, blockchain-based traceability technology enables comprehensive product tracking and traceability by integrating blockchain with the traceability system. This not only enhances the authenticity and transparency of the information but also effectively maintains data confidentiality. Research on blockchain traceability, particularly that based on union chains, has become a focal point of both domestic and international interest [21].

In the management of import and export cold chain logistics for modern flowers in Japan, Radio Frequency Identification (RFID) technology is utilized to connect information to the web, automating and electronicizing flower transactions. Producers can access order information and arrange production and shipment through the web system, while wholesalers, underwriters, retailers, and consumers can participate in bidding, placing orders, and receiving electronic invoices via mobile terminals [22]. For fruit and vegetable products, Geographic Information Systems (GIS) can be employed to construct a map of the cold chain logistics and transportation network, covering logistics and distribution centers as well as all customer points. Figure 4. Illustrates the basic topology of the cold chain transport network, consisting of a central hub and multiple customer points. By integrating multiple hubs and customer points, a transport network map containing multiple distribution centers is created, which facilitates the planning and optimization of cold chain logistics routes for agricultural fruits and vegetables [23].

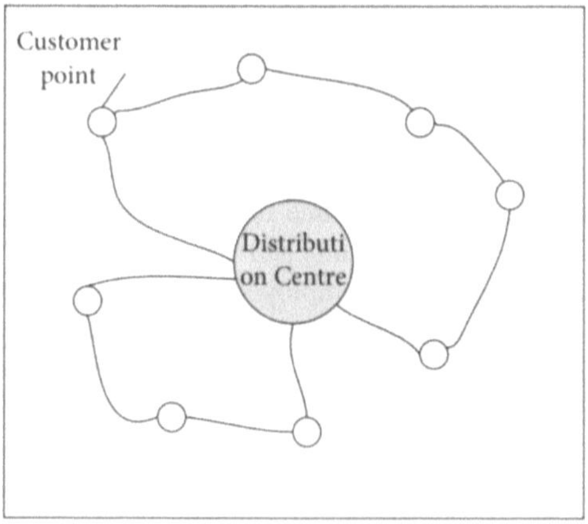

Fig. 4. Basic Topology of Cold Chain Transportation Network.

3.3 Artificial Intelligence Algorithmic Techniques

The application of algorithms, including artificial intelligence, to optimize cold chain logistics challenges within the agricultural supply chain has become a key area of contemporary technological research.

The Byzantine Fault Tolerant State Machine Replication (SMART-PBFT) algorithm demonstrates significant advantages in optimizing cold chain logistics platform management. Its communication model is illustrated in Fig. 5. Several studies have applied this algorithm to address issues related to data transparency and information sharing within agricultural logistics management systems, thereby enhancing the traceability and transparency of logistics data, optimizing the logistics management process, improving service quality, and reducing operational costs [19].

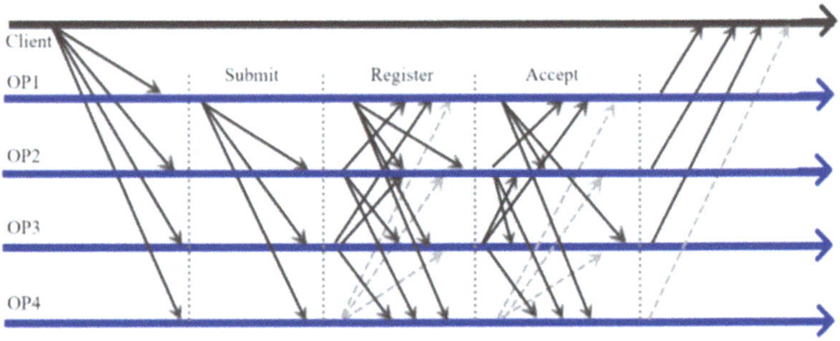

Fig. 5. The Communication Mode of SMART-PBFT Algorithm.

Cold chain logistics path optimization is a complex problem that involves multiple objectives and constraints, such as transportation cost, time, temperature control, and cargo type. Researchers commonly use methods such as the Ant Colony Optimization (ACO) algorithm, Simulated Annealing, and Particle Swarm Optimization (PSO) for path optimization. To address the issues of high cost and low vehicle utilization in cold chain logistics, some scholars have developed a multi-vehicle path optimization model considering traffic congestion, utilizing an adaptive genetic simulated annealing algorithm to solve the time-window path optimization problem. Compared to the traditional Genetic Algorithm (GA), this method reduces distribution costs by 3.52%, improves satisfaction by 29.54%, and reaches the optimal solution more efficiently [24]. In cases where achieving both the shortest time and lowest cost simultaneously is challenging for the transportation of agricultural fruits and vegetables, Jiao et al. proposed a novel cold chain transportation model. They employed an improved Ant Colony Optimization (ACO) algorithm to identify optimal transportation routes, providing a new algorithmic reference for solving cold chain transportation problems for fruits, vegetables, and agricultural products [23]. To reduce the cost of cold chain distribution for fresh and perishable agricultural products, Wang et al. proposed a two-layer planning optimization method that combines front warehouse location selection and distribution paths. In this approach, the upper layer determines candidate front warehouse locations using K-Means clustering, while the lower layer is optimized using a combination of Particle Swarm Optimization and Genetic Algorithm (PSO-GA). The results show that the hybrid APSOGA algorithm is more effective in reducing total logistics network costs than either algorithm alone [25].

In the field of grain storage safety and temperature regulation, some scholars have developed a neural network model that integrates residual networks and the self-attention mechanism. This model outperforms traditional models such as LSTM and CNN, optimizing grain bin management through intelligent ventilation decision-making and achieving balanced regulation of temperature and humidity, thereby ensuring the safe storage of agricultural products [26]. Regarding the management of risk factors in the agricultural supply chain, researchers have developed a theoretical framework for in-depth study based on Interpretative Structural Modeling (ISM) and specific modeling procedures. They systematically analyzed the sources of risk in the agricultural supply chain and established an index system for the risk factors affecting the supply chain [27].

In addition, various intelligent optimization algorithms, such as the Genetic Algorithm and Adaptive Large Neighborhood Search (ALNS) algorithm, have been widely used in the field of cold chain logistics research. Some of the principles and application scenarios of these algorithms are presented in Table 2.

Table 2. Part of The Common Algorithm Principles and Their Application Scenarios in The Field of Cold Chain Logistics.

Algorithm Name	Theory	Application
Genetic Algorithm, GA	Genetic algorithms are heuristic search methods that model the natural evolutionary process to search for optimal solutions	It can solve vehicle path optimisation problems, complex optimisation problems, vehicle path problems with nodes and arc time windows and their extensions [28]
Adaptive Large Neighborhood Search, ALNS	It is a heuristic algorithm that automatically selects good operators to destroy and repair the solution so that a better solution may be obtained	It is mainly used to solve vehicle path planning problems for time-dependent vehicle path problems [29], logistics and distribution problems with multiple distribution centres and multiple customer points [30]
K-means Clustering Algorithm	An iteratively solved cluster analysis algorithm, an unsupervised learning algorithm, which iteratively optimises the clustering centres to achieve an overall optimal clustering result	The initial clustering centre can be determined from historical distribution data and geographic information data, and the optimal distribution route for cold chain logistics can be output after iterative optimisation [31]
Simulated Annealing, SA	Simulated annealing algorithm is a probability-based algorithm for optimisation of serial structures that effectively avoids falling into local minima and eventually converges to the global optimum	It can solve optimisation problems such as spatially optimal distribution routes, shortest paths through all cities and back to the original location, and multi-temperature collaborative distribution [31]

(continued)

Table 2. *(continued)*

Algorithm Name	Theory	Application
Artificial Bee Colony Algorithm, ABC	It is an optimisation method that mimics the behaviour of bees and clusters intelligent ideas. Possible solutions to the optimisation problem are obtained by simulating the honey harvesting mechanism of bees	These multi-variable and multi-constraint optimisation problems can be handled efficiently, and the distribution plan can be adjusted at any time according to the demand, vehicle status and road conditions [32]

3.4 Challenges and Issues of Cold Chain Logistics in Agricultural Supply Chains

The digitization and automation of cold chain logistics for agricultural products must overcome the traditional model of 'focusing on research and development without practical application.' Due to the unique characteristics of agricultural products in cold chain logistics, a fully integrated intelligent service system has not yet been established. The application of advanced information technology in the actual transportation process is still limited, and the practical implementation of cold chain technology lags behind theoretical research. However, the digital and intelligent transformation of China's cold chain logistics has begun to yield results, with emerging technologies such as big data and artificial intelligence bringing positive impacts on the development of China's logistics industry. Through the adoption of digital and intelligent technologies, it is expected that by 2024, the efficiency of China's cold chain logistics will be significantly improved, and the application of digital temperature control technology will reduce loss rates to below 5% [33]. Nevertheless, in terms of the agricultural supply chain, the cold chain logistics circulation rate for most agricultural products in China remains lower than that in developed countries such as the United States and Japan, with a still-high loss rate. Despite advances in cold chain technology for agricultural products, a fully integrated supply chain that combines digitization and intelligence has not yet been formed in the circulation process of agricultural products in China. Further exploration is needed to determine how to apply existing advanced technologies in actual logistics processes.

The construction of information management systems for agricultural products remains incomplete, leading to disruptions in temperature tracking and resulting in cost losses. The technology for tracking, monitoring, and tracing information in the cold chain of agricultural products is relatively outdated, and many enterprises have yet to establish reliable logistics temperature information management systems, which frequently leads to issues such as temperature monitoring failures and chain disruptions. Empirical studies on mango cold chain logistics reveal that limited technological integration in production regions results in suboptimal cold chain management. This technological gap contributes to temperature-induced quality degradation and truncated supply chains, undermining the stability of product quality and hindering industry scalability [34]. Inadequate real-time monitoring of transportation vehicles, limited sensor coverage for critical parameters (e.g., temperature deviations and vibration intensity), and mechanical damage caused by road-induced shocks collectively exacerbate post-harvest losses and quality degradation in cold chain logistics for agricultural products.

There is a mismatch in the distribution of cold chain resources, with some economically underdeveloped areas urgently needing improvement. Low-temperature storage is a critical component of cold chain logistics in the agricultural product supply chain. Ensuring effective temperature control during the storage phase primarily depends on the environmental conditions of cold storage facilities and temperature control equipment, both of which are essential for maintaining the quality of agricultural products and minimizing losses. China is representative of this problem, with a shortage of cold storage resources in some regions that are rich in agricultural production but economically underdeveloped, and a mismatch between cold chain infrastructure and resource allocation and agricultural production regions [35]. Compared to developed countries, China exhibits a significant disparity in terms of per capita cold storage capacity. Moreover, in some of the major fruit and vegetable production regions, the ownership rate of cold storage facilities is less than 10% [36].

There is limited research on low-temperature grain storage technology, and the issue of temperature control in warehouses needs to be addressed urgently. As a core strategic material crucial to the national economy and people's livelihoods, the safety and reserve capacity of grain directly reflect the level of national governance and resource regulation. Solving the issue of low-temperature storage for grain can not only ensure the efficient operation of the national grain reserve system but also provide a solid foundation for food security, particularly in the face of extreme climate events, geopolitical conflicts, and other risks. However, some regions still face challenges such as high energy consumption and significant heat damage to grain piles during low-temperature storage. A study conducted on a regional grain and oil reserve enterprise's low-temperature warehousing practices revealed that seasonal temperature fluctuations significantly compromise grain storage stability. Maintaining consistent sub-15 °C conditions to suppress pest activity, extend storage duration, and preserve grain quality remains a critical challenge for advancing cold chain logistics in agricultural product storage systems [37].

4 Future Development Trends of Cold Chain Logistics for Agricultural Products

E-commerce has experienced rapid global growth, driven by the emergence of new consumption patterns. Consumer demand for fresh agricultural products has been increasing, and this growth is further supported by significant advances in long-distance logistics, multimodal transportation, as well as the rise of cross-border e-commerce and live-streaming sales. As a result, e-commerce for agricultural products has become a key retail channel for the agricultural sector in recent years and is expected to serve as a crucial platform for the future distribution of agricultural products. To establish long-term supply and demand partnerships, information sharing through Internet technologies, enhancing supply chain stability, and improving the quality of agricultural products and cold chain logistics are essential to ensuring the stable operation of the omni-channel supply chain in agricultural e-commerce [38].

5G technology, as the next generation of communication technology, has become a key driver in the development of cold chain logistics due to its high-speed data transmission, low latency, and extensive information connectivity. Building on 5G technology, this paper explores the future development path of intelligent logistics and warehousing informatization in the agricultural supply chain. Considering the current demand for informatization and intelligence in cold chain logistics, a model of an intelligent logistics and warehousing information system based on 5G technology has been constructed [39]. 5G technology enables seamless integration of various aspects of cold chain logistics (e.g., warehousing, pre-cooling, transportation, and distribution) through efficient information transmission and resource allocation. By connecting IoT sensors via 5G, and integrating blockchain technology, it ensures the authenticity and immutability of temperature records. Additionally, supported by a big data platform, it integrates data resources across the entire process—from warehousing to processing and transportation—enabling visualized tracking of the entire supply chain.

As a major category of agricultural product processing, the production and transportation of prepared dishes—from the raw material origin to the central processing kitchen and ultimately to consumers—must typically be conducted under cold chain conditions to ensure product freshness and quality. Prepared dishes were first developed in the United States, followed by rapid expansion in Europe and Japan. In recent years, the prepared vegetable industry has risen in China. The entire cold chain logistics process requires strict temperature control [40]. The international prepared vegetable market has matured over the years, particularly in Europe, the United States, and Japan, and is characterized by diversification and technology-driven advancements. In recent years, China's prepared vegetable industry has experienced accelerated growth, with a steady increase in market size, demonstrating substantial development potential and attracting the involvement of numerous enterprises. Studies have shown that during the cold chain transportation of prepared soups made from processed agricultural products, temperature increases due to extended transport time and changes in environmental conditions can trigger lipid oxidation, flavor changes, and microbial growth, thereby affecting product quality. By implementing precise temperature monitoring and regulation, product quality can be consistently maintained at a high level. Further in-depth studies are still needed to explore changes in flavor composition and content of prepared vegetable products during the cold chain process, the insulation properties of packaging materials, and strategies to control quality deterioration [41].

5 Conclusion

From a global development perspective, the cold chain logistics industry is moving towards scale and centralization. The integration of cold chain logistics with technologies such as big data, artificial intelligence, and the Internet of Things (IoT) will continue to deepen. Cold chain logistics technology is gradually shifting from the application of single technologies to a comprehensive model that integrates multiple technologies. Some developed countries' cold chain logistics companies have begun to widely apply satellite positioning systems, remote control technologies, and other innovations to further develop the agricultural product supply chain. In the future, e-commerce platforms for agricultural products will become key in product circulation, and cold chain logistics for prepared food products is expected to become a new growth point. Based on 5G technology, further exploration of the development of intelligent logistics and warehousing information systems in the agricultural product supply chain can be achieved, promoting standardized connections at each logistics stage and improving cold chain logistics efficiency.

It is important to strengthen the construction of cold chain logistics infrastructure, optimize industrial layouts, and improve the matching of cold chain resources with agricultural industry layouts. Furthermore, the development of cold chain logistics should be directed towards informationization and intelligence, with the widespread adoption of new technologies such as 5G, IoT, and blockchain to enhance the efficiency and security of cold chain logistics. At the same time, attention should be given to the cultivation of professional talent in cold chain logistics, providing a solid talent foundation for the development of this field.

References

1. Xu, F., Liao, J.: Research on optimization of fresh agricultural product supply chain based on blockchain technology. Logistics Sci-Tech **48**(5), 131–133 (2025)
2. Yang, Y.: Development status and comparison of cold chain logistics in China and Japan. Bus. Mag. **6**, 149–150 (2020)
3. Liu, C.: Safety guarantee system of meat cold chain logistics. Master's Thesis, Hunan Agricultural University, Changsha (2022). https://doi.org/10.27136/d.cnki.ghunu.2022.001232
4. Gu, Y.: Demand forecast of cold chain logistics of agricultural products in Beijing based on combined forecasting model. Master's Thesis, Capital University of Economics and Business, Beijing (2020). https://doi.org/10.27338/d.cnki.gsjmu.2020.000953
5. State Administration for Market Regulation of China, Standardization Administration of China: GB/T 28577—2021 Classification & basic requirement for cold chain logistics. National Standard of China, Beijing (2021)
6. Huang, S., Fang, Y., Hu, W., Yi, L., Wang, X.: Comparative study on cold logistics standards in Guangdong-Hong Kong-Macao Greater Bay Area. Stand. Sci. **5**, 108–113 (2022)
7. International Organization for Standardization: ISO 23412:2020 Indirect, temperature-controlled refrigerated delivery services—Land transport of parcels with intermediate transfer. ISO, Geneva (2020)
8. Japanese Standards Association: JSA-S1004:2020 Cold chain logistics services—Requirements for low temperature storage services and low temperature transport services. JSA, Tokyo (2021)
9. U.S. Department of Health and Human Services, Food and Drug Administration: Report to Congress on building domestic capacity to implement the FDA Food Safety Modernization Act (FSMA). U.S. Government Printing Office, Washington, D.C. (2011)
10. Ni, W., Chen, T.: Research on blockchain-based cold chain logistics integrated service platform for fresh agricultural products. Jiangsu Agric. Sci. **49**(23), 207–212 (2021)
11. Li, M., Xie, B., Li, Y., Cao, P., Leng, G., Li, C.: Emerging phase change cold storage technology for fresh products cold chain logistics. J. Energy Storage **88**, 111531 (2024)
12. Feng, T., Ji, J., Zhang, X.: Research progress of phase change cold energy storage materials used in cold chain logistics of aquatic products. J. Energy Storage **60**, 106568 (2023)
13. Jin, T., Li, B., Zhu, Z., Han, S., Wei, J.: Simulation and analysis of forced-air precooling of apples with vertical air supply. Trans. Chin. Soc. Agric. Mach. **52**(9), 369–375 (2022)

14. Morales-Quiros, A., Campabadal, C., Maier, D.E., Lazzari, S.M.N., Phillips, T.W.: Chilled aeration to control pests and maintain grain quality during summer storage of wheat in the North Central Region of Kansas. Appl. Eng. Agric. **35**(4), 657–668 (2019). https://doi.org/10.5073/JKA.2018.463.096
15. He, R., Yang, L., Hu, D.: Design and analysis of refrigeration system supplied by solar auxiliary power of refrigerator car. J. Jilin Univ. (Eng. Technol. Ed.) **48**(6), 1645–1652 (2018)
16. Su, X., Wang, B.: Life cycle simulation of ultrasonic humidification of 4 kinds of common fruits and vegetables in fresh storage and transportation. Food & Mach. **36**(2), 155–158 (2020)
17. Zheng, Q., Fan, T., Hu, B., Song, Y.: Impact of traceability technology investment on supply chains for fresh product under pre-position warehouse mode. J. Ind. Eng. Eng. Manag. **37**(4), 165–178 (2023)
18. Cao, Y., Yi, C., Wan, G., Hu, H., Li, Q., Wang, S.: An analysis on the role of blockchain-based intermediary platforms in agricultural supply chains. Trans. Res. Part E: Logis. Transp. Rev. **163** (2022)
19. Xu, X., Wah, Y.C., Koting, S.B.: Construction of a blockchain-based cold chain logistics information platform for Gannan navel oranges to enhance transparency and efficiency. Front. Sustain. Food Syst. (2024). https://doi.org/10.3389/fsufs.2024.1464918
20. Yang, G.: The literature review of agri-fresh produce supply chain management. Logis. Sci-Tech. **41**(9), 100–104+118 (2018)
21. Sun, C., Yu, H., Xu, D., Xing, B., Yang, X.: Review and prospect of agri-products supply chain traceability based on blockchain technology. Trans. Chin. Soc. Agric. Machinery **52**(1), 1–13 (2021)
22. Sun, X., Cheng, S.: The construction of Japan's modern flower cold chain logistics system and its enlightenment. World Agric. (5), 101–107+140 (2020)
23. Jiao, X., Xu, W., Duan, L.: Study on cold chain transportation model of fruit and vegetable fresh-keeping in low-temperature cold storage environment. Discret. Dyn. Nat. Soc. (2021). https://doi.org/10.1155/2021/8445028
24. Li, J., Liu, M., Liu, P.: Route optimization of multivehicle cold chain logistics for fresh agricultural products. J. China Agric. Univ. **26**(7), 115–123 (2021)
25. Wang, Y., Wang, Y., Leng, J.: A study on the vehicle routing planning method for fresh food distribution. Appl. Sci. **14**(22), 10499 (2024). https://doi.org/10.3390/app142210499
26. Zhu, Y., Li, H., Zhen, T., Li, Z.: Integrating self-attention mechanisms and ResNet for grain storage ventilation decision making: A study. Appl. Sci. **13**(13), 7655 (2023). https://doi.org/10.3390/app13137655
27. Zhao, Y.: Influencing factors of agricultural products cold chain logistics development based on ISM model. Wireless Pers. Commun. **2023**, 1–20 (2023)
28. Zhang, Y., Hua, G., Cheng, T., Zhang, J.: Cold chain distribution: How to deal with node and arc time windows? Annals of Operations Research (2018). https://doi.org/10.1007/s10479-018-3071-0
29. Xiao, Z., Hu, Z., Zhu, L.: Hybrid adaptive large neighborhood search algorithm for solving time-dependent vehicle routing problem in cold chain logistics. J. Comput. Appl. **42**(9), 2926–2935 (2022)
30. Tan, X., Wang, X., Hu, D.: Research on distribution routing optimization of multi-center cold chain logistics for replenishment along the way considering dynamic demand. J. Sichuan Univ. (Nat. Sci. Ed.) **60**(2), 70–80 (2023)
31. Li, Y.: Optimization of fresh product path for electric refrigerated trucks based on K-means and SA algorithm. Master's Thesis, North China Electric Power University, Beijing (2024). https://doi.org/10.27140/d.cnki.ghbbu.2024.000328
32. Zhang, T., Wu, T., Yu, H.: Optimization of green cold chain logistics based on improved artificial bee colony algorithm. J. Shenyang Univ. (Nat. Sci.) **36**(6), 497–506 (2024)

33. Guo, Y.: Promote China's logistics cost reduction and efficiency. Economy **3**, 36–39 (2025)
34. Yan, B., Zhang, X., Yang, W., Huang, R.: Research on countermeasures of mango logistics development in Guangxi Baise. Mark. Forum **6**, 21–26 (2023)
35. Zhang, R., Liu, Q., Liu, B., Huang, Y., Chang, Z.: Research on the construction mode of storage and preservation of cold chain facilities for agricultural products (fruits and vegetables). Jo. Chin. Agric. Mech. **45**(12), 127–132 (2024)
36. Huang, Y.: Development strategy of agricultural cold chain logistics in China from the perspective of urban-rural integration. J. Commercial Econ. **21**, 135–138 (2021)
37. Xu, Y.: Research and analysis on technical difficulties and requirements of grain storage and logistics. Sci. Technol. Cereals, Oils Foods **32**(2), 194–202 (2024)
38. Liu, N., Zhang, F.: Reverse integration and optimization of omnichannel supply chain of agricultural e-commerce. J. Commercial Econ. **22**, 153–156 (2022)
39. Han, Q.: Research on the construction of cold chain logistics intelligent system based on 5G ubiquitous Internet of Things. J. Sens. (2021). https://doi.org/10.1155/2021/6558394
40. China Federation of Commerce: Trade Logistics and Supply Chain Branch: New opportunities for cold chain logistics of China's prepared dishes from the perspective of the development of global prepared dishes. Logistics & Material Handling **28**(10), 88–91 (2023)
41. Lu, J., et al.: Optimization of prepared carrot corn rib soup and simulation of quality changes in cold chain logistics. Science and Technology of Food Industry, (2024)

Graph-Based Product2Task-Worker-Machine Mapping in Modular Construction

Jintao Xue[1], Xiao Li[1(✉)], and Chengke Wu[2]

[1] The University of Hong Kong, Hong Kong SAR, China
xuejt@connect.hku.hk, shell.x.li@hku.hk
[2] Shenzhen Institutes of Advanced Technology, Chinese Academy of Sciences, Shenzhen, China
ck.wu@siat.ac.cn

Abstract. A critical stage before work package generation in modular construction (MC) is product2task mapping. However, both the ability to perform complex reasoning and the richness of semantic information in mapped tasks still need improvement. This paper aims to address the aforementioned problems through a graph-based product2task-worker-machine mapping (P2TWM) framework (G-P2TWM). The framework first represents the data including tasks, products, workers, and machines as knowledge graphs (KGs). Then, a novel heterogeneous graph neural network for mapping in MC (HGN-MC) is employed to seamlessly extract KG data and adaptively map the products to the corresponding tasks, workers, and machines (e.g., rebar fixing, structural steel welder, and rebar bending machine), thereby enriching task-level information for the downstream process in MC (e.g. work package generation and production scheduling). The proposed G-P2TWM framework also supports flexibly adding additional heterogeneous information (e.g. spatial information) as graph nodes to enhance mapping performance. Experiments demonstrate that our method is capable of complex knowledge reasoning with high performance'.

Keywords: Modular Construction · Knowledge Graph · Product Mapping · Graph Neural Network

1 Introduction

Modular construction (MC) is a modern construction method that reduces cast in-situ works on-site through the assembly of prefabricated components from the construction factory [1]. MC is developing rapidly due to its improved quality, productivity, safety, sustainability, and reduced labor costs [2, 3], has been reasonably used in many countries such as the United States, Japan, and others, while becoming popular in Hong Kong [4, 5]. However, achieving both people's demand for personalized building products and mass production with high-level standardization presents a challenge [6]. Therefore, there is a need to develop a method to efficiently extract diverse products and adapt them for flexible mass production.

M. Li et al. (Eds.): ICLS 2025, *Proceeding of the 19th International Congress on Logistics and Supply Chain Management Systems*, pp. 18–33, 2026.
https://doi.org/10.1007/978-981-95-7700-2_3

The Work Breakdown Structure (WBS) is a paradigm that decomposes a project into a hierarchical tree structure, simplifying complex construction projects [7]. The work package is at the most detailed level, encompassing one or more fundamental tasks [8]. By breaking down a complex project into manageable work packages, thus project managers can more effectively monitor and enhance progress and performance, while also gaining additional benefits. A critical stage before work package generation in MC is product2task mapping [6], which maps data of products into fundamental tasks, thereby supporting the downstream process (e.g., work package generation, work package-based project scheduling, and production scheduling).

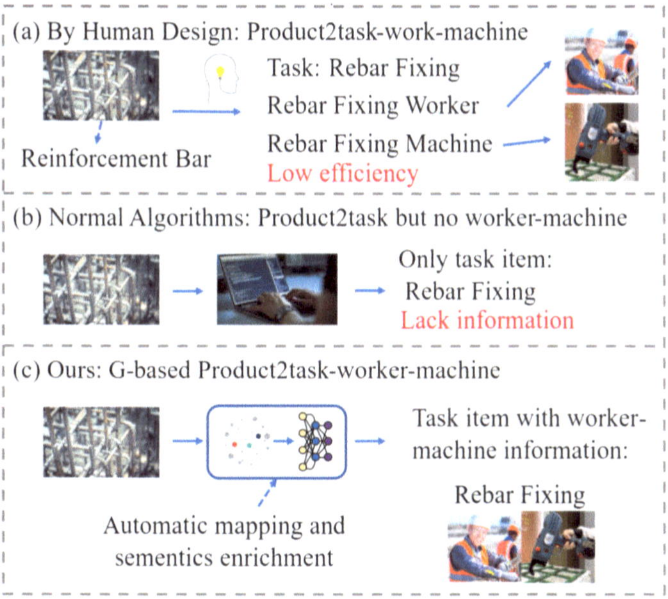

Fig. 1. Illustration comparing (a) classical human expert-based approach, (b) normal algorithm-based product2task mapping, and (c) our graph-based product2task-worker-machine method.

As shown in Fig. 1, two limitations exist in the classic methods of product2task mapping in MC. Firstly, the quality of the results of product2task significantly influences the downstream process performance. As for the downstream process, a key consideration is the type of resources required for task completion, such as the types of workers (e.g., structural steel welder) and machines (e.g., rebar bending machine) needed [9], which the raw task information might not include, requiring additional human annotation. However, the correctness of human annotation significantly impacts subsequent processes or increased workload. Secondly, another limitation is the raw product data come from multiple sources (e.g., workflow, schedule, building information modeling (BIM)) and are semi-structured or unstructured [10], and often require the manual definition of semantic mapping rules, consequently, the high complexity within this data reduces processing efficiency.

This paper aims to address the above limitations by a graph-based product2task-worker-machine (P2TWM) framework (G-P2TWM) that can process large amounts of data featuring complex structure and then be used to enrich the raw task information, facilitating better execution of subsequent processes. Specifically, as shown in Fig. 2, during the information modeling stage, we adopt the Knowledge Graph (KG) which can effectively organize the multi-source and unstructured complex raw data and represent knowledge in a heterogeneous graph structure [11]. Then, to cooperate with the characteristics of KG like graph structure and heterogeneous information, a novel heterogeneous graph neural network for mapping in MC (HGN-MC) is employed to seamlessly extract KG data and conduct knowledge reasoning over KGs that adaptively map the products to the corresponding tasks, workers and machines. Furthermore, by leveraging the graph structure advantages of KG and HGN-MC, we can easily incorporate new heterogeneous information. For instance, we introduce spatial information for products as a new type of node in KG, using edge connections to represent the relationship between products and spatial elements. This approach enriches the semantic information of KG and enhances the performance of the P2TWM mapping.

To summarize, the main contributions of this paper include the following:

- A task information enriching framework called G-P2TWM generates more helpful information for downstream processes such as work package generation, and work package project scheduling.
- A KG-based data representation approach can effectively organize the multi-source and unstructured complex raw data into a heterogeneous graph structure.
- A novel heterogeneous graph neural network for mapping in MC named HGN-MC is adapted to align with the heterogeneity and graph characteristics of KG. HGN-MC possesses robust reasoning capabilities to map products to appropriate workers and machines and allows for the flexible integration of additional heterogeneous semantic data.

2 Related Works

In this section, we review relevant information modeling and knowledge reasoning approaches in the context of MC and WBS.

2.1 Work Package Information Modeling

A large project must be systematically decomposed into smaller segments to plan and execute properly. The decomposed segments are allocated to designate organizational parts for plan and execution. This slicing approach is called the work breakdown structure (WBS) [12]. Work package is the smallest element in WBS, which may encompass a segment of the larger project management data associated with it, such as task priorities, budget, deadlines, and investment risks [7, 8]. In the context of MC, the work package may include additional information such as tools, resources, and products with geometric information [13]. BIM encompasses both geometric and non-geometric aspects. The geometric elements involve modeling products or components with multi-source geometric attributes. Additionally, it is essential to model other non-geometric information alongside modeling for product-related geometric semantics.

We summarize five paradigms of nongeometric information modeling in MC. Respectively, object-oriented [14–16], extensible markup language (XML)-based [17, 18], Petri net-based [19], ontology-based [20, 21], and KG-based [6, 22, 23]. The object-oriented paradigm involves constructing systems using collections of objects, each containing stored instances found within an object. It has the advantage of reusability, abstraction, and providing users with a ready-made, expressive visual modeling language [24]. However, this paradigm struggles with information exchange across different systems (i.e., BIM, planners, and schedulers) and lack of interoperability [15]. The XML-based paradigm provides markup language and file format for storing, transferring, and representing data. It enhances interoperability among heterogeneous systems through standardization, yet encounters difficulties in expressing implicit semantics in work packages [17, 18]. The Petri net-based paradigm employs graphical representation, consisting of components such as places, transitions, and arcs, to model discrete event systems. It also offers mathematical formulation of execution semantics for process analysis, offering benefits such as reusability and stability, [19]. However, its downside is limited interoperability. The ontology-based paradigm defines formal expression of a set of concepts, data, entities, properties, and relations that represent the entities in one subject area, but have limited flexibility and adaptability [20, 21]. The KG-based paradigm employs a graph-structured data model or topology to represent and manipulate data [11], provides rich semantic representation, and captures complex relationships within the data [6, 22]. It can also integrate data from various sources, facilitating data fusion and analysis, and can seamlessly collaborate with deep learning (DL) models for reasoning, fusion, and prediction.

2.2 Knowledge Reasoning in Modular Construction

After information modeling, the next phase is knowledge reasoning and fusion. In the context of work packages in MC, generating fundamental tasks for work package generation relies on product-to-task mapping, which encompasses knowledge reasoning. Specifically, we need to extract the information including multi-source information from diverse data (i.e., BIM, schedule) for mapping products to the corresponding tasks.

We summarize five paradigms of knowledge reasoning in modular construction (MC): rule-based [25], representation learning-based [21], neural network-based [26]–[28], and reinforcement learning (RL)-based [29]. The rule-based methods identify rules between information flows and tasks, providing high interpretability, but they are not well-suited for handling complex and large-scale data contexts [25]. The representation learning-based approach leverages knowledge-representative learning models, such as translation embedding (TransE), to initialize embeddings in work packages. However, these methods struggle with handling multi-relational semantics [21]. Additionally, deep reinforcement learning (DRL) can act as a dynamic inference method for highly efficient duplicate project planning [29], although DRL involves a high training cost. Neural network-based methods exhibit significant potential in knowledge reasoning due to their ability to handle complex and large data sets, including approaches such as recurrent neural networks (RNN) [27], convolutional neural networks (CNN) [26], and graph convolutional networks (GCN) [28], and hybrid network [6]. However, the current neural network-based methods in modular construction (MC) face challenges in efficiently processing KG with complex topological and heterogeneous structures consisting of multiple types of nodes and edges. Non-graph-based models lose topological information, while basic naive graph-based models fail to capture the heterogeneity relation of the data. The hybrid network shows improvement but requires additional models to separately extract heterogeneous features, which results in limited scalability due to increased model complexity when handling more diverse heterogeneous information [6]. Therefore, the heterogeneous graph neural network (HGNN), aims to learn representations of heterogeneous input while preserving type-specific semantics and topology structures for downstream tasks (e.g., node/edge/link prediction/classification), aligns well with the characteristics of KGs and demonstrates potential [30–32]. Recently, [33] improve the performance of HGNN based on the hierarchical attention mechanism. And [31] incorporate the residual connection and edge typing embedding in HGNN to enhance the depth of HGNN and overall performance.

3 Method

To tackle the aforementioned challenges of product2task mapping in MC, we adopt a framework called G-P2TWM, enhancing task enrichment. Then a novel graph-based framework is developed. Firstly, the framework extracts and processes raw, heterogeneous, and unstructured data into a KG-based format. Subsequently, our proposed attention and residual connection-based HGN-MC, a heterogeneous graph neural network tailored for MC, utilizes KG data to generate mapping results. HGN-MC seamlessly integrates with KG data, allowing for the flexible addition of extra information, such as product spatial data.

3.1 Problem Formulation

We give a brief description and formulation of P2TWM mapping problem. Given the multi-source data, we need to first construct task-worker-machine-product (TWMP) pairs which can be formulated as $\{t_1, t_2, \ldots, t_m : (w_1, w_2, \ldots, w_{n_1}), (m_1, m_2, \ldots, m_{n_2}), (p_1, p_2, \ldots, p_{n_3})\}$ demonstrating K-to-N multi-relations. And then use the TWMP pairs to build KG data. The constructed KG data including product information, spatial information, and so on, can be represented by a graph $\mathcal{G} = \{\mathcal{V}, \mathcal{E}, \phi, \psi\}$, where $\mathcal{V}$ represents node-set, $\mathcal{E}$ denotes edge set. Finally, we need to output corresponding task, workers, and machine (TWM) pair given graph data:

$$TWM = F(G). \tag{1}$$

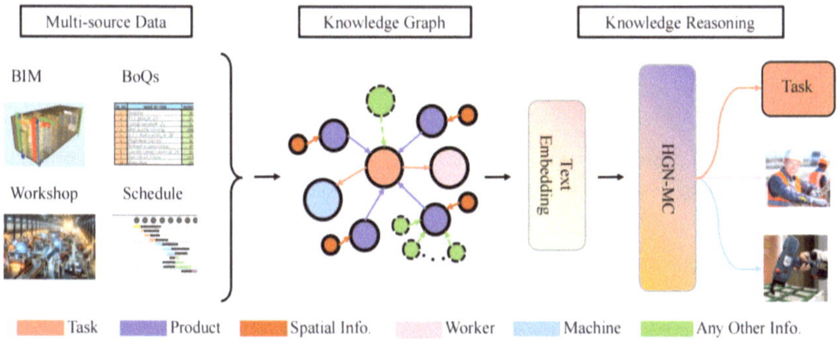

Fig. 2. Our proposed graph-based P2TWM mapping framework involves several steps. Firstly, it extracts and processes multi-source data to construct KG-based data. Next, the text-attribute KGs are converted into numerical vector graphs using pre-trained text embedding. Finally, the graph data is fed into the HGN-MC network to generate final outputs, including tasks, workers, and machines.

3.2 Knowledge Graph Data Generation

As depicted in Fig. 2, the initial step involves extracting multi-source data from various documents, encompassing products listed in bills of quantities (BoQs), tasks outlined in project schedules, spatial details extracted by interpreting the underlying data schema of BIM model, such as the position of "hinge" is within the "window interface", and supplementary worker-machine information from production workshop. Secondly, we standardize the format of the extracted raw data (e.g., word normalization, lemmatization, and stemming) to avoid ambiguity, such as "window ironmongery installation" and "install window ironmongery". Thirdly, the standardized data can be represented as TWMP, demonstrating K-to-N multi-relations. To provide rich semantic representation and capture complex relationships, we construct KG data based on TWMP pairs. And KG can efficiently incorporate any additional information, exhibiting high scalability.

3.3 Graph Neural Network-Based Knowledge Reasoning

We adopt HGN-MC to handle heterogeneous topology structures and lower-dimension semantics for P2TWM mapping, which aligns well with the characteristics of KGs. We can define a KG data as a heterogeneous graph [34], denoted as $\mathcal{G} = \{\mathcal{V}, \mathcal{E}, \phi, \psi\}$, where $\mathcal{V}$ represents the node set, $\mathcal{E}$ denotes the edge set, $\phi : \mathcal{V} \rightarrow \mathcal{T}_\vartheta$ is the node type function with $\mathcal{T}_\vartheta = \{\phi(v) : \forall v \in \mathcal{V}\}$, and $\psi : \mathcal{E} \rightarrow \mathcal{T}_e$ is the edge type function with $\mathcal{T}_e = \{\psi(e) : \forall e \in \mathcal{E}\}$. We utilize pre-trained text embeddings from GloVe [35] to convert the text-attributed data into numerical vectors. These vectors serve as the initial features of $\mathcal{G}$, denoted as node features $p_v^{(0)} \in R^{d_0}$ and edge type embedding $r_{\psi(e)}^{(0)} \in R^{d_0}$, for the input of the HGN-MC. HGN-MC aims to learn a hidden vector $p_v^{(L)} \in R^{d_L}$ for each node (e.g. product, task) of each graph layer based on the topology structure and the input features, and final layer is output. For each layer, the transformation is defined as follows:

$$p_i^{(l)} = \sigma\left(\sum_{j \in \mathcal{N}_i} \alpha_{ij}^{(l)} p_j^{(l-1)}\right), \tag{2}$$

where, σ is activation function, $p_i^{(l)}$ is the embedding of node i in l^{th} layer, $\mathcal{N}_\iota$ denotes the neighbors of node i, and $p_i^{\prime(l-1)}$ is type-specific projected feature of node j, and weight $\alpha_{ij}^{(l)}$ of edge $\langle i, j\rangle$ is learnable. The heterogeneity nodes have different feature spaces.

Table 1. The table presents examples of task-worker-machine-product (TWMP) pairs data for G-P2TWM mapping. Notably, a single task may correspond to multiple products, workers, and machines.

ID	Products	Task	Workers	Machines
0	Lysaght Bondek, Gemtree FRP Board,..., Knauf FRP Board	Board pretreatment and punching	Board processing worker	Circular saw, Plane planing
1	Corrugated profile, Composite floor slab,..., Shear stud	2D panel assembly	Floor tile mason	Electric weld-ing machine
...	...	...	...	...
27	Wall Cabinet, Toilet-Sink Cabinet,..., TV Cabinet	Cabinets installation	Mechanical Equipment Me-chanic	Electric hand drill

To cater to different types of nodes, we obtain $p_i^{\prime(l-1)}$ in the same feature dimension by type-specific projection operation:

$$p_j^{\prime(l-1)} = W_{\phi_j}^{(l-1)} p_j^{(l-1)}, \tag{3}$$

where $p_j^{(l-1)}$ and $p_j^{(l-1)}$ are the raw and mapped feature of node i, $W_{\phi_j}^{(l-1)}$ is the type specific projection matrix, $\phi_j \in \mathcal{T}_\vartheta$, where $\mathcal{T}_\vartheta$ is the node type set. Referring to [31], we incorporate both edge type embeddings and node embeddings to obtain $\alpha_{ij}^{(l)}$ through the attention mechanism. Considering a node pair $((i, j))$, and the edge-level attention $\left(\alpha_{ij}^{(l)}\right)$ which determines the significance importance weight, can be formulated as follows (we omit the layer mark (l) for simplicity):

$$\alpha_{ij} = \frac{\exp\left(\sigma\left(a^T\left[p_i' \| p_j' \| W_{\psi(\langle i,j\rangle)}^r r_{\psi(\langle i,j\rangle)}\right]\right)\right)}{\sum_{k\in\mathcal{N}_i} \exp(\sigma(a^T\left[p_i' \| p_k' \| W_{\psi(\langle i,k\rangle)}^r r_{\psi(\langle i,k\rangle)}\right]))}, \tag{4}$$

where a is learnable matrix, $p_{[\cdot]}{}'$ is the projected node feature, $r_{\psi(i,[\cdot])}$ is the type embedding for each edge $(i, [\cdot])$, $W_{\psi(i,[\cdot])}$ is the type-specific project matrix. By extending the edge information into attention weight calculation, we can better node representation during L-layer transformations. Additionally, we incorporate the classical Multi-head attention technique [36] to acquire richer and more comprehensive feature representations, thereby enhancing the model's expressive capacity:

$$\boldsymbol{p}_i^{(l)} = \|_{k=1}^{K^{(l)}} \sum_{j\in\mathcal{N}_i} \alpha_{ijk}^{(l)} \boldsymbol{p}'^{(l)}_i, l < L, \tag{5}$$

$$\boldsymbol{p}_i^{(l)} = \frac{1}{K^{(l)}} \sum_{k=1}^{K^{(l)}} \sum_{j \in \mathcal{N}_i} \alpha_{ijk}^{(l)} \boldsymbol{p'}_i^{(l)}, \tag{6}$$

where $K^{(l)}$ is the number of heads for l^{th} layers, $\|$ is the concat operation, $\alpha_{ijk}^{(l)}$ is the kth head of $\alpha_{ij}^{(l)}$, and $\alpha_{ij}^{(l)} = \|_{k=1}^{K^{(l)}} \alpha_{ijk}^{(l)} \cdot p_i'^{(l)}$ is the type specific projection feature. According to Eq. 6, we used an averaging representation for the final layer, as the dimension of the multi-heads concatenation embedding is not easily divisible by the required output dimension.

3.4 Residual Connection

Due to over-smoothing [37] and vanishing gradient problems [38], though achieving state-of-the-art (SOTA) in some tasks, most prior GNN-based methods have limited neural-network depth. Inspired by residual connections [39] and some previous work employing residual connections in GNNs [31, 40], we adopt residual connection for node and edge representation across layers to refine Eq. 2 and Eq. 4.

$$p_i^{(l)} = \sigma\left(\sum_{j \in \mathcal{N}_i} \alpha_{ij}^{(l)} p_i'^{(l-1)} + W_{\phi_i}'^{(l-1)} p_i^{(l-1)}\right) \tag{7}$$

$$\alpha_{ij}^{(l)} = (1-\beta)\hat{\alpha}_{ij}^{(l)} + \beta\alpha_{ij}^{(l-1)}, \tag{8}$$

Equation 7 extends Eq. 2 by residual connection. Where, $\left(\alpha_{ij}^{(l)}\right)$ denotes the attention scores for edge (i, j), and (σ) is an activation function. $\left(W_{\phi_i}'^{(l-1)}\right)$ means an additional type-specific projection matrix used to align features of possibly different dimensions across different layers. Following Eq. 4, after obtaining the raw attention weights $(\widehat{\alpha_{ij}})$ for edge (i, j), we introduce residual connections to them according to Eq. 8, where the hyperparameter $(\beta \in [0, 1])$ serves as a scaling factor.

3.5 Loss Definition

Given the results of HGN-MC after L-layer transformation, we only consider the nodes belonging to tasks, workers, and machines: $\mathcal{P}_\vartheta = \{\phi(i)$ is a node for prediction : $\forall i \in \mathcal{V}\Theta\}$. Instead of considering the output as classification results, we treat it as feature outputs. Subsequently, we compute the similarity ranking list of the 28 TWMP pairs' text embeddings obtained from the pre-trained text embedding matrix. Then, we use positive and negative samples for training, and we adopt the Margin Ranking Loss to compute a criterion for predicting the relative distances between inputs:

$$\mathcal{L}_{margin} = \sum_{i=1}^{N} max\big(0, m - y_i \cdot \big(f_{y_i} - h_i\big)\big), h_i \in \mathcal{P}_v, \tag{9}$$

where m represents the margin, which is set to 0. y_i denotes the flag tensor (containing 1 or -1), and f_{y_i} represents the label tensor. When y_i equals $1, f_{y_i}$ is positive and should be ranked higher than the predicted value h_i. Conversely, when y_i equals $-1, f_{y_i}$ is negative and should be ranked lower than h_i.

4 Experiments

In this section, we introduce the details of our experimental data, setup of the experimental environment, relevant settings, and validation metrics, and the experimental results prove the effectiveness of our proposed G-P2TWM framework.

4.1 Experimental Setup

We used the data from previous work [6] collected from eight MC-based production projects which are real projects held in Hong Kong, containing 684 samples of the TWMP pairs. There are 28 classes of TWMP pairs, and the partial data samples are shown in Table 1, in our setting, each task is to formulate a pair of product, human, and machine entities. The collected raw dataset is not enough for training. To generate a larger-scale dataset suitable for deep learning models, we systematically expanded the original data. Specifically, this involved uniformly sampling from the 28 classes of TWMP pairs, with reasonable variations introduced to the product sets within each data instance. Additionally, spatial information was randomly added to some products. Ultimately, we got approximately 68,400 samples for training purposes. We compare our proposed approach with three baselines, RGCN [41], Bi-LSTM, and GLSTM. RGCN is a type of convolutional neural network designed for processing highly multi-relational data, featuring average aggregation from neighbor nodes. Bi-LSTM is a commonly used recurrent neural network (RNN) model in classic natural language processing tasks, but losing the topology relationship of KG data. The GLSTM model utilizes an RGCN as a feature encoder, with the Bi-LSTM network taking the encoded features as sequential input for the mapping process. In contrast with RGCN, HGN-MC replaces the average aggregation operation with an attention-based mechanism, seamlessly integrating heterogeneous information. Additionally, we incorporate a residual mechanism to further augment the model's ability to handle complex data.

4.2 Training

We train our models using the supervised learning approach. In particular, we divide the dataset into training and test sets with an 80:20 ratio. During the training process, corresponding negative samples were generated for each positive sample at a ratio of 1:1. Positive and negative labels were assigned to each batch of data, and the P2TWM results were supervised using the Margin Ranking Loss as defined in Sect. 3.5. We utilize the Adam optimizer [42] to optimize both models. All experiments are conducted on a computer with an Intel(R) Xeon(R) Platinum 8370C CPU and NVIDIA GeForce RTX 4090.

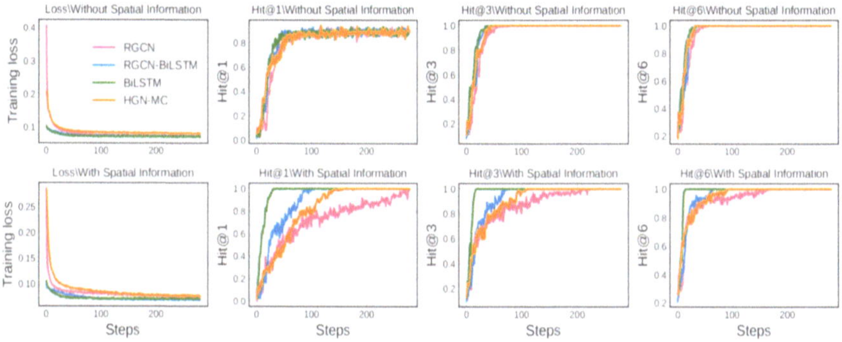

Fig. 3. The training curve of four DL models (models details are mentioned in Sect. 4.1) displays metrics including loss, hit@1, hit@3, and hit@6 with two settings: with or without spatial information.

4.3 Metrics

As mentioned in Sect. 3.5, the HGNN outputs feature vectors for various nodes. We then compute the similarity between these feature vectors and the text label embeddings obtained from the pre-trained text embedding matrix, generating a similarity ranking list. To assess our mapping performance, we utilize common evaluation metrics from the field of information retrieval: hit@1, hit@3, and hit@6, which measure the effectiveness of retrieving the desired information within the top few positions of the results. Hit@1 represents the percentage of true P2TWM pairs ranking first, and so forth for hit@3 and hit@6. In addition, we can employ common metrics used in classification tasks to analyze the results, including true positives (TP), false positives (FP), true negatives (TN), and false negatives (FN). Then we calculate Precision, Recall, F1 score, true positive rate (TPR), and false positive rate (FPR) accordingly. We use TPR and FPR to draw the receiver operating characteristic (ROC) curves. The area under the curve (AUC) is calculated. Furthermore, we examine the parameter sizes of different network models. The metric formulas are listed as follows:

$$\text{Precision} = \text{TP}/(\text{TP} + \text{FP}) \tag{10}$$

$$\text{TPR} = \text{Recall} = \text{TP}/(\text{TP} + \text{FN}) \tag{11}$$

$$\text{FPR} = \text{FP}/(\text{FP} + \text{TN}) \tag{12}$$

$$\text{F}_1 = 2 * \text{Precision} * \text{Recall}/(\text{Precision} + \text{Recall}) \tag{13}$$

4.4 Characteristics Comparison of Various Models

Table 2. Characteristics comparison of HGN-MC with three other models. Our proposed model indicated by a "†".

	Heterogeneity	Topology	Multi-tasks	Param. (MB)	Param. (with spatial)
BiLSTM				23.5	23.5
GLSTM†	√	√		25.29	25.71
RGCN	√	√	√	11.29	16.94
HGN-MC†	√	√	√	11.98	14.32

As shown in Table 2, we first compare the characteristics of HGN-MC with three other models. The BiLSTM model, commonly used for sequence input, mixes all heterogeneous data into an embedding vector, failing to consider heterogeneity and losing information about the graph data's topology. Moreover, BiLSTM cannot perform multi-task prediction. GLSTM uses RGCN as the heterogeneous feature encoder for BiLSTM input, enhancing the ability of BiLSTM to tackle heterogeneous data and topology information, but still cannot perform multitask prediction. However, HGN-MC and RGCN take the graph as input and directly update graph information by node transformation, thus supporting heterogeneity and topology. Various nodes can be supervised by various node labels during training, enabling multitask prediction. And the parameter size of the graph neural network changes with the complexity of the input graph data. Therefore, incorporating spatial information will increase the parameter size.

4.5 Performance of Product2task-Worker-Machine Mapping

We evaluate the performance of different models using the metrics mentioned in Sect. 4.3. The training curves, as shown in Fig. 3, indicated a significant improvement in performance with the inclusion of spatial data information. For the case without spatial information, the BiLSTM and GLSTM models exhibited fast convergence in most metrics. This can be attributed to the fact that sequence data typically has simpler structures and smaller state spaces, making it easier for models to learn and converge. However, the RGCN, which handles more complex graph data, exhibited poorer convergence speed and hit metrics performance. The HGN-MC showed faster convergence compared to RGCN, demonstrating the advantages of its network architecture design. However, there was little difference in hit metrics among the four models after convergence, with hit@3 and hit@6 approaching 1.0 while hit@1 remained around 0.9.

For the case with spatial information, there was a noticeable decrease in convergence speed for graph-based neural networks as the complexity of the graph data increased. However, after convergence, the performance of hit metrics further improved, indicating the significance of adding spatial information.

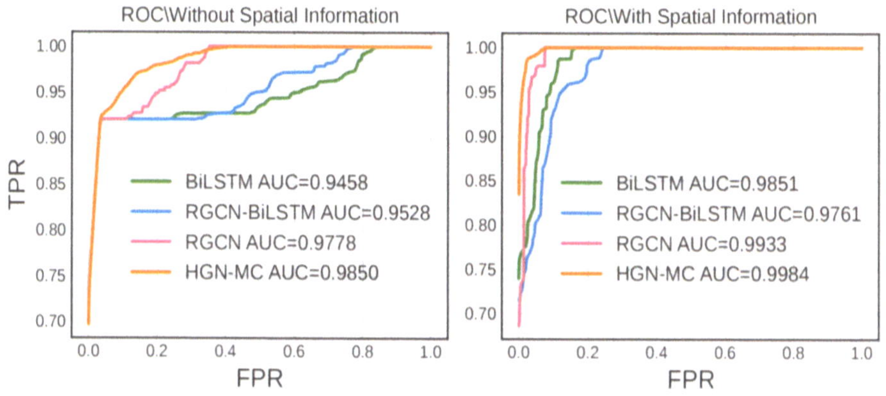

Fig. 4. The ROC curves and AUCs of four DL models (models details are mentioned in Sect. 4.1) with two settings: with or without spatial information.

We compute FPR and TPR for the test dataset. Figure 4 depicts the ROC curves and corresponding AUCs for the four DL models with two settings: with or without spatial information. All models exhibit excellent performance, with AUCs above 0.94. However, LSTM-based models perform slightly worse. These findings indicate that all four DL models excel in the task of G-P2TWM mapping in MC using the current dataset, with the incorporation of spatial information proving to be particularly beneficial.

Table 3 show some evaluation results of six metrics, including hit@1, hit@3, hit@6 and average precision (AvgPre), average recall (AvgRec), and average F1 score (AvgF1). In the absence of spatial information, Bi-LSTM and GLSTM outperform graph-based models. Bi-LSTM achieves the highest hit@1, hit@3, hit@6, and AvgRec. Regarding AvgPre and AvgF1, GLSTM performs the best.

With spatial information incorporated, all models experience a significant improvement, particularly RGCN, and HGN-MC, achieving better performance than LSTM-based models in most metrics. The HGN-MC demonstrates the most noticeable improvement, proving our model can handle heterogeneous data efficiently. Although RGCN performs well in P2TWM mapping tasks, it still needs to strengthen its ability to handle complex knowledge reasoning. These results underscore the importance of spatial information in enhancing P2TWM mapping performance.

LSTM-based models are typically used for sequence inputs, which aggregate all heterogeneous data into a single embedding vector. It does not consider heterogeneity and ignores information about graph data topology. In addition, BiLSTM cannot do multi-task prediction. In contrast, graph-based networks HGN-MC and RGCN take graphs as input and directly update graph information. This allows for greater flexibility in incorporating additional heterogeneous information beyond just spatial data.

Table 3. The table shows the percentage of predefined metrics (defined in Sect. 4.3) for two settings: with and without spatial information, note that the performance of our proposed model indicated by a "†".

Model	With Spatial Info		
	hit@1	hit@3	hit@6
RGCN	0.8960	0.9416	$\simeq 1.0$
Bi-LSTM	0.8360	0.9515	0.9722
GLSTM †	0.7346	0.8836	0.9424
HGN-MC †	**0.9720**	**0.9959**	$\simeq 1.0$
Model	Without Spatial Info		
	hit@1	hit@3	hit@6
RGCN	0.8157	0.9245	0.9383
Bi-LSTM	**0.8226**	**0.9336**	**0.9471**
GLSTM †	0.8182	0.9318	0.93795
HGN-MC †	0.8108	0.9247	0.9382
Model	With Spatial Info		
	AvgPre	AvgRec	$AvgF_1$
RGCN	0.9303	0.8953	0.8941
Bi-LSTM	0.9151	0.8326	0.8448
GLSTM †	0.8937	0.7356	0.7719
HGN-MC †	**0.9794**	**0.9720**	**0.9708**
Model	Without Spatial Info		
	AvgPre	AvgRec	$AvgF_1$
RGCN	0.8107	0.8264	0.8055
Bi-LSTM	0.7894	**0.8336**	0.7998
GLSTM †	**0.8576**	0.8320	**0.8165**
HGN-MC †	0.8008	0.8236	0.7985

5 Conclusion

This paper focuses on the challenges of product2task mapping in MC and introduces a novel graph-based framework for product2task-human-machine (G-P2TWM) mapping to handle complex knowledge reasoning. The framework can extract and process raw heterogeneous and unstructured data into a KG-based format. Then we propose a heterogeneous graph neural work in MC (HGN-MC) take in KG data, featuring multi-type nodes and relationships, and output the mapping results. The HGN-MC can seamlessly cooperate with KG-data, supporting the flexibility of adding additional information such as product spatial information. We evaluate our models and compare their performance with other models. The results demonstrate that our framework achieves high levels of automation, flexibility, and performance.

References

1. Gibb, A.G.: Off-site fabrication: prefabrication, pre-assembly and modularisation. John Wiley & Sons (1999)
2. Hong, J., Shen, G.Q., Li, Z., Zhang, B., Zhang, W.: Barriers to promoting prefabricated construction in china: A cost–benefit analysis. J. Clean. Prod. **172**, 649–660 (2018). https://doi.org/10.1016/j.jclepro.2017.10.171
3. Wuni, I.Y., Shen, G.Q.: Barriers to the adoption of modular integrated construction: Systematic review and meta-analysis, integrated conceptual framework, and strategies. J. Clean. Prod. **249**, 119347 (2020). https://doi.org/10.1016/j.jclepro.2019.119347
4. Ferdous, W., Bai, Y., Ngo, T.D., Manalo, A., Mendis, P.: New advancements, challenges and opportunities of multi-storey modular buildings–a state-of-the-art review. Eng. Struct. **183**, 883–893 (2019). https://doi.org/10.1016/j.engstruct.2019.01.061
5. Pan, W., Yang, Y., Pan, M.: Implementing modular integrated construction in high-rise high-density cities: Perspectives in Hong Kong. Build. Res. & Inf. **51**(3), 354–368 (2023). https://doi.org/10.1080/09613218.2022.2113024
6. Li, X., Wu, C., Yang, Z., Guo, Y., Jiang, R.: Knowledge graph-enabled adaptive work packaging approach in modular construction. Knowl.-Based Syst. **260**, 110115 (2023). https://doi.org/10.1016/j.knosys.2022.110115
7. Norman, S., Brotherton, S.A., Fried, R.T.: Work breakdown structures: the foundation for project management excellence. John Wiley & Sons, (2008).https://doi.org/10.1111/j.1540-5885.2010.007501.x
8. Li, C.-L., Hall, N.G.: Work package sizing and project performance. Oper. Res. **67**(1), 123–142 (2019). https://doi.org/10.1287/opre.2018.1767
9. Zhang, Y., Li, X., Teng, Y., Shen, G.Q., Bai, S.: A heuristic rule adaptive selection approach for multi-work package project scheduling problem. Expert Syst. Appl. **238**, 122092 (2024). https://doi.org/10.1016/j.eswa.2023.122092
10. Kim, K., Cho, Y.K.: Construction-specific spatial information reasoning in building information models. Adv. Eng. Inform. **29**(4), 1013–1027 (2015). https://doi.org/10.1016/j.aei.2015.08.004
11. Chen, X., Jia, S., Xiang, Y.: A review: Knowledge reasoning over knowledge graph. Expert Syst. Appl. **141**, 112948 (2020). https://doi.org/10.1016/j.eswa.2019.112948
12. Globerson, S.: Impact of various work-breakdown structures on project conceptualization. Int. J. Project Manag. **12**(3), 165–171 (1994). https://doi.org/10.1016/0263-7863(94)90032-9
13. Li, X., et al.: Swp-enabled constraints modeling for on-site assembly process of prefabrication housing production. J. Clean. Prod. **239**, 117991 (2019). https://doi.org/10.1016/j.jclepro.2019.117991
14. Shalaby, A., Ezeldin, A.S.: A model for work packages optimization in results-based-finance projects. Eng. Constr. Archit. Manag. **29**(7), 2810–2835 (2022). https://doi.org/10.1108/ECAM-10-2019-0556
15. Wang, H.-W., Lin, J.-R., Zhang, J.-P.: Work package-based information modeling for resource-constrained scheduling of construction projects. Autom. Constr. **109**, 102958 (2020). https://doi.org/10.1016/j.autcon.2019.102958
16. Xu, X., Chen, K., Cai, H.: Automating utility permitting within highway right-of-way via a generic uml/ocl model and natural language processing. J. Construct. Eng. Manag. **146**(12),. 04020135, 2020, https://doi.org/10.1061/(ASCE)CO.1943-7862.0001936

17. Liu, H., Al-Hussein, M., Lu, M.: Bim-based integrated approach for detailed construction scheduling under resource constraints. Autom. Constr. **53**, 29–43 (2015). https://doi.org/10.1016/j.autcon.2015.03.008
18. Khalili, A.: An xml-based approach for geo-semantic data exchange from bim to vr applications. Autom. Constr. **121**, 103425 (2021). https://doi.org/10.1016/j.autcon.2020.103425
19. Cheng, F., Li, H., Wang, Y.-W., Skitmore, M., Forsythe, P.: Modeling resource management in the building design process by information constraint petri nets. Autom. Constr. **29**, 92–99 (2013). https://doi.org/10.1016/j.autcon.2012.08.005
20. Li, X., Wu, C., Xue, F., Yang, Z., Lou, J., Lu, W.: Ontology-based mapping approach for automatic work packaging in modular construction. Autom. Constr. **134**, 104083 (2022). https://doi.org/10.1016/j.autcon.2021.104083
21. Wu, W., Huang, Z., Zeng, J., Fan, K.: A fast decision-making method for process planning with dynamic machining resources via deep reinforcement learning. J. Manuf. Syst. **58**, 392–411 (2021). https://doi.org/10.1016/j.jmsy.2020.12.015
22. Fang, W., Ma, L., Love, P.E., Luo, H., Ding, L., Zhou, A.: Knowledge graph for identifying hazards on construction sites: Integrating computer vision with ontology. Autom. Constr. **119**, 103310 (2020). https://doi.org/10.1016/j.autcon.2020.103310
23. Pan, Z., Su, C., Deng, Y., Cheng, J.: Video2entities: A computer vision-based entity extraction framework for updating the architecture, engineering and construction industry knowledge graphs. Autom. Constr. **125**, 103617 (2021). https://doi.org/10.1016/j.autcon.2021.103617
24. Seidl, M., Scholz, M., Huemer, C., Kappe, G.: UML@ classroom: An introduction to object-oriented modeling. Springer, (2014)https://doi.org/10.1007/978-3-319-12742-2
25. Lin, J.-R., Wu, D.-P.: An approach to twinning and mining collaborative network of construction projects. Autom. Constr. **125**, 103643 (2021). https://doi.org/10.1016/j.autcon.2021.103643
26. Zhang, C., Zhou, G., Hu, J., Li, J.: Deep learning-enabled intelligent process planning for digital twin manufacturing cell. Knowl.-Based Syst. **191**, 105247 (2020). https://doi.org/10.1016/j.knosys.2019.105247
27. Amer, F., Golparvar-Fard, M.: Modeling dynamic construction work template from existing scheduling records via sequential machine learning. Adv. Eng. Inform. **47**, 101198 (2021). https://doi.org/10.1016/j.aei.2020.101198
28. Zhou, B., Bao, J., Chen, Z., Liu, Y.: Kgassembly: Knowledge graph-driven assembly process generation and evaluation for complex components. Int. J. Comput. Integr. Manuf. **35**(10–11), 1151–1171 (2022). https://doi.org/10.1080/0951192X.2021.1891572
29. Wu, C., Wu, P., Wang, J., Jiang, R., Chen, M., Wang, X.: Developing a hybrid approach to extract constraints related information for constraint management. Autom. Constr. **124**, 103563 (2021). https://doi.org/10.1016/j.autcon.2021.103563
30. Zhang, C., Song, D., Huang, C., Swami, A., Chawla, N.V.: Heterogeneous graph neural network. In: Proceedings of the 25th ACM SIGKDD international conference on knowledge discovery & data mining, pp. 793–803 (2019). https://doi.org/10.1145/3292500.3330961
31. Lv, Q., et al.: Are we really making much progress? revisiting, benchmarking and refining heterogeneous graph neural networks. In: Proceedings of the 27th ACM SIGKDD conference on knowledge discovery & data mining, pp. 1150–1160 (2021) https://doi.org/10.1145/3447548.3467350
32. Wang, X., Bo, D., Shi, C., Fan, S., Ye, Y., Philip, S.Y.: A survey on heterogeneous graph embedding: methods, techniques, applications and sources. IEEE Trans. Big Data **9**(2), 415–436 (2022). https://doi.org/10.1109/TBDATA.2022.3177455
33. Wang, X., et al.: Heterogeneous graph attention network. In: The world wide web conference, pp. 2022–2032, (2019) https://doi.org/10.1145/3308558.3313562

34. Sun, Y., Han, J.: Mining heterogeneous information networks: a structural analysis approach. ACM SIGKDD Explor. Newsl. **14**(2), 20–28 (2013). https://doi.org/10.1145/2481244.2481248
35. Pennington, J., Socher, R., Manning, C.D.: Glove: Global vectors for word representation. In: Proceedings of the 2014 conference on empirical methods in natural language processing (EMNLP), pp. 1532–1543 (2014) https://aclanthology.org/D14-1162.pdf
36. Vaswani, A., et al.: Attention is all you need. Adv. Neural Inf. Process. Syst. **30** (2017). https://doi.org/10.5555/3295222.3295349
37. Li, Q., Han, Z., Wu, X.-M.: Deeper insights into graph convolutional networks for semi-supervised learning. In: AAAI'18, vol. 32, no. 1 (2018). https://doi.org/10.1609/aaai.v32i1.11604
38. Li, G., Muller, M., Thabet, A., Ghanem, B.: Deepgcns: Can gcns go as deep as cnns? In: Proceedings of the IEEE/CVF International Conference on Computer Vision, pp. 9267–9276, (2019) https://doi.org/10.1109/TPAMI.2021.3074057
39. He, K., Zhang, X., Ren, S., Sun, J.: Deep residual learning for image recognition. In: Proceedings of the IEEE Conference on Computer Vision and Pattern Recognition, pp. 770–778 (2016)
40. Li, G., Muller, M., Ghanem, B., Koltun, V.: Training graph neural networks with 1000 layers. In: International Conference on Machine Learning. PMLR, pp. 6437–6449 (2021). https://proceedings.mlr.press/v139/li21o.html
41. Schlichtkrull, M., Kipf, T.N., Bloem, P. Van Den Berg, R., Titov, I., Welling, M.: Modeling relational data with graph convolutional networks. In: The semantic web: 15th International Conference, ESWC 2018, Heraklion, Crete, Greece, June 3–7, 2018, Proceedings 15. pp. 593–607, Springer, Cham (2018). https://doi.org/10.1007/978-3-319-93417-438
42. Kingma, D.P., Ba, J.: Adam: A method for stochastic optimization. In: ICLR (Poster) (2015). https://arxiv.org/abs/1412.6980

Decoding Market Signals with Self-adaptive Temporal Modeling in Multi-period Decision-Making

Zhuomin Liang[1], Tongtong Xie[2], Zelong Yi[1], and Yelin Fu[1](✉)

[1] College of Economics, Shenzhen University, Shenzhen, China
liangzhuomin2019@email.szu.edu.cn, {yizl,msylfu}@szu.edu.cn
[2] College of International Studies, Shenzhen University, Shenzhen, China
xietongtong2018@email.szu.edu.cn

Abstract. The volatility of agricultural commodity prices presents substantial challenges for resource allocation and strategic planning in multi-period decision-making within supply chains. However, the complex and non-stationary, non-linear nature of agricultural price dynamics renders these fluctuations difficult to model and predict effectively. To address this challenge, we introduce an AI-driven predictive framework that integrates attention mechanisms with random forests (AM-RF). Leveraging a decade-long observation period (from July 26, 2013, to July 25, 2023), we integrate approximately 21,000 news headlines with macroeconomic indicators, while innovatively incorporating the Chain-of-Thought (CoT) strategy to automatically extract sentiment signals from news content using large language models (LLMs). Our results demonstrate that our AM-RF model significantly outperforms benchmark models in multi-step forecasting across various time horizons, short-term (1 day, 5 days), mediu mterm (60 days), and long-term (180 days) with superior accuracy and robustness. Furthermore, our model captures differences in the time-series contribution of external environmental factors. Specifically, market sentiment emerges as the most influential factor in short- and medium-term price forecasting, while the economic environment assumes a more prominent role in long term predictions. In contrast, market fundamentals and price costs exhibit relatively marginal contributions, especially in longer forecasting windows. Our study highlights the potential of AI and LLM in addressing the complexities of dynamic market environments and provides robust evidence to support data driven decision-making frameworks within agricultural supply chains.

Keywords: Agricultural Commodity Prices · Multi-period Forecasting · Large Language Models (LLMs) · Self-adaptive Artificial Intelligence · Chain of Thought (CoT) Prompt Engineering

M. Li et al. (Eds.): ICLS 2025, *Proceeding of the 19th International Congress on Logistics and Supply Chain Management Systems*, pp. 34–46, 2026.
https://doi.org/10.1007/978-981-95-7700-2_4

1 Introduction

With the rapid expansion of the global agricultural commodity market, not only has the landscape of food production and supply chains been reshaped, but it has also provided new opportunities for investors, producers, and policymakers to strategically position themselves in a complex economic environment. However, the volatility of prices for major agricultural commodities (such as soybeans, corn, and wheat) affects global food security, agricultural sustainability, and the economic strategies of multiple countries (e.g., [1]), thus posing significant challenges for resource allocation and long-term planning. In this context, accurate price forecasting becomes crucial for understanding market dynamics, optimizing supply chain resources, and formulating effective policies [2].

Agricultural commodity prices not only reflect supply and demand dynamics but are also influenced by multiple external factors, including macroeconomic fluctuations, policy changes, and market sentiment (e.g., [3]). However, the complex interactions and dynamic changes of these factors make price forecasting exhibit complex multi-period characteristics across both the time dimension and decision-making scenarios. First, there exist non-stationarity and dynamics. Agricultural commodity prices are often driven by various external factors (e.g., macroeconomic fluctuations), leading to significant non-stationary and dynamic changes in their time series [2]. Traditional static models struggle to capture these complex time series patterns, thus limiting their forecasting performance. Second, there exists high dependency in time series. The key to multi-period forecasting lies in its forecast decision chain: the prediction result for each period directly affects decision optimization for subsequent periods. This high temporal dependency places greater demands on the model's ability to handle the time dimension [4]. Finally, there is the dynamic adjustment of feature contributions. In longterm forecasts, the impact of different factors (or features) on price changes significantly varies over time. For instance, the influence of international economic conditions, policy uncertainty, and market sentiment signals may dominate at different time windows. An effective forecasting model must possess the flexibility to adjust feature weights in order to accurately capture the complex dynamics of price fluctuations over long time spans [3, 5].

In agricultural commodity price forecasting, traditional methods such as AutoRegressive Integrated Moving Average (ARIMA) and machine learning (ML) techniques like Support Vector Regression (SVR) perform well in simple scenarios, but face significant limitations in multi-period decision-making, and complex dynamic environments (See [6]). Recently, the development of AI has opened new possibilities for adaptive forecasting modeling. Deep learning (DL) techniques, particularly Recurrent Neural Networks (RNNs) and their improved variants, i.e., Long Short-Term Memory (LSTM) and Gated Recurrent Units (GRU), overcome the gradient vanishing problem inherent in traditional RNNs through gating mechanisms, allowing these models to capture long-term dependencies in time series data (e.g., [7]). This capability enables LSTM and GRU models to perform exceptionally well in forecasting complex dynamics and nonlinear price signals. Notably, the attention mechanism (AM) effectively integrates heterogeneous data sources (such as news texts, financial indicators, and macroeconomic variables), breaking through the limitations of traditional methods in feature selection and time-varying processing.

In this paper, we propose an AI-driven forecasting framework for agricultural commodity price prediction. We first select a Random Forest (RF) model, which has the ability to capture multivariate interactions. Considering the dynamic weighting of factors and cross-dependencies in multi-period prediction scenarios, we introduce an attention mechanism that allows the model to identify key time points and the dynamic impact of exogenous variables, such as policy uncertainties and market sentiment fluctuations. This mechanism provides greater flexibility in accurately predicting price changes across multiple time periods (e.g., [8]). Based on this, we construct a model combining attention mechanisms and RF. Additionally, we use a large language model (LLM) to perform semantic analysis and sentiment quantification on industry news texts. By incorporating the Chain-of-Thought (CoT) prompting, LLM can assess the potential market impact of news headlines based on context and generate a dynamic sentiment index. For evaluation, we use 10-year observational data from 2013 to 2023, including (1) online news website focused on the agricultural industry, which provides high-granularity real time market dynamics and regional production supply and demand signals, and (2) a set of macroeconomic and financial indicators (e.g., S&P 500 Index). These data provide the framework with a broad economic context and, combined with micro-sentiment signals, support the multidimensional dynamic modeling of agricultural commodity prices. The forecasting target of the model is the S&P Goldman Sachs Commodity Index (GSCI) Agriculture Total Return Index, which integrates the price changes of several key agricultural commodities and is an ideal dependent variable for capturing multi-period market dynamics.

Specifically, we conduct a comprehensive model evaluation in multi-step window scenarios (1 day, 5 days, 60 days, 180 days), and the results demonstrate that our model shows significant advantages both in short-term agility and long-term trend-capturing accuracy. This can be attributed to (1) the attention mechanism, which allows the model to dynamically focus on key moments and important features in the time series; (2) RF's Bagging strategy to optimize the ability to model the complex interrelationships of factors across multiple time windows. Furthermore, we conduct an in-depth analysis of the key factors of agricultural commodity price fluctuations and their dynamic variations across different time windows. The study reveals that, while macroeconomic indicators exhibit a significant cumulative effect on price predictions in the medium and long term, market sentiment plays a crucial role in the short- and medium-term, with its sensitivity to price fluctuations surpassing that of other macroeconomic factors. This finding underscores the critical importance of market sentiment in short-term price volatility, especially in the context of sudden events or market sentiment shocks, where the sentimental reactions of market participants can directly influence price movements. However, as the forecasting horizon extends, the marginal effect of market sentiment gradually diminishes. Particularly in the 180-day forecast window, macroeconomic factors and energy costs exhibit stronger predictive power.

2 AI-Driven Prediction Framework

2.1 Problem Description

Multi-period decision-making requires forward-looking predictions of price trends over multiple future time steps, providing references for long-term strategy planning and resource allocation. In the agricultural commodity market, prices are influenced by multiple factors, including historical price trends, macroeconomic and financial conditions, as well as market sentiments. Let the target commodity price time series be denoted as $\{p_t\}_{t=1}^{T}$, where p_t represents the price at time t. We consider a macro feature sequence $\{x_t\}_{t=1}^{T}$, where $x_t \in \mathbb{R}^D$ represents indicators related to macroeconomic and financial markets. Simultaneously, at each time step t, sentiment analysis of news text using LLM yields a sentiment variable $s_t \in \mathbb{R}$, quantifying the market impact of the news at that moment.

Given a historical window length τ, at time t, we utilize the past τ steps of prices, macro features, and news sentiment variables $(p_{t-\tau}, \ldots, p_t)$, $(x_{t-\tau}, \ldots, x_t)$, $(s_{t-\tau}, \ldots, s_t)$ to predict the price $p_{t+\Delta}$ at future time $t + \Delta$, where $\Delta \geq 1$ denotes the forecast horizon. Formally, we aim to find a predictive function $F(\cdot)$ such that:

$$F{:}(\underbrace{p_{t-\tau},\ldots,p_t}_{past\ prices};\ \underbrace{x_{t-\tau},\ldots,x_t}_{macro\ features};\ \underbrace{s_{t-\tau},\ldots,s_t}_{news\ sentiment})\mapsto\hat{p}_{t+\Delta}. \tag{1}$$

However, the agricultural futures market is a typical complex dynamic system characterized by irregularity, non-stationarity, and high volatility, which extremely challenges accurate prediction. In particular, influenced by the complex environment, the intricate nonlinear relationships between input variables may lead to error accumulation in multi-step forecasts. Therefore, it is crucial to accurately identify the contribution of each feature, avoid information redundancy, and improve prediction accuracy. Although deep learning approaches take significant advantages in addressing this issue, they mainly focus on single-step prediction, and often overlook the weight differences of variables at different time steps (e.g., [7]), thus limiting their ability to provide sufficient information for multi-period decision-making. To address this, we introduce an attention mechanism to adaptively extract the corresponding weights of features at different time steps. We also integrate Random Forest to further explore the complex interactions between features and enable multi-period forecasting.

2.2 Time Series Forecasting Model with Attention Mechanism and Random Forest

In this study, we propose a time series forecasting model that integrates the Attention Mechanism (AM) and Random Forest (RF) for multi-horizon forecasting of agricultural commodity prices. Although existing deep learning methods (such as LSTM and GRU) have achieved some success in time series forecasting, they still face significant limitations in long-term dependency modeling, computational complexity, and interpretability. On the other hand, traditional machine learning methods (such as Random Forest and Gradient Boosting Decision Trees) are structurally better suited to capture nonlinear relationships, but they lack the adaptive feature extraction ability when dealing with complex time series data. Therefore, we combine AM (for dynamic feature extraction capability) and RF (for robust nonlinear regression capability) as a novel forecasting framework AM-RF, aiming to improve the effectiveness of time series modeling (See Fig. 1).

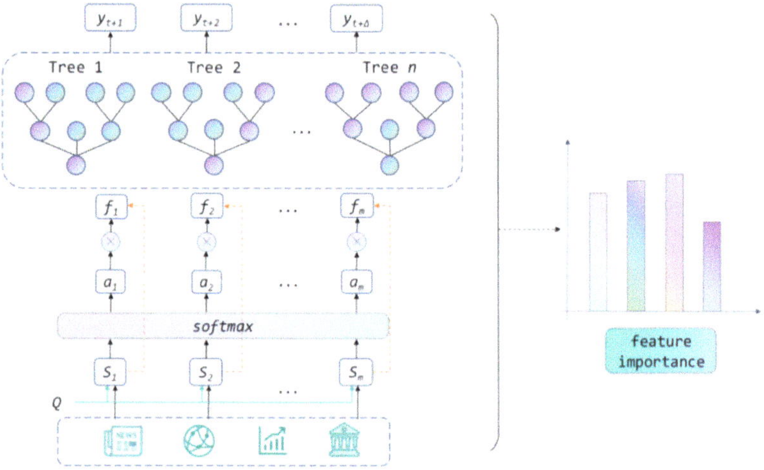

Fig. 1. AM-RF model framework.

In this model, AM serves as a data preprocessing module that dynamically computes the importance weights of time steps for the multivariate time series data to reduce the interference of redundant information and enhance the influence of key time segments. Specifically, AM calculates the weighted contributions of different time steps to form new feature representations, replacing the traditional equal-weight sliding window inputs. This not only highlights the historical information most crucial for the prediction target but also flexibly adapts to the dependency patterns across different time scales, improving the model's generalization ability. Subsequently, we employ RF as the final forecasting model. As an ensemble learning method based on Bagging (i.e., Bootstrap Aggregation), RF leverages the collective output of multiple decision trees for prediction. Compared to a single decision tree, RF improves prediction stability and reduces overfitting that may arise in single-model approaches through multiple sampling and model fusion. Building on this, this study further integrates the attention mechanism with the Bagging structure to deeply refine and represent the underlying patterns and interactive effects of time series data at multiple levels. To validate the effectiveness of the proposed model, we compare it against multiple benchmark models (SVR, LSTM, Bi-LSTM, GRU) to comprehensively assess its performance in multi-step prediction tasks.

We adopt two commonly used metrics to assess predictive performance: the Root Mean Squared Error (RMSE) and the Mean Absolute Error (MAE). For a test set of size N with true values $\{y_n\}_{n=1}^{N}$ and predictions $\{\hat{y}_n\}_{n=1}^{N}$, these metrics are defined as:

$$RMSE = \sqrt{\frac{1}{N}\sum_{n=1}^{N}(y_n - \hat{y}_n)^2}, \tag{2}$$

$$MAE = \frac{1}{N}\sum_{n=1}^{N}|y_n - \hat{y}_n|. \tag{3}$$

RMSE penalizes larger deviations more heavily, making it sensitive to outliers, while MAE provides a more direct, scale-dependent measure of average error magnitude. By reporting both RMSE and MAE, we gain a more nuanced understanding of the models' accuracy and robustness, ensuring a fair and standardized basis for comparison.

2.3 Data

We employ a dataset spanning a ten-year observation period (July 26, 2013, to July 25, 2023), integrating two primary data sources: (1) News headlines from the *The Packer* (www.thepacker.com) website, which specializes in the U.S. agricultural market and provides high-granularity industry dynamics, i.e., micro-level news channels. As a news platform focusing on the U.S. fruit and vegetable industry, it continuously tracks and reports on various dynamics across the supply chain, covering multiple dimensions such as cultivation, seasonal supply-demand changes, etc. Compared to macroeconomic media, this platform provides news information that directly reflects changes and trends in core segments of the supply chain, thus enabling researchers to capture signals such as logistical disruptions and to complement micro-market dynamics that traditional macroeconomic indicators cannot reveal. Following the most up-to-date sentiment analysis method, we adopt LLMs to extract hidden sentiment information from each news headline (e.g., [9]). We introduce the CoT strategy to enhance reasoning capabilities in NLP tasks, improving the accuracy of solving complex problems. The core of CoT is to simulate human thought processes by step-by-step deduction, progressively generating reasoning chains to explicitly express the logical relationships and solution paths, thereby achieving more accurate and interpretable results (e.g., [9]). With CoT, LLMs perform internal reasoning to clarify logical linkages before generating sentiment and impact analysis results, providing transparent and interpretable justifications. (2) Macroeconomic time series indicators, including the S&P 500 Index (S&P 500), Dow Jones Industrial Average (DJIA), Citi U.S. Economic Surprise Index, Nasdaq Composite Index, Crude Oil ETF Volatility Index, and Economic Policy Uncertainty Index (EPU Index).

For the dependent variable, we focus on the overall market trend by selecting the S&P Goldman Sachs Agriculture Total Return Index. This index integrates prices and roll returns of key agricultural commodity futures such as soybeans and corn, reflecting the overall value trend of the global agricultural market over extended periods. Compared to single commodity prices, this index is more adaptable and captures the dynamic characteristics of diversified commodity portfolios, making it more suitable for multi-horizon forecasting and long-term decision optimization research.

Table 1. Description of Variables.

Variable	Definition	Data Range	Category
S&P GSCI Agriculture Total Return Index	Reflecting the overall performance of the broad commodity market, including agricultural commodities	[1.16, 5185.2]	Dependent Variable
Sentiment	Based on headlines from *The Packer* website, reflecting market expectations from various micro-entities (e.g., producers, suppliers, consumers) in the agricultural supply chain	{-0.8, 0.8}	Market Sentiment
S&P 500 Index	Reflecting the overall performance of the US stock market, representing the macroeconomic environment and stock market trends	[2.12, 4796.56]	Market Fundamentals
Dow Jones Industrial Average	Demonstrating the stock market performance of 30 major US companies, indicating macroeconomic and stock market health	[17.36, 36799.65]	
NASDAQ Composite Index	The overall performance of companies listed on the NASDAQ stock exchange, with a high weighting of technology stocks	[4.98, 15993.71]	

(*continued*)

Table 1. *(continued)*

Variable	Definition	Data Range	Category
Crude Oil ETF Volatility Index	Measures the volatility of oil prices, reflecting the potential impact of energy prices on production and transportation costs	[2, 325.15]	Price Volatility Cost
Economic Policy Uncertainty Index	Measures economic policy uncertainty, reflecting the stability of the economic environment and the unpredictability of future economic trends	[1, 861.1]	Economic Policy & Macro Environment
Citi Economic Surprise Index	Measures the difference between actual economic data and market expectations, revealing the deviation between actual economic performance and forecasts	[-144.6, 259.1]	

Finally, we aggregate results extracted from the news sentiment of the same day (2 for negative, 0 for neutral, and 1 for positive) to generate a daily sentiment index. This index, along with macroeconomic signals and the dependent variable S&P Goldman Sachs Agriculture Total Return Index, forms a multidimensional time series dataset. Based on this dataset, we conduct the subsequent predictive modeling and analysis (see Table 1). These indicators are proxies for four main categories of agricultural commodity market elements: (1) market fundamentals, which mainly include S\&P 500, DJIA, and the Nasdaq Composite Index, to reflect the macroeconomic environment and the performance of the stock market; (2) market sentiment, i.e., news-driven market expectations, which capture the potential impacts by quantifying the sentiment fluctuations of market participants; (3) cost of price volatility, such as the Crude Oil ETF Volatility Index, which measures the potential impact of energy price volatility on production and transportation costs; and (4) economic policy and macro-environment, which includes the EPU Index and the Citi U.S. Economic Surprise Index, to portray the stability of the economic environment. Based on this dataset, we launch the later work on forecast modeling and analysis.

3 Results and Analysis

To assess the performance of the proposed AM-RF model, we compare it with several benchmark models to predict the future values of the return index for 1-day, 5-day, 60-day, and 180-day time horizons, and conduct a comprehensive analysis in terms of prediction accuracy and interpretability. Specifically, the AM-RF model demonstrates superior predictive ability across different time windows, especially excelling in the short-to-medium-term predictions.

3.1 Predictive Performance of Self-Adaptive AM-RF Model

To evaluate the performance of the proposed AM-RF model, we compare it with various benchmark models, including traditional time series models (e.g., SVR) and advanced deep learning models (LSTM, Bi-LSTM, GRU, etc.). The prediction tasks cover four time windows: 1, 5, 60, and 180 days, using RMSE and MAE to evaluate the accuracy and stability of each model across different forecasting windows (see Table 2). All experiments are conducted using the deep learning framework PyTorch in Python for model training and testing.

Table 2. Performance Comparison of Models Across Time Windows.

Model	1-day		5-days		60-days		180-days	
	RMSE	MAE	RMSE	MAE	RMSE	MAE	RMSE	MAE
SVR	0.803	0.547	0.806	0.550	0.802	0.546	0.786	0.544
LSTM	0.733	0.501	0.777	0.536	0.750	0.512	0.831	0.698
BiLSTM	0.713	0.490	0.723	0.497	0.771	0.530	0.807	0.648
GRU	0.784	0.542	0.823	0.582	0.793	0.555	0.880	0.743
AM-RF	**0.532**	**0.422**	**0.526**	**0.425**	**0.543**	**0.433**	**0.533**	**0.424**

In the 1-day forecast, the shortest time window, the AM-RF model outperforms (RMSE = 0.532, MAE = 0.422) than the traditional SVR model (RMSE = 0.803, MAE = 0.547), demonstrating its superiority in short-term predictions. Compared to other deep learning models, AM-RF further enhances the information extraction and feature selection capabilities, enabling it to predict short-term fluctuations more accurately.

In the 5-day time window, AM-RF continues to exhibit excellent performance (RMSE = 0.526, MAE = 0.425). Compared to the SVR model (RMSE = 0.806, MAE = 0.550), AM-RF reduced RMSE by 34.7% and MAE by 22.6%, and significantly outperforms LSTM (RMSE = 0.777, MAE = 0.536) and Bi-LSTM (RMSE = 0.723, MAE = 0.497). This indicates that, in the medium-term time window, the AM-RF model benefits from the ensemble learning advantage of random forests, showing a clear advantage in capturing complex features and feature interactions.

In the 60-day time window, AM-RF achieves an RMSE of 0.543 and an MAE of 0.433. Compared to SVR (RMSE = 0.802, MAE = 0.546), AM-RF shows a noticeable reduction in both RMSE and MAE, further confirming its effectiveness in medium-term predictions. While the performance of LSTM and Bi-LSTM remains relatively stable, AM-RF maintains lower errors over a longer time span by leveraging the strengths of multiple decision trees.

In the longest time window, the 180-day forecast, AM-RF still exhibits strong performance (RMSE = 0.533, MAE = 0.424). Compared to SVR (RMSE = 0.786, MAE = 0.544), AM-RF reduces RMSE by 32.1% and MAE by 34.9%. Although deep learning models such as Bi-LSTM (RMSE = 0.807, MAE = 0.648) and LSTM (RMSE = 0.831, MAE = 0.698) show stable performance in the long-term time window, AM-RF still demonstrates powerful long-term forecasting ability by integrating the predictive advantages of multiple tree models.

Table 3. Performance Comparison of Models Across Time Windows.

Absence of	1 day		5-days		60-days		180-days	
	RMSE	ER (%)	RMSE	ER (%)	RMSE	ER (%)	RMSE	ER (%)
Market Sentiment	0.543	1.34	0.544	3.09	0.548	2.66	0.542	0.16
Market Fundamentals	0.538	0.33	0.538	2.00	0.547	2.59	0.554	2.48
Price Cost	0.535	-0.27	0.536	1.52	0.538	0.91	0.543	0.38
Economic Environment	0.525	-1.99	0.515	-2.31	0.526	-1.48	0.517	-4.50
	MAE	ER (%)	MAE	ER (%)	MAE	ER (%)	MAE	ER (%)
Market Sentiment	0.430	1.18	0.434	2.60	0.437	2.88	0.434	1.95
Market Fundamentals	0.425	-0.04	0.427	0.94	0.434	2.00	0.436	2.44
Price Cost	0.422	-0.69	0.427	0.85	0.429	1.02	0.429	0.58
Economic Environment	0.416	-2.22	0.417	-1.61	0.421	-0.88	0.413	-2.98

3.2 What Should We Focus on at Different Time Windows?

In a multi-period decision-making environment, the prediction of agricultural commodity prices requires the integration of dynamic information from multiple input features. These features include macroeconomic indicators, financial market signals, and micro-level sentiment variables, among others, and their contribution and influence across different time scales may vary significantly. This challenge is particularly prominent in multi-period forecasting applications (e.g., [7, 10]). Therefore, this study utilizes feature importance analysis to quantify the relative contribution of different features in the prediction process, aiming to reveal the patterns of information utilization in multi-period decision-making (c.f. [11]). We calculate the baseline errors (viz., the RMSEs and MAEs when all features are included in the model prediction). We also calculate Effectiveness Rate (ER) to serve as a reference for evaluating the impact on model performance after removing specific features (c.f. [12]).

$$ER_{RMSE} = \frac{RMSE_{absence} - RMSE_{baseline}}{RMSE_{baseline}} \times 100 \tag{4}$$

$$ER_{MAE} = \frac{MAE_{absence} - MAE_{baseline}}{MAE_{baseline}} \times 100 \tag{5}$$

where $RMSE_{baseline}$ and $MAE_{baseline}$ are the baseline errors with all features included. $RMSE_{absence}$ and $MAE_{absence}$ is the error after removing a specific feature category. If ER is positive, it means that removing the feature category results in an increase in the model error, indicating that the category of features contributed positively to the performance of the prediction model. Negative ER demonstrates a decrease in error after removal, indicating that the feature category may have added noise or unnecessary complexity in some way.

From Table 3, we can draw the conclusions that market sentiment plays a crucial role in short- and medium-term predictions, particularly in the 5-day and 60-day windows. The exclusion of market sentiment leads to a significant increase in forecast errors, suggesting that it has the greatest impact on the model in these time windows. Its volatility reflects short-term market dynamics, and also increasingly affects medium-term predictions, especially in uncertain market environments where sentiment responses play a decisive role in price movements. Furthermore, the importance of the economic environment becomes increasingly significant in the long-term forecast window. Its exclusion leads to a marked increase in RMSE and MAE, highlighting the profound long-term influence of the economic environment. In contrast, the impact of market fundamentals and price costs on forecast performance remains relatively stable. Although their effects vary across different time windows, their contribution to model accuracy is relatively smaller, especially in the medium and long-term windows, where their influence appears secondary.

4 Conclusion

In the agricultural commodity market, the complexity of multi-cycle decision-making scenarios necessitates precise forecasting of future market trends to support investment optimization, supply chain management, and policy formulation. However, the realization of these decisions is often influenced by the significant complexity of price fluctuations, which arise from the dynamic interaction of multi-dimensional factors such as macroeconomic trends, micro-market signals, and policy uncertainty. To address this challenge, we propose an AI-driven forecasting model that integrates attention mechanisms with random forest (AM-RF). Compared to traditional forecasting models (e.g., SVR), our model achieves notable improvements in efficiently extracting important time series features and capturing the nonlinear dynamic interactions among multiple variables with significant predictive performance across different time windows.

Based on feature importance analysis, we reveal the dynamic effects of factors (such as policy uncertainty) at various time scales. Specifically, our findings provide valuable operational insights for managers. In the short term, managers should rely on high-frequency data and real-time market sentiment analysis, particularly through sentiment resources (such as news and social media) and analysis tools, to quickly capture shifts in market trends. However, macroeconomic factors become increasingly influential as the forecasting window extends, especially in the medium- and long-term forecasts. The economic environment's impact on agricultural commodity prices gradually strengthens in these time windows, with macro variables (such as policy changes, inflation rates, and international economic conditions) significantly improving their explanatory power for long-term price fluctuations. Thus, agricultural managers should enhance their tracking and evaluation of macroeconomic trends in medium- to long-term planning, and formulate corresponding production and supply chain strategies based on the evolving economic environment. Additionally, our study highlights the growing influence of production cost factors, such as energy prices and raw material costs, in long-term forecasts. As such, when formulating long-term supply chain and production strategies, agricultural managers should place special emphasis on energy price fluctuations. They should consider strategically utilizing risk hedging tools (such as futures contracts and energy supply chain diversification) to mitigate the uncertainties associated with energy markets.

Despite our study being among the few AI-driven forecasting models, we acknowledge that there are many directions worth exploring. First, while this study reveals the correlation between feature variables and agricultural commodity price fluctuations, it does not further explore potential bidirectional causality. Future research could further validate the causal mechanisms through which feature variables influence price fluctuations, thereby enhancing the theoretical explanatory power of the forecasting model. Additionally, the training of this model was conducted independently on a single market and a single commodity, whereas agricultural commodity markets exhibit high cross-correlations and regional interdependencies. Future studies could model the interdependencies between different commodities and markets to improve the model's generalization performance and cross-market adaptability.

Acknowledgement. This research is financially supported by the National Natural Science Foundation of China (Nos. 72031004, 72222019,72171154 72101098), the Guangdong Provincial Planning Project of Philosophy and Social Sciences (No. GD25CYJ67). And it is also supported by the Special Fund for the Cultivation of Independent Innovation Achievements of Postgraduate Students at Shenzhen University (No. 000066010705).

References

1. Lu, H., Ma, X., Ma, M., Zhu, S.: Energy price prediction using data-driven models: a decade review. Comput. Sci. Rev. **39**, 100356 (2020)
2. Kalimuthu, T., Kalpana, P., Kuppusamy, S., Sreedharan, V.R.: Intelligent decision-making framework for agriculture supply chain in emerging economies: research opportunities and challenges. Comput. Electr. Agric. **219**, 108766 (2024)

3. Behzadi, G., O'Sullivan, M.J., Olsen, T.L., Zhang, A.: Agribusiness supply chain risk management: a review of quantitative decision models. Omega, 79, 21--42 (2017)
4. Li, X., Wang, X., Feng, Z.: Dynamic repositioning in bike-sharing systems with uncertain demand: an improved rolling horizon framework. Omega **126**, 103047 (2024)
5. Cuellar-Usaquén, D., Ulmer, M.W., Gomez, C., Álvarez-Martínez, D.: Adaptive stochastic lookahead policies for dynamic multi-period purchasing and inventory routing. Eur. J. Oper. Res. **318**(3), 1028–1041 (2024)
6. Luo, R., Liu, J., Wang, P., Tao, Z., Chen, H.: A multisource data-driven combined forecasting model based on internet search keyword screening method for interval soybean futures price. J. Forecast. **43**(2), 366–390 (2023)
7. Chakraborty, S., Jagabathula, S., Subramanian, L., Venkataraman, A.: Frontiers in operations: News Event-Driven forecasting of commodity prices. Manuf. Serv. Oper. Manag. **26**(4), 1286–1305 (2024)
8. Huang, Z., Wang, D., Yin, Y., Li, X.: A spatiotemporal bidirectional attention-based ride-hailing demand prediction model: a case study in Beijing during COVID-19. IEEE Trans. Intell. Transp. Syst. **23**(12), 25115–25126 (2022)
9. Yu, X., Chen, Z., Ling, Y., Dong, S., Liu, Z., Lu, Y.: Temporal data meets LLM – Explainable financial time series forecasting, arXiv preprint arXiv:2306.11025. (2023)
10. Saxena, R., Paul, R.K., Kumar, R.: Transmission of price shocks and volatility spillovers across major onion markets in India. Agric. Econ. Res. Rev. **33**(1), 45 (2020)
11. Yi, Z., Liang, Z., Xie, T., Li, F.: Financial risk prediction in supply chain finance based on buyer transaction behavior. Decis. Support. Syst. **170**, 113964 (2023)
12. Li, J., Li, G., Liu, M., Zhu, X., Wei, L.: A novel text-based framework for forecasting agricultural futures using massive online news headlines. Int. J. Forecast. **38**(1), 35–50 (2020)

A Quasi-Natural Experiment Study on the Impact of China's Energy-Consuming Rights Trading (ECRT) on Corporate Financial Performance

Pei Zheng[1(✉)], Jingyi Zhang[1], Wen Wen[1], and Kin Keung Lai[2]

[1] Business School of Hunan University, Changsha 410082, China
{zp,zjy2002}@hnu.edu.cn

[2] International Business School of Shanxi, Normal University, Xian 710119, China

Abstract. To achieve the "Dual Carbon" goals and advance energy consumption control, China introduced the Energy-Consuming Rights Trading (ECRT) system as a market-based environmental governance mechanism following its carbon emissions trading policy. While existing studies predominantly focus on theoretical or ex-ante analyses, this research employs a Propensity Score Matching–Difference in Differences (PSM-DID) model with panel data from 1,973 A-share listed firms (2013–2023). Using Tobin's Q as a proxy for financial performance and green innovation as the mediator, the study controls for firm fundamentals (capital structure, solvency, growth capacity, operational efficiency, and technological level) to conduct an ex-post evaluation of ECRT's impact. Results indicate: (1) ECRT significantly enhances corporate financial performance, with effects intensifying annually, urging firms to actively participate in market development. (2) ECRT indirectly suppresses financial performance by reducing green innovation, partially offsetting its direct positive effect; this masking effect diminishes when green innovation is controlled. (3) Heterogeneity tests reveal that ECRT benefits energy-intensive firms, non-state-owned enterprises (non-SOEs), and eastern regions, while non-energy-intensive firms, SOEs, and central/western regions show insignificant responses. Thus, policymakers should adopt region-specific measures, avoid uniform implementation, and provide targeted subsidies to incentivize broader participation and ensure balanced regional development.

Keywords: Energy-Consuming Rights Trading · Financial Performance · Propensity Score Matching First Section

Supported by National Social Science Foundation of China (Grant No. 25BGL210), the Hunan Provincial Natural Science Foundation of China (Grant No. 2024JJ5099) and the Hunan Provincial Social Science Foundation of China (Grant No. 22YBA040).

M. Li et al. (Eds.): ICLS 2025, *Proceeding of the 19th International Congress on Logistics and Supply Chain Management Systems*, pp. 47–66, 2026.
https://doi.org/10.1007/978-981-95-7700-2_5

1 Introduction

Since the establishment of the global climate governance framework under the 2015 Paris Agreement, China has been advancing systemic reforms to drive the world's largest energy transition. In 2020, President Xi Jinping announced China's "3060 Dual Carbon" goals at the 75th UN General Assembly, committing to peak carbon emissions by 2030 and achieve carbon neutrality by 2060. By 2024, the State Council's White Paper on *China's Energy Transition* further outlined a clean, low-carbon, safe, and efficient energy system under the "Four Revolutions and One Cooperation" strategy. These measures demonstrate China's commitment to environmental governance and reinforce its role as a global leader in climate action.

As the world's largest emitter of greenhouse gases and energy consumer, China views reducing fossil fuel use as fundamental to addressing environmental challenges, making energy revolution a core component of carbon neutrality. This has led to the emergence of "Energy-Consuming Rights Trading (ECRT)", a market-based mechanism for cross-regional energy quota allocation under total energy consumption control. Unlike the Western green/white certificate systems prevalent, China's ECRT was first proposed in the 2015 Ecological Civilization Reform Plan, with pilot programs launched in Zhejiang, Fujian, Henan, and Sichuan in 2016. Subsequent policies, including the 2021 Dual-Control Improvement Plan and the 2024 Energy Conservation Action Plan, have accelerated national market development and cross-provincial trading mechanisms.

To ensure effective implementation and scaling of EUR trading, evaluating pilot program outcomes is critical. However, due to data limitations and reporting lags, most existing research remains theoretical or simulation-based, with limited empirical post-policy analysis. This study addresses this gap by analyzing 2013–2023 panel data from 31 Chinese provinces using Propensity Score Matching–Difference in Differences (PSM-DID) to examine:(1) Whether EUR trading enhances or threatens firms' market competitiveness post-policy, (2) The mechanisms driving these effects, and (3) How outcomes vary by region, ownership, or industry. The findings will inform government policy, guide corporate strategy and investment decisions, and provide new insights for global research on market-based environmental regulation tools.

2 Theoretical Foundations, Literature Review, and Research Hypotheses

2.1 Theoretical Foundations and Literature Review

To conserve resources and protect the environment, governments often implement environmental regulations to control or intervene in corporate activities. Direct administrative interventions are termed command-and-control environmental regulation, while indirect measures combining administrative and market mechanisms fall under market-incentive environmental regulation. With the emergence of eco-labeling and environmental certification systems, voluntary corporate initiatives in environmental protection or energy efficiency—classified as voluntary environmental regulation—have also into the regulatory framework [1]. Current research on the efficacy of environmental regulation remains inconclusive. Some scholars argue, based on the Porter Hypothesis, that moderate environmental regulation enhances corporate development [2, 3]. Others contend that it inhibits growth [4, 6, 7], while a third perspective highlights context-dependent effects, citing nonlinear relationships due to corporate heterogeneity [8–11] or divergent impacts from macro-political contexts and regulatory tools. For instance, market-incentive regulations demonstrate more significant positive effects on firm value compared to command-and-control measures [12–14]. Consequently, research on market-based mechanisms—such as carbon emissions trading and pollution discharge rights trading—has garnered widespread scholarly attention.

Energy Consumption Rights Trading (ECRT), also referred to as Energy Use Rights Trading, is an innovative market-driven policy mechanism. Under this system, participants trade legally allocated energy consumption quotas within a capped framework, incentivizing efficiency and conservation [15]. As China is the first proposer of ECRT, most existing studies are domestically initiated and generally follow three directions:

First, legal research focuses on designing ECRT mechanisms, improving regulatory clauses [16] to integrate law and policy [17], and refining legal norms through pilot practices [18–20]. Second, studies explore synergies between ECRT and overlapping policies like energy consumption taxes[21–23], energy-saving trading, and carbon emissions trading (CET), particularly how firms strategically maximize profits under dual ECRT-CET regimes [24, 25].Third, policy effect analyses include ex-ante simulations (e.g., Wang et al. [26] used DEA models to show ECRT reduces energy intensity and total consumption; Liu et al. [27] demonstrated combined ECRT-CET enhances provincial economic benefits and emission cuts; Zhang et al.[15] highlighted ECRT's superior economic/energy-saving potential over command-control policies) and limited ex-post evaluations such as Zhang et al. [28] found ECRT lowers regional energy intensity via PSM-DID; Li et al. [29] linked ECRT to corporate low-carbon innovation). Overall, ECRT research remains theoretical or macro-level, with scarce micro-level firm analyses.

2.2 Research hypothesis

Market-based environmental regulations require firms to internalize environmental costs [30, 31], increasing cost pressures. As profit-maximizing entities, firms must optimize resource allocation, improve operational efficiency, or reduce energy inputs to enhance financial performance under such constraints [32]. However, some studies suggest that environmental regulations raise compliance costs, directly reducing revenue [33] and causing economic losses, particularly for firms exceeding emission quotas under market-based mechanisms [34]. Based on this, we propose the following hypothesis:

H1: ECRT as a market-based environmental regulation, improves corporate financial performance.

Under market-based regulations, While simply increasing environmental expenditures or reducing output is unsustainable, firms can leverage environmental management to establish competitive advantages and boost financial performance [35]. Green innovation, as a pillar of sustainable development, can generate new profit growth and facilitate industrial upgrading [36]. Nevertheless, some research indicates that the costs of green innovation may outweigh its benefits, potentially squeezing operational performance

[37].Green innovation is driven by internal factors such as corporate resource capabilities [38], executive cognition [39], and green absorptive capacity [36], as well as external factors including government oversight [40], policy shocks [41, 42], market competition, and consumer demand [38, 43]. Environmental regulations also serve as a critical external driver [44]. Thus:

H2: ECRT influences corporate financial performance via green innovation.

The policy effects of ECRT may vary depending on firm ownership, geographic location, and industry. Under China's mixed-ownership system, state-owned enterprises (SOEs) and private firms have different operational objectives. Regional disparities, particularly between the more developed eastern regions and the central and western regions, as well as differences in energy intensity across industries, further contribute to heterogeneous effects. Accordingly, we propose:

H3a: ECRT's effect on financial performance is more pronounced in private firms than SOEs.

H3b: ECRT's effect is stronger in eastern firms than central/western firms.

H3c: ECRT's effect is more significant in energy-intensive industries than non-energy-intensive ones.

3 Research Methods and Data Description

3.1 Data Sources

This study uses all Chinese A-share listed companies from 2013 to 2023 as the initial sample, covering 31 provinces. Firms from Zhejiang, Fujian, Henan, and Sichuan—the four pilot provinces—are designated as the treatment group, while those from other provinces serve as the control group. The National Development and Reform Commission (NDRC) proposed the launch of ECRT pilot construction in September 2016, completing its top-level design and preparatory work that year. The pilot officially commenced in 2017; thus, we define 2017 onward as the implementation period and 2016 and prior as the pre-implementation period. After excluding (1) firms listed after 2013, (2) financial sector firms, (3) delisted, ST, and ST* firms, and (4) samples with missing data, the final sample comprises 1,973 firms with 18,752 observations. All data are sourced from the China Stock Market & Accounting Research Database (CSMAR) and the Chinese Research Data Services Platform (CNRDS).

3.2 Variable Selections

Existing literature primarily employs two variables to measure financial performance: return on assets (ROA) and Tobin's Q. ROA evaluates corporate profitability from an accounting perspective, while Tobin's Q reflects firm value from a market-based viewpoint. As an incentive-based market policy, the ECRT mechanism aligns more closely with market-oriented metrics. Therefore, this study adopts Tobin's Q as the dependent variable representing financial performance.

The difference-in-differences (DID) approach involves three dummy explanatory variables: a time dummy distinguishing pre- and post-implementation periods, a regional dummy indicating pilot provinces, and their interaction term (the DID estimator), which serves as the core indicator for assessing ECRT's policy effects.

The impact of ECRT pilot implementation on corporate financial performance may be influenced by other factors. Drawing on commonly used control variables from existing literature [45–49], we include: (1) basic firm characteristics - firm age and size. Older firms tend to have greater maturity, more experience in responding to market changes, and better risk control capabilities, leading to improved financial performance. Larger firms typically have better access to information and resources, though their more extensive operations may present management challenges, both affecting financial performance; (2) capital Structure variables including ownership concentration and property rights nature, as different shareholder structures and ownership types lead to varied business strategies and financial outcomes; (3) corporate capability indicators representing debt-paying ability (current ratio and asset-liability ratio), growth potential (revenue growth rate), technological level (R&D expenditure to revenue ratio), and operational efficiency (current asset turnover rate). Detailed variable definitions are provided in Table 1.

Table 1. Variable definitions

Variable Type	Variable Name	Variable Symbol
Explained Variable	Tobin's Q	*TobinQ*
Explanatory Variable	Time Dummy Variable	*year*
	Regional Dummy Variable	*prov*
	DID Estimator	*EU*
Control Variables	Firm Age	*age*
	Firm Size	*size*
	Equity Concentration	*SOE*
	Nature of Corporate Ownership	*Ftype*
	Current Ratio	*CR*
	Asset-Liability Ratio	*LR*
	Revenue Growth Rate	*IR*
	Current Asset Turnover Ratio	*CAT*
	R&D Expense to Revenue Ratio	*R&D*
Mediating Variable	Green Patents	*GP*

3.3 Research Methodology

The Difference-in-Differences (DID) Method. The DID method represents a widely used quasi-natural experimental approach in policy evaluation. Its fundamental principle involves comparing the pre-post policy change in the treatment group (affected by the policy) with that in the control group (unaffected), under the parallel trends assumption, to isolate the policy's net effect. In examining the impact of ECRT on corporate financial performance, enterprises in pilot provinces constitute the treatment group while those in non-pilot provinces serve as the control group. The following DID model is established to assess the net effect of the ECRT pilot policy:

$$TobinQ_{it} = \alpha_0 + \alpha_1 EU_{it} + \sum_{k=2}^{10} \alpha_k Controls_{it} + u_i + v_t + \varepsilon_{it} \quad (1)$$

In Equation (1), EU_{it} represents the interaction term, where EU_{it}=year$_t$*prov$_i$ .Here, year$_t$ denotes the time dummy variable and prov$_i$ represents the province dummy variable, with prov$_i$=1 indicating that the firm is located in a pilot region and year$_t$=1 signifying the post-implementation period of the pilot program. α_1 of the EU term captures the net effect of ECRT on financial performance. $Controls_{it}$ refers to the control variables, while u_i and v_t represent individual and time fixed effects respectively, and ε_{it} stands for the error term.

The Propensity Score Matching-Difference in Differences (PSM-DID) Method. This is employed to address potential selection bias, given that pilot regions were selected based on comprehensive government assessments of regional economic development, energy structures, and industrial characteristics[28], rather than through random assignment. The PSM approach first identifies characteristic variables that may influence group assignment, then uses a logit model (probit models are also commonly used) to estimate propensity scores representing the probability of control group units being selected into the treatment group. This study adopts the standard logit model for propensity score estimation. Matching is then performed based on these propensity scores using the 1:3 caliper nearest neighbor matching method, with alternative matching approaches (kernel matching, radius caliper matching, etc.) used for robustness checks. Post-matching balance tests confirm that the matched groups exhibit no significant differences except for policy exposure, effectively mitigating self-selection bias. This validated matching enables subsequent DID analysis [49].

The Dynamic Effects Model. It is employed to examine the year-specific impacts of policy implementation. This approach decomposes the aggregate effect into annual components, serving dual purposes of assessing yearly policy effects and conducting parallel trend tests. The model specification replaces the interaction term in Eq. (1) with interactions between year-specific dummy variables and regional dummies, formally expressed as:

$$\text{TobinQ}_{it} = \beta_0 + \sum_{2013}^{2023} \beta_t year_t{*}prov_i + \sum_{k=2}^{10} \beta_k Controls_{it} + u_i + v_t + \varepsilon_{it} \quad (2)$$

Mediation Effect Model. This study employs the improved stepwise method with lower error rates to conduct joint significance tests for mediation effects [32, 50, 51]. The mediation model is constructed with $TobinQ_{it}$ as the dependent variable, green innovation GP_{it} as the mediator, and ECRT implementation EU_{it} as the independent variable, specified as follows:

$$GP_{it} = \gamma_0 + \gamma_1 EU_{it} + \sum_{k=2}^{10} \gamma_k Controls_{it} + u_i + v_t + \varepsilon_{it} \tag{3}$$

$$TobinQ_{it} = \delta_0 + \delta_1 EU_{it} + \delta_2 GP_{it} \sum_{k=3}^{11} \gamma_k Controls_{it} + +u_i + v_t + \varepsilon_{it} \tag{4}$$

The testing procedure involves three steps: First, examining coefficient α_1 in Eq. (1) to verify the existence of direct effects. A significant α_1 indicates notable policy effects of EU_{it} warranting further mediation analysis. Second, testing coefficients γ_1 in Eq. (3) and δ_2 in Eq. (4) to confirm whether the mediator is both influenced by the independent variable and affects the dependent variable. Significant γ_1 demonstrates EU_{it}'s impact on GP_{it}, while significant δ_2 shows GP_{it}'s effect on $TobinQ_{it}$. The joint significance of both coefficients establishes the mediation pathway [52]. Finally, examining δ_1's significance in Eq. (4) determines the mediation type: insignificant δ_1 suggests complete mediation; significant δ_1 with the same sign as $\gamma_1 * \delta_2$ indicates partial mediation, while opposite signs imply a suppression effect [51, 53].

4 Empirical Analysis

4.1 Descriptive Statistics

Table 2. Descriptive statistics

Variable	Sample Size	Mean	Standard Deviation	Minimum	Maximum
TobinQ	18752	2.072505	1.85223	0.61125	92.24998
year	18752	2018.131	3.15568	2013	2023
EU	18752	0.1385452	0.3454805	0	1
size	18752	2.42e+10	1.09e+11	5.41e+07	2.73e+12
age	18752	20.52725	6.129911	4	67
SOE	18752	54.90787	15.15204	4.3831	101.16
ftype	18752	2.491303	9.023173	0	87.6912
CR	18752	2.225037	2.961449	0.07885	144.0001
LR	18752	0.4413644	0.202526	0.07969	1.956558
IR	18752	0.2553647	4.789033	0.98535	429.0361

(continued)

Table 2. *(continued)*

Variable	Sample Size	Mean	Standard Deviation	Minimum	Maximum
CAT	18752	1.313859	1.071325	0.006185	22.17983
RD	18752	0.0437675	0.0522194	0	1.3745
GP	18752	10.92982	50.3681	0	1603

Table 2 presents the descriptive statistics of key variables. The mean Tobin's Q for the sample firms is 2.072, with values ranging widely from 0.611 to 92.24, indicating substantial variations in corporate financial performance across firms. To mitigate potential multicollinearity issues, logarithmic transformations were applied to control variables [54]. After transformation, all correlation coefficients between variables remained below 0.5, effectively addressing heteroskedasticity concerns.

4.2 The Overall Impact of ECRT on Corporate Financial Performance.

Prior to PSM, we conducted six DID estimations to analyze the impact of ECRT on corporate financial performance, progressively incorporating control variables and accounting for year, firm, province, and industry fixed effects. The results consistently show no statistically significant effect of ECRT on financial performance, regardless of model specifications. This non-significance may stem from substantial heterogeneity among firms. We therefore employ PSM to eliminate dissimilar observations and enhance comparability between treatment and control groups.

Using the DID estimator EU as the dependent variable and variables from the control set as covariates, we performed PSM with caliper nearest neighbor matching, retaining only samples within the common support region. As shown in Fig. 1, post-matching standardized mean differences for all covariates were below 5%, with significantly reduced absolute bias compared to pre-matching results. Previously significant covariates (lnage, lntype, lnsize, etc.) showed no significant differences after matching, satisfying the balance test requirements. After excluding 86 samples outside the common support region, we conducted DID analysis on the remaining 1,887 matched samples.

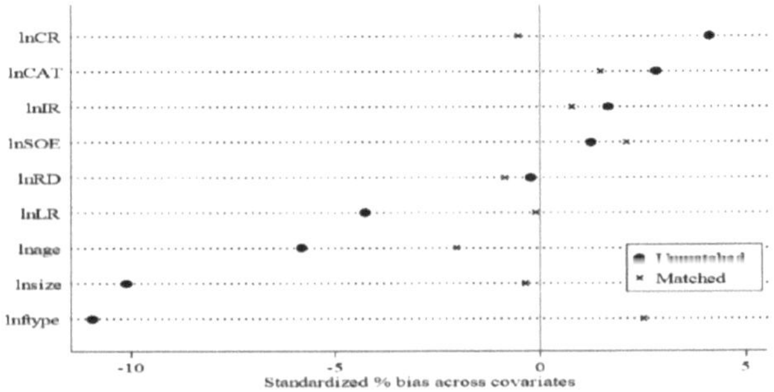

Fig. 1. Balance Test for Propensity Score Matching

As shown in Columns (1) and (2) of Table 3, the ECRT policy demonstrated no statistically significant impact on the financial performance of Chinese listed companies when control variables were excluded, even after accounting for firm and year fixed effects. Column (3) indicates that after incorporating control variables while considering only year fixed effects, the policy's effect remained insignificant. However, Columns (4) through (6) reveal that when controlling for both firm and year fixed effects alongside other covariates, the policy exerted a significantly positive overall impact on corporate financial performance, with the pilot program contributing to an average 0.168% improvement. This effect remained robust at 0.192% (significant at the 5% level) after further controlling for industry and province fixed effects, thereby validating Hypothesis 1.

While prior research has established that ECRT contributes to environmental improvement and supports carbon neutrality goals, this study demonstrates its additional benefit of enhancing corporate economic performance, providing empirical evidence for the policy's dual economic-environmental benefits under current political conditions. This finding contrasts with studies on similar market-based mechanisms like carbon emissions trading, which despite environmental benefits [55, 56], have shown negative financial impacts [37]. We attribute the positive financial effect of ECRT to its late-mover advantage, having benefited from the institutional experience of carbon emissions trading while sharing similar policy designs and objectives. This enabled the ECRT pilot to rapidly stimulate market incentives, simultaneously addressing environmental concerns while improving corporate financial performance.

The results further illuminate the effects of other control variables on financial performance. Firm age, ownership concentration, current ratio, asset-liability ratio, revenue growth rate, and current asset turnover ratio all positively influence financial performance, suggesting that concentrated ownership facilitates decisive decision-making, while greater maturity and stronger operational capabilities enhance stability and performance - findings consistent with theoretical expectations. Conversely, firm size and state ownership exhibited significant negative effects, indicating that larger scale may complicate operational control and adversely affect market value, while state-owned enterprises bear greater financial risks in ECRT, reflecting their political and social responsibilities. Interestingly, R&D intensity shows no significant impact.

Table 3. PSM-DID Regression results

Variable	(1) *TobinQ*	(2) *TobinQ*	(3) *TobinQ*	(4) *TobinQ*	(5) *TobinQ*	(6) *TobinQ*
EU	−0.0698	0.111	−0.0531	0.168**	0.168**	0.192**
	(0.0703)	(0.0789)	(0.0664)	(0.0778)	(0.0779)	(0.0778)
lnage			−0.450***	−0.820***	−0.820***	−0.796***
			(0.0484)	(0.0993)	(0.0994)	(0.102)
lnSOE			0.327***	0.789**	0.789**	0.695**
			(0.120)	(0.350)	(0.350)	(0.350)

(*continued*)

Table 3. (*continued*)

Variable	(1) *TobinQ*	(2) *TobinQ*	(3) *TobinQ*	(4) *TobinQ*	(5) *TobinQ*	(6) *TobinQ*
lnsize			0.254**	0.208*	0.208*	0.202*
			(0.0988)	(0.121)	(0.121)	(0.118)
lnftype			−0.0822***	−0.0532***	−0.0532***	−0.0541***
			(0.0281)	(0.0156)	(0.0156)	(0.0157)
lnCR			0.273***	0.170**	0.170**	0.138*
			(0.0710)	(0.0782)	(0.0783)	(0.0783)
lnLR			0.0936	0.332***	0.332***	0.296**
			(0.102)	(0.120)	(0.121)	(0.116)
lnIR			0.149***	0.258***	0.258***	0.274***
			(0.0559)	(0.0838)	(0.0839)	(0.0880)
lnCAT			0.0696	0.0260	0.0260	0.00270
			(0.112)	(0.0522)	(0.0523)	(0.0467)
lnRD			5.776***	1.072	1.072	1.281
			(1.491)	(1.272)	(1.274)	(1.307)
cons	2.121***	2.062***	9.947***	17.45***	17.45***	17.20***
	(0.0323)	(0.0258)	(1.200)	(2.311)	(2.314)	(2.362)
Individual FixedEffects	no	yes	no	yes	yes	yes
Year Fixed Effects	yes	yes	yes	yes	yes	yes
Province Fixed Effects	no	no	no	no	yes	yes
Industry Fixed Effects	no	no	no	no	no	yes
R-squared	0.064	0.613	0.207	0.638	0.638	0.651
Observations	11,736	11,736	11,736	11,736	11,736	11,736

4.3 Mechanism of Effect

Table 3 demonstrates that the implementation of ECRT policies contributes to the improvement of corporate financial performance. To examine the underlying mechanisms, we employ green innovation as a mediating variable while controlling for covariates, individual fixed effects, and year fixed effects. Green innovation is measured by the total number of green patents applied for by enterprises in a given year, including independently and jointly filed invention patents and utility model patents. The specific regression results of the mechanism test are presented in Table 4. Column (1) of Table 4 shows that coefficient γ_1 in Equation (3) is statistically significant, confirming the impact of ECRT on green innovation. Column (2) reports that coefficient δ_2 in Equation (4) is positive and significant ($\delta_2 = 0.0006$), while the coefficient δ_1 of EU maintains the same direction as the direct effect coefficient α_1 in Column (4) of Table 3. However, the direct effect coefficient α_1 is smaller than δ_1 due to a suppression effect. Specifically, ECRT indirectly reduces financial performance by lowering green innovation levels, which partially offsets (suppresses) its direct positive effect on financial performance. After controlling for green innovation, this suppression effect disappears, revealing an enhanced positive impact of ECRT on financial performance.

Table 4. Mediation effect results

Variable	*(1) GP*	*(2) TobinQ*
EU	−3.220**	0.138*
	(1.492)	(0.0799)
GP		0.000639***
		(0.000218)
cons	−242.1***	2.066***
	(72.00)	(0.0180)
R-squared	0.759	0.621
Observations	11,736	11,736

These results validate Hypothesis 2, demonstrating that green innovation serves as a mediating channel through which ECRT enhances corporate financial performance. The mediation effect size is calculated as 0.0145 ($|\gamma_1 * \delta_2|/\delta_1$).

4.4 Heterogeneity Tests

Building upon the aggregate analysis of ECRT's impact on corporate financial performance, we conduct subgroup regressions to examine potential heterogeneity effects.

Table 5. Heterogeneity test on the impact of ECRT policy on corporate financial performance

Variable	*(1a) TobinQ*	*(1b) TobinQ*	*(2a) TobinQ*	*(2b) TobinQ*	*(2c) TobinQ*	*(3a) TobinQ*	*(3b) TobinQ*
EU	−0.0501	0.222**	0.201*	0.0787	0.106	0.291**	0.0885
	(0.190)	(0.0950)	(0.104)	(0.0993)	(0.216)	(0.115)	(0.104)
_cons	33.73**	17.03***	18.33***	14.32***	21.47***	13.01***	20.40***
	(14.77)	(2.107)	(2.753)	(2.995)	(4.517)	(2.435)	(2.859)
Individual Fixed Effects	yes	yes	yes	yes	yes	yes	yes

(continued)

Table 5. *(continued)*

Variable	*(1a) TobinQ*	*(1b) TobinQ*	*(2a) TobinQ*	*(2b) TobinQ*	*(2c) TobinQ*	*(3a) TobinQ*	*(3b) TobinQ*
Year Fixed Effects	yes	yes	yes	yes	yes	yes	yes
Control Variables	yes	yes	yes	yes	yes	yes	yes
R-squared	0.652	0.638	0.615	0.759	0.651	0.698	0.625
Observations	1,205	10,143	8,004	2,085	1,647	3,480	8,202

Ownership Heterogeneity Test. The analysis divides firms into SOEs and non-SOEs based on state ownership. Table 5 (columns 1a–1b) shows non-SOEs achieved a significant 0.222% financial improvement post-policy (supporting Hypothesis 3a), while SOEs showed insignificant negative effects. This divergence reflects SOEs' dual economic-social mandates and institutional support that reduce policy responsiveness, contrasting with non-SOEs' market-driven adaptability which enabled effective strategic adjustments and performance gains under the new policy environment.

Regional Heterogeneity Test. We conducted regional subgroup analysis As shown in Columns (2a)–(2c) of Table 5 the regression results for eastern, central, and western firms demonstrate distinct patterns of policy impact. Table 5 shows eastern firms exhibit significant financial improvement (10% level) from the policy, while central/western firms show no effects (supporting Hypothesis 3b). This disparity reflects eastern China's more developed economic environment and firms' stronger adaptive capacity. Dynamic analysis (Table 5, columns (1)–(3) for eastern, central, and western regions respectively). Dynamic analysis reveals western firms had only a transient effect in 2016 (policy announcement year), whereas eastern firms demonstrated immediate (2017) and sustained benefits, peaking in 2020 (0.353% improvement) and persisting through 2023. These results suggest the policy's effectiveness depends on regional economic conditions and firms' responsiveness (Table 6).

Table 6. Year regression results by region

Variable	*(1) GP*	*(2) TobinQ*
EU	−3.220**	0.138*
	(1.492)	(0.0799)
GP		0.000639***
		(0.000218)
cons	−242.1***	2.066***
	(72.00)	(0.0180)
R-squared	0.759	0.621

(continued)

Table 6. (*continued*)

Variable	*(1) GP*	*(2) TobinQ*
Observations	11,736	11,736

Industry Heterogeneity Test. In accordance with the Benchmark and Baseline Energy Efficiency Levels for Key Industrial Sectors (2023 Edition) policy document and the Guidelines for Industry Classification of Listed Companies (CSRC, 2012), energy-intensive industries (CSRC codes B06-09, C25-32, D44-45) include coal, petroleum, steel, nonferrous metals, chemicals, building materials, and power generation. Table 5 shows significant industry heterogeneity: energy-intensive firms improved financial performance by 0.1529% (1% significance) post-policy, mitigating energy constraint risks, while non-energy-intensive firms showed no significant effects (supporting Hypothesis 3c). This confirms market-based regulations primarily impact energy-dependent sectors with greater mitigation potential.

4.5 Robustness Tests

The Parallel Trends Test. The dynamic effects model tests parallel trends using year-treatment interactions. Excluding 2013 (to avoid multicollinearity), Fig. 2 shows no significant pre-treatment differences before 2016 (period -1). Post-announcement divergence and sustained post-implementation effects confirm parallel trends.

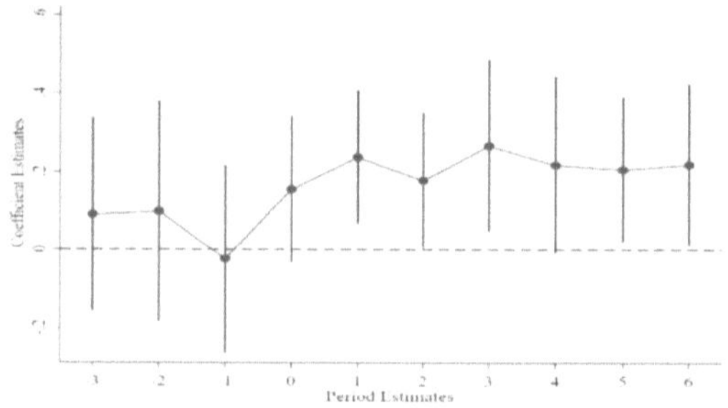

Fig. 2. The Parallel Trends Test Plot

The Placebo Test. Random reassignment (1,000 iterations) excluded confounders. Fig. 3's t-density plot shows simulated coefficients within 10% bounds (dashed), with the actual estimate (solid) as an outlier. Normally distributed p-values near zero (p > 0.035) confirm robustness.

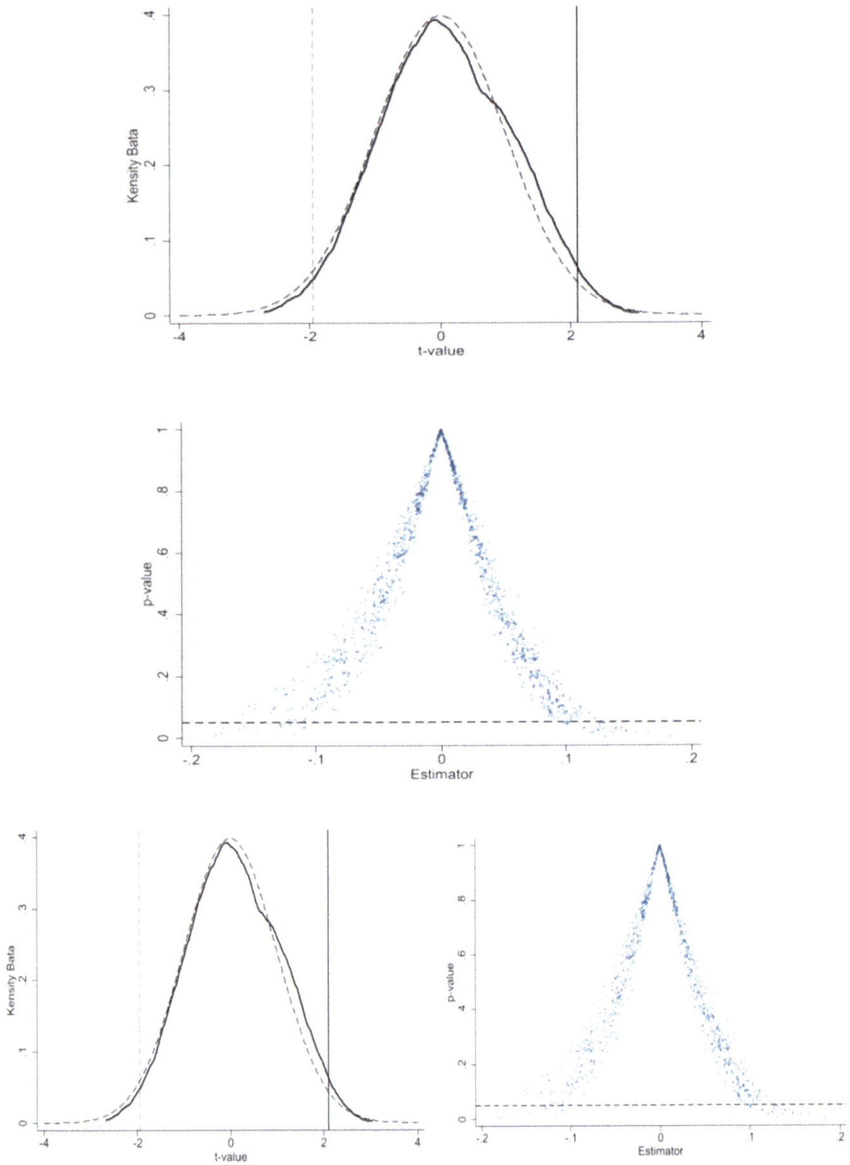

Fig. 3. t- value Kernel Density Plot and p-value Scatter Plot

The Propensity Score Matching Verification. Multiple matching methods (caliper radius, kernel matching) consistently eliminated 86 extreme outliers outside common support regions (Fig. 4). The materially equivalent results across all three approaches demonstrate methodological robustness.

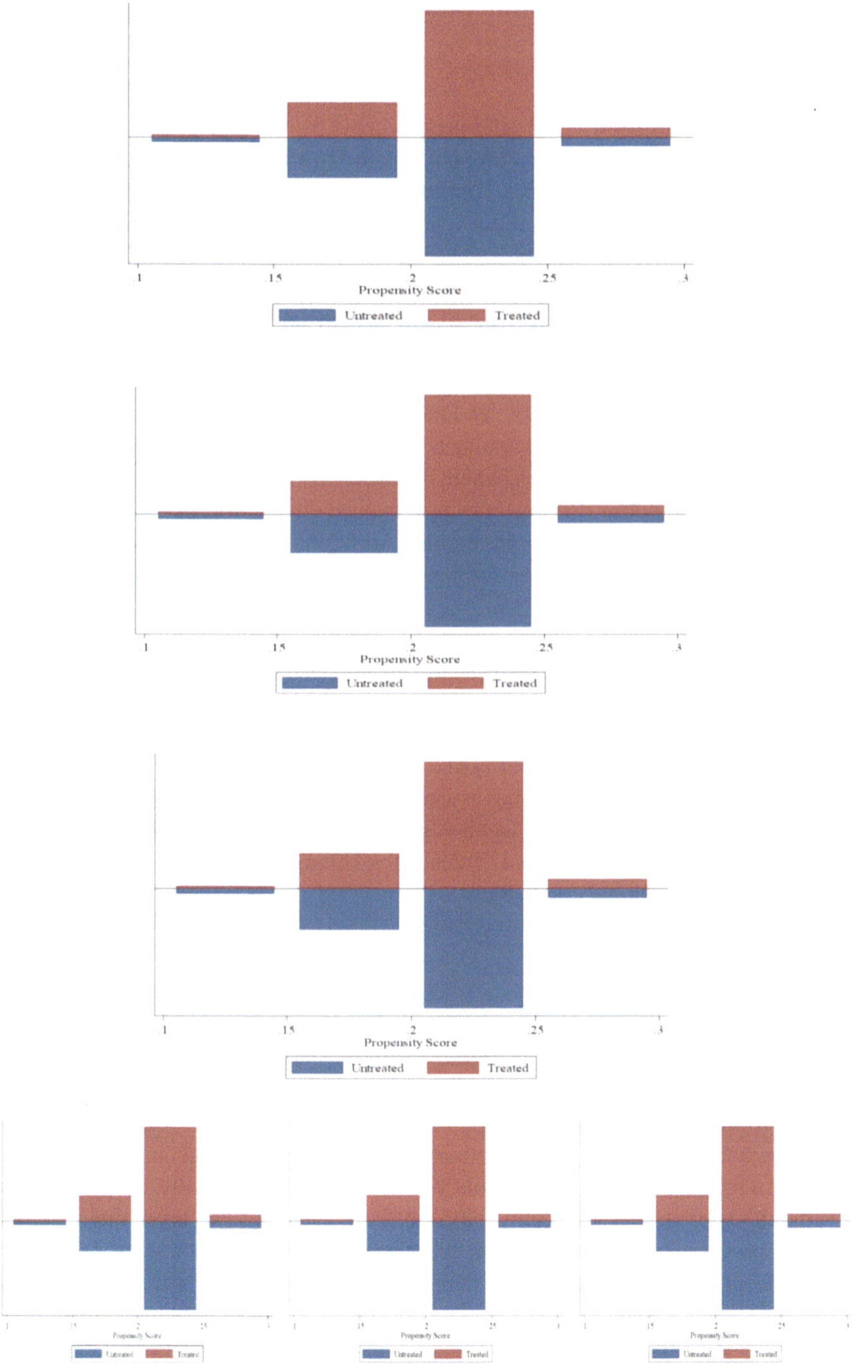

Fig. 4. Comparison of Matching Results: Caliper Nearest Neighbor, Caliper Radius, and Kernel Matching

5 Conclusions and Recommendations

5.1 Conclusions

Based on panel data from 1,973 enterprises across 31 Chinese provinces from 2013 to 2023, this study employs the PSM-DID method to examine the impact of ECRT on corporate financial performance. The main findings are as follows: (1) The implementation of ECRT policies has a positive effect on corporate financial performance, increasing it by an average of 0.168%. The regression results are robust. (2) Mechanism tests reveal a masking effect in the "ECRT–green innovation–corporate financial performance" pathway. Specifically, while ECRT directly improves financial performance, this effect is partially offset by its indirect suppression of green innovation, leading to a slight attenuation of the overall impact. (3) Heterogeneity analysis indicates that corporate ownership, geographic location, and industry type significantly influence the financial incentives of ECRT. Notably, non-state-owned enterprises exhibit marked financial improvement post-implementation, whereas state-owned enterprises remain unaffected. Geographically, the policy demonstrates pronounced effects in eastern China but negligible impacts in central and western regions. Additionally, energy-intensive industries experience significant financial performance gains, while non-energy-intensive firms show no improvement.

This study makes dual contributions to the literature. Methodologically, it addresses the scarcity of micro-level evidence by analyzing post-2017 pilot data from actual market participants (enterprises), overcoming the macro-level focus and data recency limitations in existing research. Theoretically, it pioneers the investigation of financial performance impacts—a dimension largely overlooked in prior policy evaluations predominantly focused on environmental outcomes—while elucidating the synergistic mechanisms between energy conservation and technological innovation pathways. The heterogeneity analyses further provide nuanced evidence for differential policy effectiveness across organizational and regional contexts.

5.2 Recommendations

The above findings provide theoretical support for the further implementation of ECRT and corporate strategic adjustments. Based on this, we propose the following managerial recommendations: (1) For government authorities, it is essential to deepen the implementation of ECRT, expand its coverage, and explore synergies with other environmental regulation policies. Regional coordination between eastern, central, and western China should also be considered to ensure policy flexibility and adaptability, avoiding a "one-size-fits-all" approach. Additionally, targeted fiscal subsidies and economic incentives should be provided to mitigate potential negative financial impacts on state-owned enterprises, encourage participation from non-energy-intensive firms, and stimulate green innovation to enhance corporate confidence. Moreover, the successful implementation of ECRT offers a "China solution" to global environmental challenges. (2) For enterprises, amid China's increasingly stringent energy regulations, firms should proactively support the development of the ECRT market and actively participate in it, turning challenges into opportunities. Strategies include adjusting business plans in response to policy shifts, exploring green sectors, developing eco-friendly products, upgrading energy-efficient production lines, and enhancing corporate image to attract consumers and investors. By optimizing industrial structure, firms can improve financial performance. Furthermore, enterprises should engage constructively with policymakers, providing feedback based on their operational needs.

This study provides a detailed analysis of the impact of ECRT on corporate financial performance. However, since the policy was launched in 2017 and currently covers only four provinces (Zhejiang, Fujian, Henan, and Sichuan), the sample data have limitations in both time span and geographic scope. The study did not distinguish between pilot and non-pilot firms in the trial regions, which could be explored in future research. Additionally, the sample selection was restricted to A-share listed companies, which, while simplifying data collection, may introduce selection bias by excluding non-listed firms. Furthermore, given the coexistence of multiple environmental regulations in practice, the synergistic effects between ECRT and other policies warrant further investigation.

References

1. Zhu, G., Zhang, S.: Ecological Civilization Construction Dictionary, vol. 1, pp. 466–67. Jiangxi Science & Technology Press, Nanchang (2016)
2. Yang, S., Wang, C., Zhang, H., Lu, T., Yi, Y.: Environmental regulation, firms' bargaining power, and firms' total factor productivity: evidence from China. Environ. Sci. Pollut. Res. **29**(6), 9341–9353 (2022)
3. Zheng, C., Zhang, Y., Chen, K.: Corporate innovation and capacity utilization in China's coastal areas: governance under the context of environmental regulation. J. Coast. Res. **109**(SI), 197–205 (2020)
4. Fabrizi, A., Gentile, M., Guarini, G., Meliciani, V.: The impact of environmental regulation on innovation and international competitiveness. J. Evol. Econ. **34**(1), 169–204 (2024)
5. Yu, H., Lyu, Q., Jiang, Y.: Environmental Regulation, regional finance development and enterprises' cross-regional capital flow. Int. Rev. Econ. Financ. **99**, 103984 (2025)
6. Li, M., Dong, L., Luan, J., Wang, P.: Do environmental regulations affect investors? Evidence from China's action plan for air pollution prevention. J. Clean. Prod. **244**, 118817 (2020)
7. Fang, J., Liu, C., Gao, C.: The impact of environmental regulation on firm exports: evidence from environmental information disclosure policy in China. Environ. Sci. Pollut. Res. **26**(36), 37101–37113 (2019)
8. Wang, Q., Xu, X., Liang, K.: The impact of environmental regulation on firm performance: evidence from the Chinese cement industry. J. Environ. Manag. **299**, 113596 (2021)
9. Pang, R., Shi, M., Zheng, D.: Who comply better? The moderating role of firm heterogeneity on the performance of environmental regulation in China. Environ. Dev. Sustainabil. **24**(5), 6302–6326 (2022)
10. Fang, J., Gao, C., Lai, M.: Environmental regulation and firm innovation: evidence from National Specially Monitored Firms program in China. J. Clean. Prod. **271**, 122599 (2020)
11. Yang, M., Yuan, Y., Yang, F., Echeverri, D.: Effects of environmental regulation on firm entry and exit and China's industrial productivity: a new perspective on the Porter Hypothesis. Environ. Econ. Policy Stud. **23**, 915–944 (2021)
12. Chen, L.: Research on the value compensation effect of environmental regulation on enterprises: a comparison based on different environmental regulation tools. Contemp. Econ. **11**, 114–119 (2021)

13. Zhang, A., Li, X., Jin, J., Wu, W., Yang, X.: Environmental regulation, agency costs and corporate performance: empirical evidence from listed companies in the chemical industry. Account. Res. **08**, 83–93 (2021)
14. Zhao, X., Zhao, Y., Zeng, S., Zhang, S.: Corporate behavior and competitiveness: impact of environmental regulation on Chinese firms. J. Clean. Prod. **86**, 311–322 (2015)
15. Zhang, N., Zhang, W.: Can China's energy-consuming rights trading achieve a win-win situation for economic dividends and energy conservation? Econ. Res. J. **54**(01), 165–181 (2019)
16. Zhou, H.: Examining and breaking through the legal supervision system of energy-consuming rights trading from the perspective of 'Responsive Law'. J. Gansu Univ. Polit. Sci. Law (03), 92-99+123 (2019)
17. Wang, X.: The implementation path of energy-consuming rights trading system from the perspective of legal policy. J. Henan Univ. Technol. (Soc. Sci. Ed.) **37**(05), 44–51+93 (2021)
18. Hu, N., Pei, Q.: Improving the energy-consuming rights trading system to promote energy efficiency. Macroecon. Manag. **12**, 43–49 (2020)
19. Wang, X.: Exploration of energy-consuming rights trading mechanism in environmental rights markets. Sci. Technol. Innov. Prod. (02), 1–3+7 (2021)
20. Zhao, Q.: Research on China's Legal System of Energy Use Rights. Beijing Institute of Technology (2017)
21. Chen, Z.F.: Coordinated use of energy consumption tax and energy-consuming rights trading system. Res. Sci. **41**(12), 2205–2215 (2019)
22. Yao, Q.: Comparative Analysis and Policy Recommendations on Energy Tax and Energy-Consuming Rights Trading. Jiangxi University of Finance and Economics (2018).
23. Liu, M.: On the institutional coordination dimension of building China's energy-consuming rights trading system. China Popul. Res. Environ. **27**(10), 217–224 (2017)
24. Li, Y., Zhu, L.: Synergistic effects of energy-consuming rights trading and carbon markets: strategic research on high-energy-consumption industries. Indu. Technol. Econ. **38**(07), 136–142 (2019)
25. Bi, J.: Constructing a linkage mechanism between energy use rights and carbon emission rights. Legal Person **05**, 33–35 (2021)
26. Wang, B., Lai, P., Du, M.: Can the energy-consuming rights trading system achieve "Dual Control" of total energy consumption and intensity?. China Popul. Res. Environ. **1** (2019)
27. Liu, H., Wang, Y.: Economic dividend effects under the policy combination of tradable energy use rights and carbon emission rights. China Popul. Resour. Environ. **29**(05), 1–10 (2019)
28. Zhang, Y., Guo, S., Shi, X., Qian, X., Nie, R.: A market instrument to achieve carbon neutrality: is China's energy-consumption permit trading scheme effective? Appl. Energy **299**, 117338 (2021)
29. Li, S., Zhao, C.: The driving effect of energy-consuming rights trading system on corporate low-carbon technological innovation. China Popul. Res. Environ. **33**(10), 124–134 (2023)
30. Zhou, W., Tao, L.: Regional heterogeneity of environmental regulation's impact on China's labor employment: an empirical test based on industrial structure threshold effects. West. Forum **30**(01), 100–110 (2020)
31. Hu, Z., Li, Y.: Environmental regulation and China's industrial green technology efficiency: empirical evidence from provincial panel data. J. Hunan Univ. (Soc. Sci. Ed.) **31**(05), 42–48 (2017)
32. Xuan, D., Ma, X., Shang, Y.: Can China's policy of carbon emission trading promote carbon emission reduction? J. Clean. Prod. **270**, 122383 (2020)
33. Liu, M., Zhou, C., Lu, F., Hu, X.: Impact of the implementation of carbon emission trading on corporate financial performance: evidence from listed companies in China. PLoS ONE **16**(7), e0253460 (2021)

34. Brouwers, R., Schoubben, F., Van Hulle, C., Uytbergen, S.: The initial impact of EU ETS verification events on stock prices. Energy Policy **94**, 138–149 (2016)
35. Gallego-Álvarez, I., Segura, L., Martínez-Ferrero, J.: Carbon emission reduction: the impact on the financial and operational performance of international companies. J. Clean. Prod. **103**, 149–159 (2015)
36. Zhou, L., Cao, C.: The hybrid drive effects of green innovation in Chinese coal enterprises: an empirical study. Kybernetes (2019)
37. Liu, C., Fang, J., Xie, R.: Energy policy and corporate financial performance: evidence from China's 11th five-year plan. Energy Econ. **93**, 105030 (2021)
38. Jiao, J., Zhang, X., Tang, Y.: What factors determine the survival of green innovative enterprises in China?–a method based on fsQCA. Technol. Soc. **62**, 101314 (2020)
39. Zhao, S., Zhang, B., Shao, D., Wang, S.: Can Top management teams' academic experience promote green innovation output: evidence from Chinese enterprises. Sustainability **13**(20), 11453 (2021)
40. Gong, M., Dai, A.: Multiparty evolutionary game strategy for green technology innovation under market orientation and pandemics. Front. Public Health **9** (2021)
41. Yu, C., Wu, X., Zhang, D., Chen, S., Zhao, J.: Demand for green finance: resolving financing constraints on green innovation in China. Energy Policy **153**, 112255 (2021)
42. Xie, Q., Zhang, Y., Chen, L.: Does green credit policy promote innovation: a case of China. Manag. Decis. Econ. (2022)
43. Liao, Z., Xu, C., Cheng, H., Dong, J.: What drives environmental innovation? A content analysis of listed companies in China. J. Clean. Prod. **198**, 1567–1573 (2018)
44. Yu, X., Xu, Y., Sun, M., Zhang, Y.: The green-innovation-inducing effect of a unit progressive carbon tax. Sustainability **13**(21), 11708 (2021)
45. Zhang, Y., Liu, J.: Does carbon emissions trading affect the financial performance of high energy-consuming firms in China? Nat. Hazards **95**(1), 91–111 (2019)
46. Qin, Y., Sun, L., Feng, X.: Impact of the 'Belt and Road' initiative on financial performance of construction enterprises: a PSM-DID approach. J. Beijing Univ. Civil Eng. Arch. **37**(03), 86–93 (2021)
47. Muhammad, N., Scrimgeour, F., Reddy, K., Abidin, S.: The relationship between environmental performance and financial performance in periods of growth and contraction: evidence from Australian publicly listed companies. J. Clean. Prod. **102**, 324–332 (2015)
48. Akbar, A., Jiang, X., Qureshi, M., Akbar, M.: Does corporate environmental investment impede financial performance of Chinese enterprises? The moderating role of financial constraints. Environ. Sci. Pollut. Res. **28**(41), 58007–58017 (2021)
49. Zhang, Y., Wang, W.: How does China's carbon emissions trading (CET) policy affect the investment of CET-covered enterprises? Energy Econ. **98**, 105224 (2021)
50. Baron, R.M., Kenny, D.A.: The moderator–mediator variable distinction in social psychological research: conceptual, strategic, and statistical considerations. J. Pers. Soc. Psychol. **51**(6), 1173 (1986)
51. Wen, Z., Ye, B.: Mediation effect analysis: methods and model development. Adv. Psychol. Sci. **22**(05), 731–745 (2014)
52. Qi, B., Du, Y., Sun, Z.: Capital market liberalization and corporate tax avoidance: a quasi-natural experiment based on Shanghai-Hong Kong and Shenzhen-Hong Kong stock connect. Finan. Trade Res. **32**(08), 82–98 (2021)
53. Ai, X., Hao, L., Li, G.: The impact of financial knowledge on urban and rural residents' entrepreneurial activities: empirical analysis based on CHFS data. J. Hunan Univ. Sci. Technol. (Soc. Sci. Ed.) **24**(02), 71–79 (2021)
54. Tang, K., Liu, Y., Zhou, D., Qiu, Y.: Urban carbon emission intensity under emission trading system in a developing economy: evidence from 273 Chinese cities. Environ. Sci. Pollut. Res. **28**(5), 5168–5179 (2021)

55. Shen, J., Tang, P., Zeng, H.: Does China's carbon emission trading reduce carbon emissions? Evidence from listed firms. Energy Sustain. Dev. **59**, 120–129 (2020)
56. Chen, S., Shi, A., Wang, X.: Carbon emission curbing effects and influencing mechanisms of China's emission trading scheme: the mediating roles of technique effect, composition effect and allocation effect. J. Clean. Prod. **264**, 121700 (2020)

Design and Improvement of Vibration Tooling Based on Finite Element Analysis

Lijuan Cai, Bin Zhou, Jiazhen Zhang(✉), Jiaxi Lu, and Xiaotian Zhu

Shanghai Aerospace Control Technology Institute, Shanghai 201109, China
wkdxzsw@163.com

Abstract. In the vibration test of large volume tooling, due to different product types and uses, the size is also different, in order to further improve the design level of tooling fixture, improve its performance, on the basis of the use of finite element analysis, through the use of ANSYS software, the designed tooling fixture is analyzed, and the natural frequency of the fixture is determined. To meet the relevant standards and requirements of enhanced vibration test. The results show that the proposed vibration test method effectively verifies the validity and reliability of fixture simulation, and provides valuable engineering data for the later scientific design of fixture.

Keywords: ANSYS · Simulation · Tooling · Design

1 Introduction

Vibration tool is a kind of process equipment used to connect the vibration table with the product to be shaken, and transfer the vibration of the vibration table to the product to be shaken. Its performance directly affects the authenticity and reliability of the vibration test. In order to transfer the motion and energy of the shaking table to the product without distortion, the shaking table must not only have good strength and stiffness, but also have a high natural frequency. If the vibration tooling is not designed properly, the tooling itself will resonate in the range of test frequency, which will cause the product to bear undue load and destroy, and the test will get wrong results. Therefore, the reasonable design of large-scale vibration tooling is an extremely important work in the process of product structure development.

2 General Requirements for Vibration Tooling Design

2.1 Fixture Design Requirements

The fixture designed in this paper is mainly used for the later vibration test. The excitation source used in the whole test presents a random vibration state and carries out random vibration along the vertical and horizontal directions. During the vibration test, the

M. Li et al. (Eds.): ICLS 2025, *Proceeding of the 19th International Congress on Logistics and Supply Chain Management Systems*, pp. 67–76, 2026.
https://doi.org/10.1007/978-981-95-7700-2_6

test profile is mainly composed of two sections, namely magnitude profile and spectral density profile. Among them, magnitude profile is a typical stepping stress profile, and its magnitude value gradually increases from low to high. When the extreme magnitude of the shaking table is reached, its magnitude stops increasing, so the vibration intensity is generally high. In addition, the stress spectral density profile usually shows a high broadband characteristic, which can quickly find and deal with more sensitive fuze defects, so during the setting of the frequency range of the motor station, it is necessary to set its range between 5 Hz and 3 000 Hz along the vertical direction, along the horizontal direction. Set the value range to 5 Hz to 2000 Hz [1].

In addition, it is necessary to carry out a scientific and standardized design of the fixture in strict accordance with the following fixture design requirements [2]: ① Each connection point corresponding to the fixture and the connecting surface must maintain the same response speed, so that the excitation input corresponding to the test shows high stability and uniformity. ② To improve the rigidity of the fixture as much as possible to ensure that it can withstand high vibration strength. ③ During the actual movement of the fixture, it is necessary to ensure its stability along the transverse motion amplitude. ④ When the fixture and the specimen are installed and fixed on the vibration test bench at the same time, it is necessary to ensure that the distance between the vibration table and the fixture is minimized, so that the center of gravity of the fixture becomes lower and lower, so as to ensure the stability and reliability of the fixture. ⑤ The damping of the fixture should be as large as possible, and the degree of waveform distortion should be as small as possible. ⑥ To ensure that the designed fixture has stable mechanical properties, it is necessary to strictly simulate the current installation effect of the specimen in accordance with the requirements for the use of the specimen. At the same time, it is necessary to scientifically control the center of gravity position of the fixture in strict accordance with the installation and fixing steps of the vibration test equipment. In addition, it is necessary to ensure that the designed fixture shows a certain versatility, easy processing, economy and other characteristics. ⑦ When controlling the quality of the fixture, it is necessary to reduce the quality of the fixture as much as possible on the basis of meeting the vibration test conditions to ensure that it shows the characteristics of light quality. In short, in order to further improve the design level and effect of fixtures, designers must strictly follow the above design principles to improve the performance of fixtures.

2.2 Fixture Material Selection

At present, the more commonly used fixture materials mainly include the following: ① Aluminum: Aluminum usually shows a small density of high stiffness, stable performance and other characteristics, the material is widely used in fixtures, and has achieved good application results. ② Steel: Steel shows a high density and quality, but its damping is relatively small, resulting in the steel fixture corresponding to the natural frequency is generally low, does not meet the high frequency fixture design requirements [3, 4]. ③Magnesium material: Magnesium material shows the characteristics of light weight, large damping, simple welding, etc., can produce more high-quality fixture materials, but magnesium material has a certain flammability, therefore, it can not be used in the production of fixture. Through comprehensive comparison and analysis of the characteristics of fixture materials, the LY12 aluminum alloy material is set as the fixture manufacturing material. The characteristics of LY12 aluminum alloy material are shown in Table 1.

Table 1. Characteristics of LY12 aluminum alloy material

Item	Parameter value
Modulus of elasticity	7.2×1010 N·m^{-2}
Poisson's ratio	0.34
Density	2700 kg·m^{-3}

2.3 Fixture Preliminary Design

On the basis of fully combining the appearance characteristics of fixture, in strict accordance with the relevant standards and requirements of fixture design, using SolidWorks software, the three-dimensional diagram of fixture is preliminarily designed, and the three-dimensional diagram of fixture is shown in Fig. 1.

Fig. 1. A 3D graphics of fixture

The preliminary design principles of the fixture are as follows: (1) The symmetrical design of the fixture is preferred in the fixture design; (2) the center of gravity of the fixture is reduced to a minimum; (3) The shaking table can be safely and reliably transferred to the fixture. The fixture can be effectively and stably connected with the shaking table by using hex screws, and the corresponding threaded holes are set in the middle to ensure the connection between the fixture and the shaking table. By setting the fixture in this structure, the center of gravity of the fixture in the whole test can be reduced to ensure that the fixture exhibits stable frequency response characteristics and good lateral movement [5].

3 Finite Element Analysis Method Based on ANSYS

3.1 ANSYS Modal Analysis

3.1.1 Meshing

During the vertical random vibration of the tool, the fixture can be combined to obtain the series spring property, and during the horizontal random vibration, the fixture can obtain the parallel spring property. During the modal analysis of fixture using subspace iterative method, once the fixture cannot meet the relevant standards and requirements, it needs to be improved, and then the modal analysis of the improved fixture is carried out. Because the fixture entity usually shows a certain simplicity, so by using tetrahedral units, the scientific division of the fixture can be achieved, so as to fully understand and grasp the actual situation of the physical model, at the same time, but also to ensure the simplicity of the calculation process. In the process of division, there are many lines and surfaces in the structure, which is difficult to control, so the intelligent grid division method is adopted in the tooling structure. The fixture structure diagram after grid division is shown in Fig. 2.

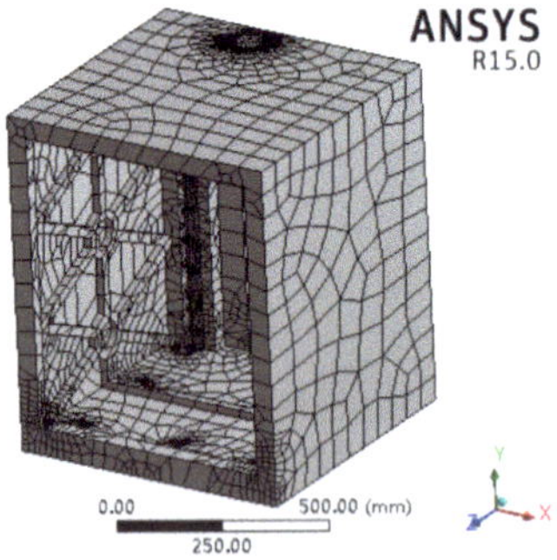

Fig. 2. Finite element mesh model of fixture

3.1.2 Imposed Boundary Condition

Tooling plays a connecting role in the process of use. During the analysis of its structure, a rigid connection is formed between the tooling and the workbench through eight bolts in a circumferential direction. If the contact deformation between the tooling and the workbench is ignored, and the influence of damping and inertia is not considered, then the bolted joint surface of the tooling structure can be considered as a full constraint. At this time, the boundary conditions of tooling structure constraints are shown in Fig. 3.

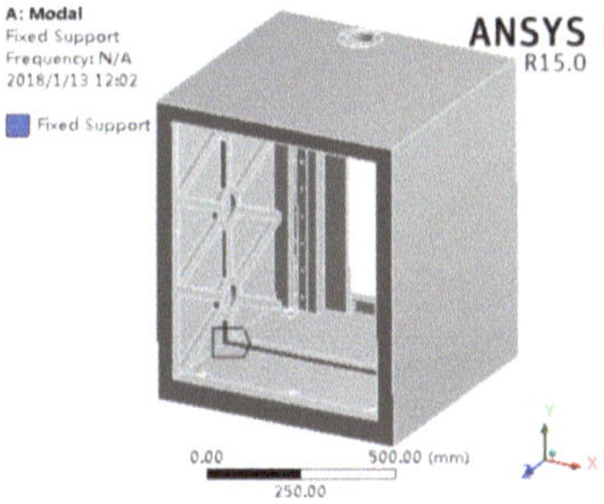

Fig. 3. Constrained boundary conditions of tooling

3.1.3 Modal Analysis Results

During the modal analysis of the tool, only the dynamic characteristics of the lower-order modes of the tool structure are still selected, that is, the first 6 order dynamic characteristics of the structure are still selected. Figure 4 is the first 6 modal modes of the tool structure studied in this topic, and Table 2 is the tool simulation natural vibration frequency of the tool structure.

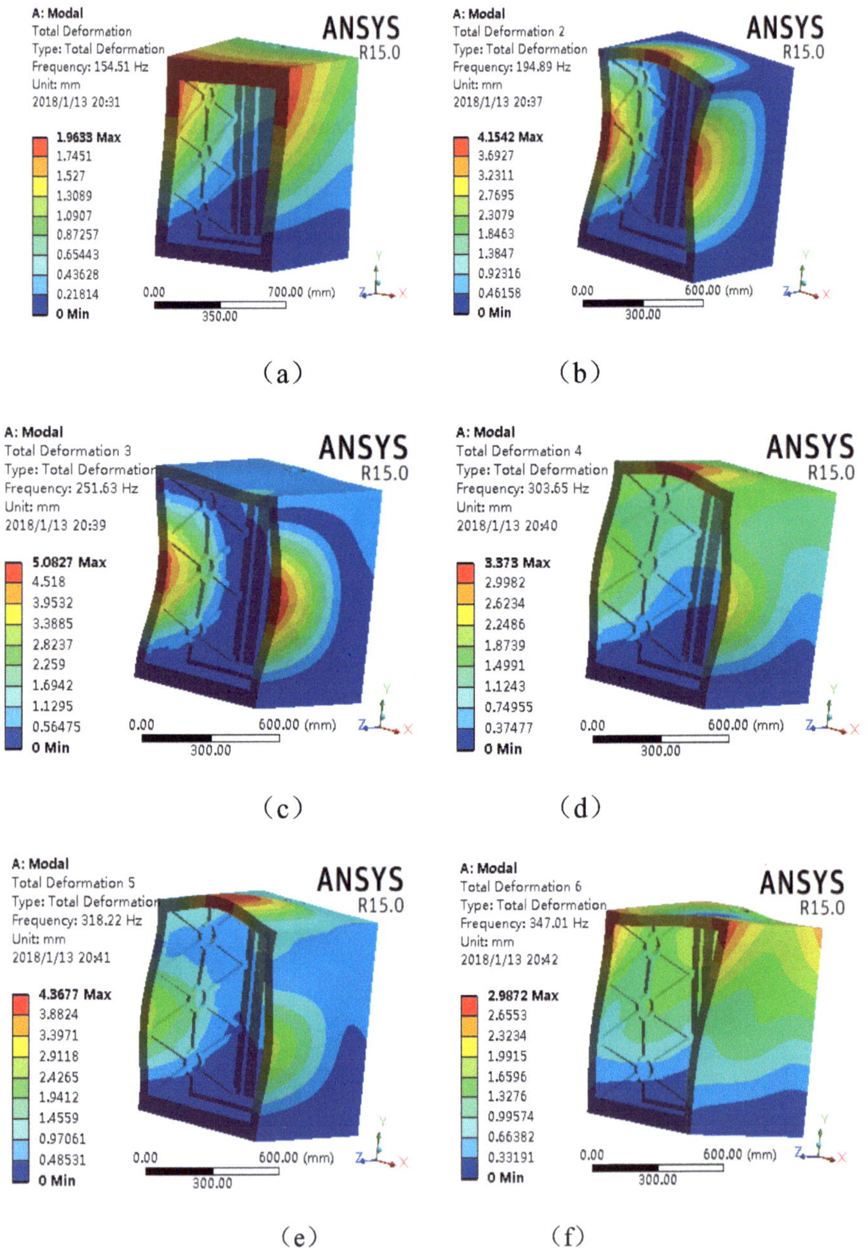

Fig. 4. Deformation cloud image of the first 6 modes (a) 1st order mode cloud image (b) 2nd order mode cloud image (c) 3rd order mode cloud image (d) 4th order mode cloud image (e) 5th order mode cloud image (f) 6th order mode cloud image

Table 2. Tool simulation of natural vibration frequency

Rank	Vertical vibration direction/Hz	Horizontal vibration direction/Hz
1	4165	4365
2	4197	6109
3	6278	6602

It can be seen from the data in Table 2 that through the modal analysis of the fixture using ANSYS software, it can be found that the designed fixture can not meet the relevant standards and requirements of vibration test. Therefore, it is necessary to improve the frame structure and the layout of the stiffened plates to further improve the rigidity and stability of the structure.

4 Redesign of Vibration Fixture

In order to improve the shortcomings of the stiffness and stability of the tooling structure, the layout form of the tooling structure and the dimensional change of the thickness of the tooling were optimized under the premise that the overall dimension of the tooling was basically unchanged, and the influence of various layout forms of the tooling and the dimensional change of the tooling structure was analyzed. It provides a good foundation for the further optimization design of tooling structure. In modal analysis, the entire dynamic performance of the tooling structure depends on the low-order modal dynamic characteristics of the structure. Therefore, in the optimization scheme of the tooling structure, the first six natural frequencies of the tooling structure are still selected as the optimization target. The structural optimization scheme made by changing the reinforcement layout form of the tooling structure is as follows: (a), (b), (c), (I), (II), (III), etc. The specific reinforcement layout is shown in Fig. 5.

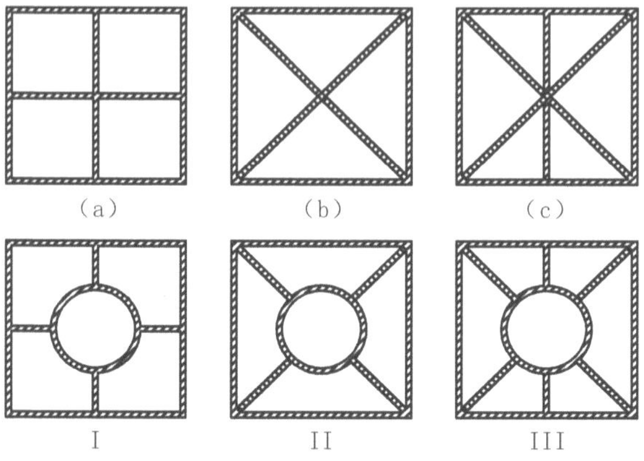

Fig. 5. Six different rib layouts

In the tooling structure, the natural frequency of the tooling structure can be affected to different degrees by using the above six kinds of reinforcement layout. Based on the analysis and comparison of the above six optimization schemes, this optimization scheme selects a better reinforcement layout form. The influence of the above six different reinforcement layout forms on the vibration modes of the column structure is shown in Fig. 6 below.

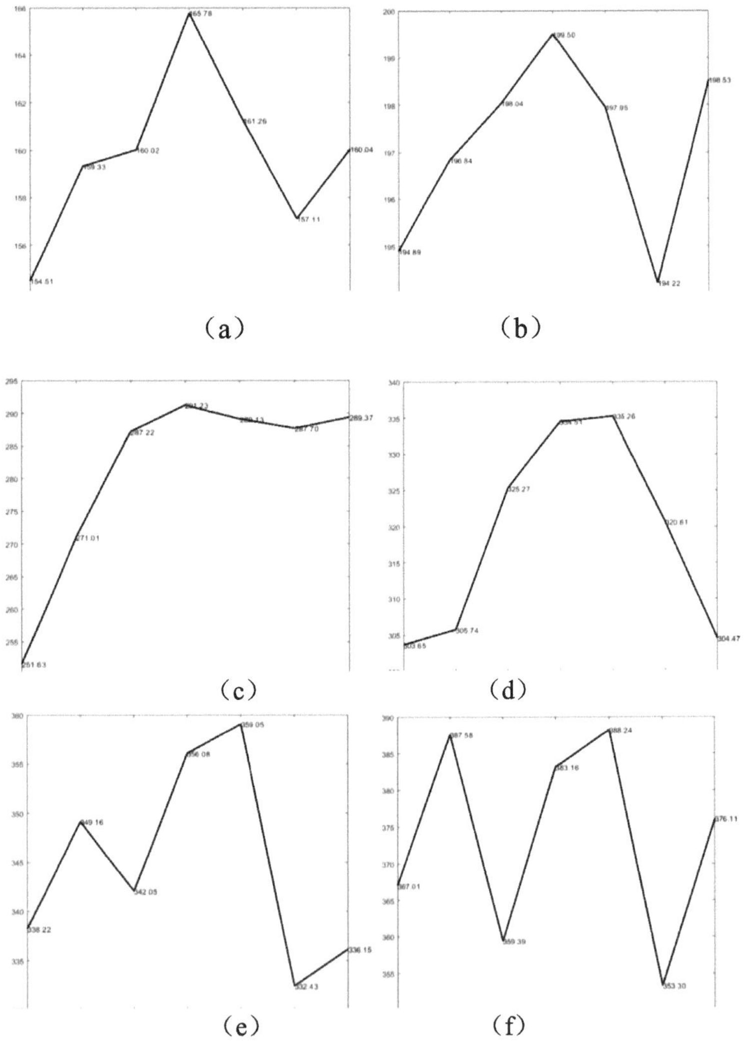

Fig. 6. Line chart of the influence of different reinforcement layout on each order mode (a) Line diagram of the 1st mode (b) Line diagram of the 2nd mode (c) Line diagram of the 3rd mode (d) Line diagram of the 4th mode (e) Line diagram of the 5th mode (f) Line diagram of the 6th mode

The higher the natural frequency of the tool structure, the better the dynamic stiffness. As can be seen from Fig. 6: In the tooling structure, if the "(c)" reinforcement plate is used in the first 3 orders of natural frequency, it is much better than the other forms of reinforcement plate, but the "(I)" reinforcement plate is much better than the other forms of reinforcement plate in the last 3 orders of natural frequency. In the design and optimization of tooling structure, it is only necessary to pay attention to the first 3 modes of its structure, so the layout form of "(c)" in the six different reinforcement layout forms should be used as the basis for further analysis and optimization of tooling structure.

In addition, there are many factors that lead to the resonance phenomenon, mainly the fixture itself, the shaking table moving ring, the test piece and the connection between the various parts. Under the existing conditions, in order to successfully complete the high frequency vibration test, it can only be solved by increasing the natural frequency of the specimen. The main factors affecting the natural frequency of the specimen are the material of the manufacturing fixture, the weight of the fixture, the rigidity of the fixture, the connection form of the fixture and the moving coil, etc. Their effects on the natural frequency are as follows [6–8]:

a. During vibration, if the excitation frequency increases, then the system no longer moves like an object, and some parts begin to show resonance amplification. The smaller the damping, the higher the resonance amplification value; conversely, the larger the damping, the lower the resonance amplification value. Aluminum and magnesium have better damping characteristics than steel.
b. The previous fixture structure is a semi-cavity fixture, which has the advantages of simple structure and low cost, but in the vibration process, the vertical plate is easy to resonate at some vibration frequencies, and the center of gravity of the fixture is difficult to maintain consistency with the center of the product, according to the clamping characteristics, the use of the back fixture structure is more suitable for vibration requirements. In addition to the advantages of simple structure and low cost, it can also effectively avoid the shortcomings of tooling fixtures;
c. In order to enhance the stiffness of the fixture and avoid bolt resonance, the tightness of the connection between them should be ensured, and the relative movement between the fixture will not be generated during the vibration process, so the number of connecting bolts between the fixture should be increased as much as possible, if possible, the stiffness of the bolt should also be calculated to be less than the stiffness required to limit the rotation of the rigid body. The compression of the fixture should be greater than the elongation of the bolt [9, 10].

According to the above vibration theory and the requirements of the tooling, we have improved the structure of the tooling, replaced the tooling material, and redesigned the tooling fixture. After the tooling is produced, in order to obtain more test data and accumulate data and experience for the future tooling fixture design, We used the data collector DSP for product testing to compare the natural frequencies of new and old vibration fixtures and found that: The natural frequency of the old vibration fixture is about 3000 Hz, and the controller is more difficult to control the vibration, the new vibration fixture natural frequency is 9300 Hz, the controller is easier to control the vibration, that is, theoretically speaking, the new tooling can meet the requirements of high-frequency vibration, when re-conducting high-frequency vibration test, in order to be careful, First of all, the no-load test of the fixture was carried out, and the vibration test was successfully completed. Then, the product was installed on the fixture, and the vibration was simulated in the actual condition.

5 Conclusion

In summary, ANSYS software is used to carry out modal analysis of the designed fixture, and the natural frequency of the fixture is calculated, and the reliability and effectiveness of the simulation of the fixture is verified by test. The results show that the validity and reliability of the final calculation results can be guaranteed by using finite element analysis. In addition, through the use of finite element software, the simulation of the fixture after design or before production can effectively improve and optimize the structure and materials of the fixture to ensure that the fixture meets the relevant performance requirements, so as to obtain the best design scheme, in order to shorten the purpose of the fixture design cycle.

References

1. Zheng, S., Chang, S.: Vibration test fixture design research. Reliabil. Design Process Control **24**(5), 146–217 (2016)
2. Wang, D., Ren, W., Liu, Q.: Vibration test fixture resonance frequency set Requirement study. Spacecraft Environ. Eng. **35**(1), 11–16 (2017)
3. Xiong, W.: Design and natural frequency analysis of a large-size LCD vibration test tool. Environ. Technol. **37**(6), 181–184 (2019)
4. Wu, W., Qin, Y., Xu, G.: Analysis of influence of complex vibration tooling design on test. Environ. Technol. **35**(1), 11–16 (2017)
5. Sun, X., Yang, Z., Peng, Z.: Application of ANSYS software in thermal cell random vibration tooling design. Power Technol. **44**(1), 132–134 (2020)
6. Siciliano, B., Sciavicco, L., Villani, L., et al.: Robotics: modelling, planning and control. Adv. Textb. Control Signal Process. **4**(12), 76–82 (2019)
7. Hefei. The Concept and Techniques of Network Numerical Control System. China Mechanical Engineering, pp. 12–14 (2021)
8. Dexter, R.J.: The finite element method: linear static and dynamic finite element analysis by Thomas J. R. Hughes. Religion **6**(2), 222 (2020)
9. Williamson, M.P.: Finite-element analysis. Comput.-Aided Eng. J. **2**(2), 66–69 (2021)
10. Malkin, S.: Grinding Technology: Theory and Applications of Machining with Abrasives. Halsted Press, E. Horwood (2019)

Low-Altitude Logistics with Physical Internet

Shenle Pan(✉)

Centre for Management Science, I3 - UMR CNRS 9217, PSL University, Mines Paris, 60 Boulevard Saint-Michel, Paris, France
shenle.pan@minesparis.psl.eu

Abstract. This paper explores the integration of Low-Altitude Logistics (LAL), primarily enabled by drones and unmanned aerial vehicles (UAVs), within the Physical Internet (PI) paradigm to address the evolving demands of city logistics. LAL offers rapid and flexible last-mile delivery capabilities, while PI aims to restructure logistics networks through modularity, openness, and hyperconnectivity. Although both concepts have garnered increasing attention independently, their combined application remains underexplored. Based on recent literature, this study identifies the operational, regulatory, and infrastructural challenges involved in deploying delivery drones and evaluates how PI principles and key components, such as PI-containers, PI-hubs, and PI-routing protocols, can mitigate these barriers. Several use cases and implementation scenarios are presented to illustrate how PI-based infrastructure can facilitate the effective integration of drones and strengthen the resilience of urban logistics networks. The paper concludes by emphasizing the need for further research on the deployment strategies, digital infrastructure, and policy frameworks required to support this convergence.

Keywords: low-altitude economy · low-altitude logistics · logistics operations · physical internet · smart cities · sustainability

1 Introduction

The Low-Altitude Economy refers to the economic activities that occur in the lower airspace (e.g., below 1,000 m) utilizing low-altitude airspace resources through technologies like aerial drones and unmanned aerial vehicles (UAVs) (hereafter referred to simply as drones since ground-based drones are outside the scope of this paper [1]), electric vertical take-off and landing (eVTOL) aircraft, low-altitude air mobility systems, for various applications like rescues, inspections, surveys, and delivery of goods and passengers [2]. It represents a new frontier in integrating airspace with economic and commercial use. According to the Ministry of Transport of China[1], the scale of China's Low-Altitude Economy market is expected to reach 1.5 trillion RMB by 2025 and is likely to reach 3.5 trillion RMB by 2035. Logistics applications are expected to play a significant role in this market.

[1] www.mot.gov.cn/jiaotongyaowen/202503/t20250306_4165146.html

M. Li et al. (Eds.): ICLS 2025, *Proceeding of the 19th International Congress on Logistics and Supply Chain Management Systems*, pp. 77–88, 2026.
https://doi.org/10.1007/978-981-95-7700-2_7

For city logistics operations, the increasing demand for rapid, eco-efficient, and flexible delivery systems in both urban and rural areas is accelerating the application of low-altitude drones and UAVs. The research on low-altitude logistics (LAL) operations has been increasing. The first wave of research on drones for city logistics can be traced back to the Amazon Prime Air program in 2013, which explored the use of drones at low altitudes (below 400 feet at that time) for freight distribution in cities. As of now, the company offers air deliveries in Texas and Arizona in the United States[2]. More examples can be found in the survey in [3]. LAL has also been rapidly developing in China. Giant logistics players have invested and deployed their own LAL systems during recent years, such as SF Express, JD Logistics, and Meituan.

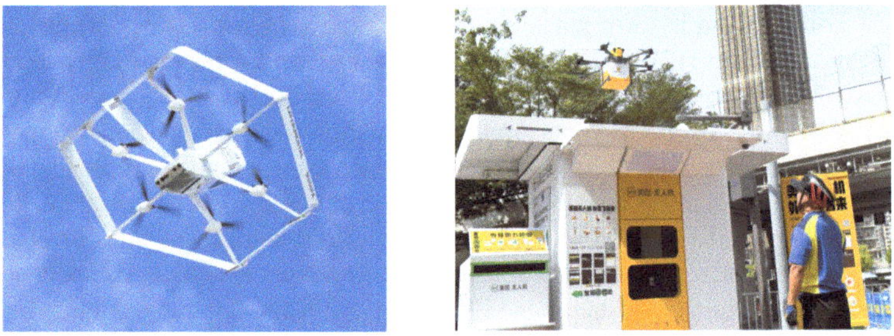

Fig. 1. Examples of modern low-altitude logistics systems. Left: Amazon Prime Air system in the United States (Source: Amazon in 2025); Right: Meituan food delivery system in Shenzhen China (Source: Meituan in 2025).

Compared to other civil applications of the Low-Altitude Economy, such as search and rescue, tourism and mobility, humanitarian or emergency logistics, where drones offer distinct advantages in speed and accessibility to restricted areas, the use of drones for freight distribution remains more questionable. On one hand, drones may enhance the speed and equity of logistics services; on the other hand, its efficiency and sustainability have been significantly challenged when compared to traditional truck or electric vehicle (EV) deliveries [4, 5]. Additionally, regulatory and safety concerns remain major obstacles to scaling up drone applications in urban environments [6].

In addition to recent technological developments, the drone logistics literature has shown rapidly growing interest in innovative urban freight distribution schemes that leverage the advantages of drones while improving overall efficiency. One of the most extensively studied topics is the design of multi-echelon multi-modal networks, for example, integrating drones with traditional trucks [7, 8], autonomous vehicles [9], or human couriers [10]. Other research focuses on order management and scheduling, for example, [11] propose the use of drones for high-priority deliveries while conventional vehicles handle standard orders; [12] develop optimization models for parcel delivery scheduling using drones, taking into account payload and battery constraints. While significant attention has been given to operational planning problems in drone delivery, its integration with other emerging and transformative logistics paradigms, such as the Physical Internet, has received relatively little discussion in the existing literature.

[2] https://www.aboutamazon.com/news/transportation/amazon-drone-delivery-arizona.

This paper discusses the combined application of the Physical Internet (PI) and drone to create a dynamic and resilient system for city logistics. PI is a transformative paradigm of logistics and supply chain management, aimed at the effective and seamless interconnection of heterogeneous logistics systems and services to enable effective, efficient, sustainable, and resilient logistics systems [13, 14]. The paradigm may cover the end-to-end logistics services including the last mile where drone delivery has been mostly investigated. PI is redefining how physical objects move, using concepts from the digital Internet such as modularity (e.g., goods are encapsulated in standard and modular containers), interoperability (e.g., seamless intermodal transfers), and routing intelligence (e.g., intermodal route planning). In such context, the combination of drone and PI creates a highly efficient logistics system where drones act as PI-container mover in city logistics network, capable of providing flexible, effective, and resilient delivery.

Next, Sect. 2 provides a brief review of the research foci of LAL and PI, focusing on the most relevant advancements. Section 3 discusses how PI may support drone delivery by overcoming the major barriers of adoption. Section 4 concludes the work and presents some use cases showing the potential to leverage simultaneously LAL and PI systems' advantages.

2 Background and Technological Foundations

2.1 Low-Altitude Logistics

Recent technological and research advancements have significantly broadened the scope of LAL, also known as drone delivery or last-mile drone. The section discusses only the logistics-related topics, and other topics like drone design and propulsion system engineering, communication protocols and standards, are excluded. A recent review [15] identifies the most extensively studied challenges related to logistics as routing optimization, followed by drone battery management, cargo distribution optimization and scheduling, data communication technologies, and environmental concerns (e.g., air pollution, energy consumption). These challenges are critical to the effective deployment of drone delivery systems in urban logistics operations and have spurred the development of innovative drone-based delivery schemes. For instance, several recent studies have proposed hybrid distribution models that integrate trucks and drones within a depot–van–drone–destination framework [3, 7], harnessing the complementary advantages of both transport modes. This approach is particularly advantageous given the typical operational range of drones, which is generally limited to approximately 10-20km for small drones and up to 100km for large drones [5, 16]. In this vein, most research efforts have focused on optimization problems related to drone routing [8], order scheduling [7, 11], or drone facility location [1].

Another major stream of research focuses on comparing the performance of drone delivery systems with traditional transportation modes and ground-based unmanned delivery vehicles, such as Automated Guided Vehicles (AGVs), to assess their applicability and advantages. Overall, the literature indicates that drone delivery does not consistently outperform these alternatives across all use cases or evaluation criteria. For instance, [17] employ the method of Continuous Approximation Analysis to compare truck-launched delivery drones (i.e., drones deployed from heavy-duty vehicles to final destinations) with inner-city hub-based ground autonomous delivery vehicles (i.e., AGVs dispatched from neighborhood hubs). Their findings suggest that, in terms of operational costs, drone delivery is more advantageous in large and low-density service areas, whereas ground-based AGVs perform better in dense urban environments. In addition, [4] argue that, when the drone range exceeds 100 km and the payload capacity is high (e.g., fixed-wing drones), drones can become more cost-efficient than trucks for inter-city cargo delivery, mainly thanks to the absence of staff costs and much lower life cycle cost than electric or diesel trucks. This further highlights the advantages of drones in cargo consolidation scenarios, consistent with the results in [5], which show that integrating consolidation processes with drone delivery can enhance parcel distribution cost savings within urban contexts.

Regarding city logistics externalities, the greenhouse gas (GHG) emissions problem has been often jointly studied with economic aspects, but the outcome depends closely on the scope and parameters of analysis. For instance, [4] reveal that E-trucks generate much lower use phase and life cycle GHG compared to (electric) drones, mainly due to low energy demand per km. However, the environmental performance of drones may improve gradually when the delivery distance increases, due to the reduced energy demand per km. [18] provide a different conclusion when comparing life cycle GHG per package delivered for drone and trucks, with a wider scope covering emissions from warehouse, battery production. In such context, drones become very competitive and may reduce GHG emissions and energy consumption when it is carefully deployed with adaptive distribution schemes, as their analysis suggests. In terms of service level, most studies concur that drones offer advantages in service time and delivery speed. However, other externalities [19], such as congestion and accidents, remain underexplored. To some extent, it can be assumed that drones generate fewer of these externalities compared to ground-based transportation, although further empirical research is needed to confirm this assumption.

Overall, the related literature indicates that drone delivery has strong potential to serve as an economically and environmentally friendly solution; however, its efficiency and effectiveness depends heavily on deployment strategies, use-case contexts, and the logistics schemes tailored to support it. In addition, significant adoption barriers need to be further addressed [6]. Section III will discuss how PI may help overcome key adoption barriers.

2.2 The Physical Internet Paradigm

The Physical Internet (PI), as a metaphor for the digital internet, envisions a globally integrated logistics system based on the principles of openness and interconnectivity across logistics networks and services. This vision is enabled by standardized collaboration protocols, modular containers, and interoperable planning interfaces [13, 14]. The objective of the PI is to enhance the efficiency and sustainability of existing logistics and supply chain operations. Recent advancements in PI research have been extensively reviewed, for example [20–22].

This section focuses specifically on key PI components with the potential to support and facilitate drone-based delivery systems, which are PI-containers, PI-hub, and PI-routing protocols. As a core pillar of the PI framework, PI-containers are modular and standardized units designed to encapsulate and transport goods [23]. The concept is analogous to maritime containers, whose global interoperability and efficiency have been well established. However, PI-containers are specifically intended for inland, multimodal transportation, aiming to extend the same level of standardization and efficiency across diverse transportation modes and standards. Recent research has concentrated on the conceptualization and prototyping of PI-containers [24], as well as on their intelligent design to support planning and monitoring [25]. A state-of-the-art example of PI-containers is the SMART Box[3] which has been recently introduced in the European retail sector.

PI-hubs form the backbone of the PI network by supporting the diverse logistics functions required by both the system and its users. They serve as open-access logistics hubs for the consolidation and sorting of cargo (PI-containers), including modal shift operations [26], akin to the role of routers in the digital Internet. From a network topology perspective, PI-hubs aim to connect heterogeneous service networks by acting as exchange points for flows between different service providers—functionally analogous to Internet Exchange Points (IXPs) on the Internet. In terms of design, the typology of PI-hubs varies according to their functionality and role, ranging from large multimodal platform-like hubs [27] to inner-city micro-hubs that serve as relay points for urban transportation [28]. The core operations performed within PI-hubs include consolidation, sorting, and bundling of cargo, as well as route planning (either determining the next hop or the full path to the final destination).

Inspired by data packet routing protocols on the Internet, the PI-routing protocol can be seen as a standardized framework for planning freight routes and coordinating transport across logistics networks, regardless of whether they are operated by the same or different carriers. Routing decisions, including route planning and modal shift choices, are made at PI-hubs, either at the point of origin or at intermediate layover hubs. Recent research further explores these mechanisms and their implementation within the PI framework, see the recent works discussed in [22].

In addition to physical infrastructure and planning, the PI also heavily relies on digital interoperability. The development of a robust digital backbone is essential for the effective deployment of the PI system. Recent studies have proposed the integration of advanced technologies, such as smart APIs, blockchain and smart contracts, semantics and ontologies, to enhance digital interoperability within PI networks and among all stakeholders [14, 29]. More recently, [20] suggest the integration of Digital Twin and Cyber-Physical Systems (CPS) technologies to develop PI framework towards the Cyber-Physical Internet (CPI). Built on interoperable systems, CPI aims to integrate and synchronize physical and digital networks to improve the agility and effectiveness of decision making.

This aspect is particularly critical for the integration of drones into PI systems, as it ensures the trackability and traceability of cargo across different transport modes, as well as the safety and integrity of the products. The next section provides further detail on these aspects.

---

[3] https://www.gs1belu.org/sites/gs1belu/files/2021-04/GS1%20Innovation%20Café%20GS1%20SMART-Box.pdf.

3 Overcoming Barriers to Drone Logistics with PI

In addition to the economic and environmental performance issues discussed above, recent research has identified 34 major barriers to the implementation of drone logistics, based on expert surveys and an extensive literature review [6], as shown in Table 1. This section examines the potential of the PI to address the most significant and relevant of these barriers from the perspective of logistics operations.

Table 1. PI Impact on Barriers to Drone Adoption in Logistics (based on [6]).

Main Category	Sub-Category	PI Impact
Threat to privacy and security (Th)	Unauthorized photography (Th1)	Irrelevant
	Identification of non-authorized drones (Th2)	High
	Surveillance and privacy (Th3)	Irrelevant
	Violating rights (Th4)	Irrelevant
	Physical attacks, jamming and spoofing (Th5)	Irrelevant
	Intentional hacking and cyber-attacks, terrorism (Th6)	Irrelevant
Regulations (R)	Accountability for drone owners (R1)	High
	Drone's route (R2)	High
	Insurance obligations (R3)	High
	Pilot certification and training (R4)	High
	Crowding airspace for manned aircrafts (R5)	Medium
	Determination of liability (R6)	High
Public perception and psychological (P)	Higher the perceived risk (P1)	Medium
	Transparency (P2)	High
	Societal anxiety about automation (P3)	Medium
	Awareness about drone technology (P4)	High
	Drones and theft (P5)	Irrelevant
	Public annoyance (P6)	Low
	Private sector use of drones (P7)	Medium
Environmental issues (En)	CO2 emissions (En1)	High
	Harming wildlife (En2)	Irrelevant
	Visual pollution and sound pollution (En3)	Low
	Create debris (En4)	Irrelevant
Economic aspects (Ec)	Uneven distribution of income (Ec1)	Irrelevant

(continued)

Table 1. (*continued*)

Main Category	Sub-Category	PI Impact
	Higher Initial costs (Ec2)	High
	Economy and employment (Ec3)	High
	Disrupt trucking industry (Ec4)	High
Technical issues (Te)	Short flight range (Te1)	Irrelevant
	Navigation (Te2)	Irrelevant
	Obstacle avoidance and mid–air collisions (Te3)	Irrelevant
	Bad weather conditions (Te4)	Irrelevant
	Tracking of drones (Te5)	High
	Delivery and performance risk (Te6)	Irrelevant
	Limited carrying capacity (Te7)	High

- Threat to privacy and security (Th): PI is generally not directly relevant to this group of barriers, except Identification of non-authorized drones. This exception is justified by the reasonable assumption that freight delivery operations would involve only commercial and licensed drones. PI plays a role in ensuring cargo traceability and trackability within logistics systems, which includes associating shipments with authorized transportation modes such as drones. The remaining sub-categories under this barrier are either less applicable to logistics operations or can be effectively addressed through appropriate business practices and adherence to regulatory requirements.
- Regulations (R): According to [6], regulatory issues represent the most significant barrier to the adoption of drone delivery, surpassing concerns related to privacy and security. PI is expected to play a key role in supporting regulatory compliance for drone operations. First, PI facilitates the standardization of business processes, data exchange formats, and communication protocols, thereby enhancing the accountability and liability of drones within delivery services. In addition, seamless business-to-business (B2B) or object-to-object communication enabled by PI may introduce a new paradigm for managing and coordinating drone routes and airspace. Nevertheless, regulatory constraints ultimately remain within the purview of policymakers, and their decisions are critical to shaping the regulatory landscape. Finally, with broader adoption of drones potentially driven by PI, a corresponding increase in demand for well-trained drone pilots is anticipated.
- Public perception and psychological (P): This category is more closely related to the general applications of drones, including freight delivery. People tend to believe that drones without an onboard pilot are more vulnerable to cyberattacks or are primarily used for surveillance or military purposes [6]. If PI helps promote drone delivery, more people will gain experience with the service and become more aware of the positive aspects of the technology in commercial application. Additionally, the rise of the Smart City paradigm presents excellent opportunities to integrate PI and drone technology into urban infrastructure, thereby facilitating greater public acceptance.

- Environmental issues (En): Drone delivery has been a subject of ongoing debate regarding its environmental impact. As previously discussed, the emissions footprint of drone delivery depends heavily on the specific use case and logistical arrangements. Public Involvement (PI) will play a vital role in improving overall performance by facilitating more flexible and efficient cooperative transportation schemes that help maximize the benefits of drone solutions. Furthermore, it is important to include other negative externalities, such as visual pollution, congestion, land use, noise, and accidents [19], in the environmental performance analysis to provide a comprehensive comparison between drones and other delivery options.
- Economic aspects (Ec): Similar to environmental aspects, PI is expected to significantly enhance the economic performance and feasibility of drone delivery systems, particularly in terms of operational costs and service effectiveness. For instance, PI may facilitate the deployment of plug-and-play logistics hubs that enable drones to bypass congested urban routes, thereby reducing both delivery times and costs in densely populated areas. Likewise, PI can support service extension to rural regions lacking reliable road infrastructure, functioning in a manner analogous to ad-hoc networks, which can reduce both capital and operational expenditures (CAPEX and OPEX), as well as improve service level. Additionally, PI's emphasis on asset standardization and modularization, particularly through the use of PI-containers, enables dynamic and seamless cargo transfers across different transport modes, which can lead to further reductions in operational expenses in cooperative transportation.
- Technical issues (Te): This category pertains to technological developments aimed at enhancing drone performance, particularly under challenging constraints such as adverse weather, energy consumption, range, and cargo handling. While the PI, as a logistics paradigm, is not directly associated with all the technical challenges outlined in [6], it may still contribute to mitigating some of them. Specifically, PI's advanced object-tracking capabilities can improve drone monitoring, while its emphasis on cooperative transportation can aid in capacity management, for example, large drones for inter-city transportation and small drones for last-mile operations. Furthermore, the digital interoperability inherent in the PI framework supports enhanced performance monitoring across systems and assets. Nevertheless, communication protocols and standards still require further research and development.

This section offers a forward-looking discussion on how PI may help address key barriers of drone adoption in freight transportation. While PI may not be directly relevant to every challenge, it primarily contributes to operations management by helping reduce overall costs as well as societal and environmental impacts. Figure 2 summarizes the key benefits of PI in supporting drone delivery.

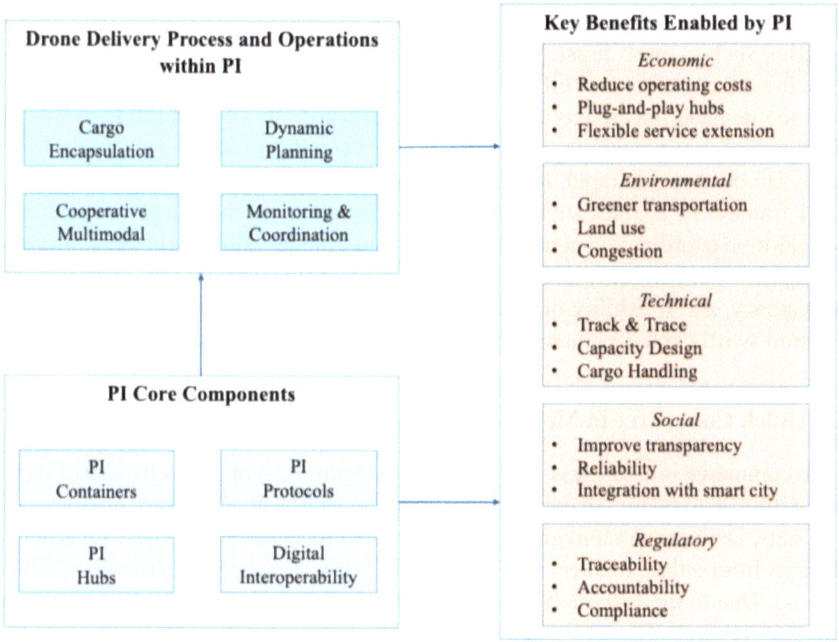

Fig. 2. Drone delivery operations supported by Physical Internet.

4 Conclusion and Future Directions

This study examined the potential synergies between Low-Altitude Logistics (LAL) and the Physical Internet (PI) paradigm, highlighting how the integration of these two emerging concepts can address the critical challenges of drone-based city logistics. While drones offer promising capabilities in terms of delivery speed, customer accessibility, and service flexibility, their widespread adoption is currently constrained by technical limitations, regulatory barriers, economic and environmental challenges. The PI, with its principles of modularity, interoperability, and systemic coordination, presents a viable pathway to overcome many of these limitations.

Despite its transformative potential, the integration of PI with drone logistics remains underexplored in both academic research and practical deployment. Future research should focus on developing interoperable standards, simulation frameworks, and pilot projects that empirically validate the proposed models. As urban and rural logistics needs continue to evolve, the convergence of PI and LAL may become a cornerstone of sustainable and intelligent freight transport in smart cities. Here we present only use cases and scenarios that are expected to attract increased research interest and practical attention in the near future.

4.1 Emergency and Relief Logistics

Drones have been widely investigated for emergency and relief logistics, which refers to the planning, coordination, and execution of transporting and distributing aid and resources in response to emergencies, disasters, or humanitarian crises. This includes scenarios such as post-disaster response, urgent medical deliveries, and first aid services. In such contexts, time efficiency and service effectiveness are critical, particularly given the demand uncertainty and potential inaccessibility of road infrastructure. The integration of drone technology with the PI offers significant advantages for these operations. Drones provide rapid, flexible access to hard-to-reach or damaged areas, while the PI framework enables standardized cargo handling, modular logistics operations, and real-time coordination across diverse transport modes and stakeholders. Moreover, PI's digital interoperability and object tracking capabilities enhance the responsiveness, transparency, and reliability of emergency logistics, ensuring that critical supplies are delivered swiftly and accurately when and where they are needed most.

4.2 Quick Commerce in Metropolitan Areas

Quick commerce is a business model centered on ultra-fast and effective delivery, typically within 30 to 60 min. It encompasses services such as meal delivery platforms (e.g., Uber Eats, Deliveroo), rapid grocery delivery from local stores, and next-hour delivery offerings from online retailers (e.g., Amazon's Prime Now, FNAC's two-hour delivery in Paris). Due to the extremely short lead times and narrow time-windows, order consolidation is rarely feasible, often resulting in single-order or even single-item home deliveries. This approach significantly increases labor costs, raising concerns about the long-term viability of the quick commerce model, especially in large metropolitan areas. Automation presents a promising solution to reduce delivery costs. Ground-based AGVs and aerial drones are among the most frequently proposed technologies, exemplified by Meituan's food delivery drones currently operating in Shenzhen, China (see Fig. 1). With growing academic interest in this area, further research is needed to assess the optimal deployment of these solutions across different contexts and environments.

4.3 Multi-echelon Multi-modal Network

As highlighted in the existing literature, delivery drones represent a promising complement to conventional and modern transportation systems within distribution networks. Key challenges lie in determining the optimal deployment strategies, specifically where and how to deploy them. For instance, large drones capable of transporting consolidated shipments over long distances may demonstrate superior economic and environmental performance. In contrast, the effectiveness of smaller drones is more sensitive to factors such as demand density and urban area conditions. This suggests that larger drones may be better suited for inter-city logistics, for example, the Rhaegal cargo drone from Sabrewing in the United States, and the Air White Whale in China. Conversely, smaller drones may face limitations in last-mile delivery within urban environments due to regulatory and infrastructural constraints. Designing multi-echelon, cooperative multi-modal transportation networks will be critical to fully leveraging drone capabilities, combined with e-trucks or delivery AGVs. In this context, the core components of the PI may provide essential flexibility and interoperability, both physical and digital, to enable the integration and coordination of such networks.

4.4 Rural Zone Logistics Services

Rural areas often suffer from inadequate freight delivery services due to the high operating costs associated with low demand density or frequency, and long delivery distance. In some developing countries, inadequate road infrastructure further limits the feasibility of conventional ground-based delivery. In such contexts, drone delivery can offer a more efficient alternative, as demonstrated by the startup Zipline's operations in Rwanda, which have contributed to improved service equity in the region. The PI framework may support the deployment of drones in rural areas by providing shared digital and physical infrastructure and services, such as PI-containers and PI-hubs, thereby reducing both operating and upfront investment costs.

Acknowledgments. This research is supported by FEDERATEUR AVICAR Carnot M.I.N.E.S. and the Physical Internet Chair at, Mines Paris, PSL University in France.

References

1. Dukkanci, O., Campbell, J.F., Kara, B.Y.: Facility location decisions for drone delivery with riding: a literature review. Comput. Oper. Res. **167**, 106672 (2024)
2. Huang, C., Fang, S., Wu, H., Wang, Y., Yang, Y.: Low-altitude intelligent transportation: system architecture, infrastructure, and key technologies. J. Ind. Inf. Integr. **42**, 100694 (2024)
3. Boysen, N., Fedtke, S., Schwerdfeger, S.: Last-mile delivery concepts: a survey from an operational research perspective. OR Spect. (2020). https://doi.org/10.1007/s00291-020-00607-8
4. Raghunatha, A., Lindkvist, E., Thollander, P., Hansson, E., Jonsson, G.: Critical assessment of emissions, costs, and time for last-mile goods delivery by drones versus trucks. Sci. Rep. **13**, 11814 (2023)
5. Chu, X., Chen, S., Wang, K., Wu, L., Xu, G.: A cost-efficiency analysis of drones in revolutionizing intra-city express services. Adv. Eng. Inf. **65**, 103324 (2025)
6. Sah, B., Gupta, R., Bani-Hani, D.: Analysis of barriers to implement drone logistics. Int. J. Log. Res. Appl. **24**, 531–550 (2021)
7. Zhao, J., Long, Y., Xie, B., Xu, G., Liu, Y.: A matheuristic solution for efficient scheduling in dynamic truck–drone collaboration. Expert Syst. Appl. **267**, 126218 (2025)
8. Long, Y., Xu, G., Zhao, J., Xie, B., Fang, M.: Dynamic Truck–UAV collaboration and integrated route planning for resilient urban emergency response. IEEE Trans. Eng. Manag. **71**, 9826–9838 (2024)
9. Imran, N.M., Mishra, S., Won, M.: A-VRPD: automating drone-based last-mile delivery using self-driving cars. IEEE Trans. Intell. Transp. Syst. **24**, 9599–9612 (2023)
10. Chen, J., Wan, P., Xu, G.: Cooperative learning-based joint UAV and human courier scheduling for emergency medical delivery service. IEEE Trans. Intell. Transport. Syst. **26**, 935–949 (2025)
11. El-Adle, A.M., Ghoniem, A., Haouari, M.: The cost of carrier consistency: last-mile delivery by vehicle and drone for subscription-based orders. J. Oper. Res. Soc. **75**, 821–840 (2024)
12. Torabbeigi, M., Lim, G.J., Kim, S.J.: Drone delivery scheduling optimization considering payload-induced battery consumption rates. J. Intell. Rob. Syst. **97**, 471–487 (2020)
13. Ballot, E., Pan, S.: The physical internet and logistics. In: Vickerman, R. (ed.) International Encyclopedia of Transportation, pp. 479–487. Elsevier, Oxford (2021). https://doi.org/10.1016/B978-0-08-102671-7.10288-X

14. Pan, S., et al.: Digital interoperability in logistics and supply chain management: state-of-the-art and research avenues towards Physical Internet. Comput. Ind. **128**, 103435 (2021)
15. Eskandaripour, H., Boldsaikhan, E.: Last-mile drone delivery: past, present, and future. Drones **7**, 77 (2023)
16. Agatz, N., Bouman, P., Schmidt, M.: Optimization approaches for the traveling salesman problem with drone. Transp. Sci. **52**, 965–981 (2018)
17. Lemardelé, C., Estrada, M., Pagès, L., Bachofner, M.: Potentialities of drones and ground autonomous delivery devices for last-mile logistics. Transport. Res. Part E: Logist. Transport. Rev. **149**, 102325 (2021)
18. Stolaroff, J.K., et al.: Energy use and life cycle greenhouse gas emissions of drones for commercial package delivery. Nat. Commun. **9**, 409 (2018)
19. European Commission. Handbook on the External Costs of Transport - Version 2019 (2019)
20. Wu, H., et al.: Towards cyber-physical internet: a systematic review, fundamental model and future perspectives. Transport. Res. Part E: Logist. Transport. Rev. **197**, 104051 (2025)
21. Münch, C., Wehrle, M., Kuhn, T., Hartmann, E.: The research landscape around the physical internet – a bibliometric analysis. Int. J. Prod. Res. 1–19 (2023) https://doi.org/10.1080/00207543.2023.2205969
22. Pan, S., Ballot, E., Huang, G.Q.: Operations with physical internet. In: Reference Module in Social Sciences. Elsevier (2025). https://doi.org/10.1016/B978-0-443-28993-4.00171-2
23. Montreuil, B.: Toward a Physical Internet: meeting the global logistics sustainability grand challenge. Logist. Res. **3**, 71–87 (2011)
24. Landschützer, C., Ehrentraut, F., Jodin, D.: Containers for the Physical Internet: requirements and engineering design related to FMCG logistics. Logist. Res. **8**, 8 (2015)
25. Sallez, Y., Pan, S., Montreuil, B., Berger, T., Ballot, E.: On the activeness of intelligent Physical Internet containers. Comput. Ind. **81**, 96–104 (2016)
26. Montreuil, B., Meller, R.D., Ballot, E.: Towards a Physical Internet: the impact on logistics facilities and material handling systems design and innovation, pp. 1–23 (2010)
27. Chargui, T., Ladier, A.-L., Bekrar, A., Pan, S., Trentesaux, D.: Towards designing and operating physical internet cross-docks: problem specifications and research perspectives. Omega **111**, 102641 (2022)
28. Chen, C., Pan, S., Wang, Z., Zhong, R.Y.: Using taxis to collect citywide E-commerce reverse flows: a crowdsourcing solution. Int. J. Prod. Res. **55**, 1833–1844 (2017)
29. Pan, S.: Blockchain technology for logistics collaboration in physical internet. In: 2024 International Conference on Automation in Manufacturing, Transportation and Logistics (ICaMaL), pp. 1–9 (2024). https://doi.org/10.1109/ICaMaL62577.2024.10919774

Measuring the Performance of Logistics Enterprises Using a Multi-Criteria Decision-Making Model

Dang Thanh Tuan[1](✉), Ho Thanh Phong[1], Nguyen Ngoc Ai Thy[2], and Le Minh Thuan[1]

[1] Hong Bang International University, Ho Chi Minh City, Vietnam
tuandt@hiu.vn

[2] Industrial University of Ho Chi Minh City, Ho Chi Minh City, Vietnam
nguyenngocaithy@iuh.edu.vn

Abstract. The logistics industry in Vietnam plays a pivotal role in the national economy, yet it continues to face significant challenges related to operational efficiency, high costs, and limited competitiveness. Developing a comprehensive, objective, and practically relevant set of performance evaluation criteria for logistics enterprises has become necessary. This study proposes a multi-criteria decision-making (MCDM) model that integrates the CRITIC and TOPSIS methods to assess the performance of six prominent logistics enterprises in Vietnam. The CRITIC method is employed to determine the objective weights of 11 criteria covering economic, social, and service level dimensions, while the TOPSIS method is applied to rank the operational performance of the selected companies. The results indicate that the PetroVietnam Transportation Corporation (PVTrans) achieved the highest performance score, while Tan Cang Logistics maintained the most stable ranking across different scenarios. Additionally, both Transimex Logistics and PVTrans demonstrated a significant dependency on inventory turnover and scope of operation. This research contributes to developing a practical tool to support managers in resource allocation and performance improvement strategies, thereby enhancing the competitive advantage of logistics enterprises.

Keywords: operational performance · evaluation criteria · multi-criteria decision-making · CRITIC · TOPSIS

1 Introduction

In the context of global economic volatility, Vietnam's import-export market achieved impressive figures in 2024. The country's export turnover reached USD 405.53 billion, marking a 14.3% increase compared to the previous year, while import turnover rose by 16.7% to USD 380.76 billion [1]. The total import-export turnover in 2024 amounted to USD 786.29 billion, surpassing the record level set in 2022. Notably, exports exceeded

M. Li et al. (Eds.): ICLS 2025, *Proceeding of the 19th International Congress on Logistics and Supply Chain Management Systems*, pp. 89–103, 2026.
https://doi.org/10.1007/978-981-95-7700-2_8

the USD 400 billion milestone for the first time in three years, representing a significant achievement in Vietnam's efforts toward international trade development. These results placed Vietnam 17th among the world's 20 largest trading economies [2].

The logistics industry is considered the "backbone" of the economy and is increasingly affirming its crucial role in the development of Vietnam's import-export market. According to the Vietnam Logistics Business Association (VLA), in 2022, the logistics sector contributed approximately 15% to the country's GDP. The total volume of goods handled through Vietnam's seaport system exceeded 570 million tons, up 14% compared to 2023. Notably, Quang Ninh province reached a record of nearly 150 million tons of goods, an increase of 7.8% over the previous year [3]. In addition, according to data from the General Statistics Office, in the first nine months of 2024, nearly 6,500 logistics enterprises were newly registered (accounting for 5.33% of the total number of new enterprises nationwide), an increase of 13.5% compared to the same period last year, with a total registered capital of VND 36.55 trillion [4]. The increase in the number of enterprises indicates the strong growth of the Vietnamese logistics industry. However, compiled data from the General Statistics Office also shows that 4,519 businesses suspended operations, and nearly 600 enterprises were dissolved [4]. This poses challenges regarding performance management in logistics businesses.

Organizations and enterprises are increasingly seeking effective methods to evaluate their performance and make informed decisions. The ability to measure and assess various aspects of business operations is crucial for driving growth, enhancing competitiveness, and ensuring sustainability. Developing a performance evaluation system helps logistics enterprises identify the key factors that affect operational efficiency and propose appropriate improvement solutions [5]. Recent studies have also focused on establishing systems of performance measurement and evaluation criteria. However, most of these studies concentrate on financial indicators [6].

Therefore, this research is essential for assessing operational efficiency based on a comprehensive set of criteria, including financial, service delivery, and social aspects. This research has significant implications for enhancing the competitiveness of Vietnamese logistics enterprises. The results will provide a scientific, objective, and industry-specific performance evaluation system, helping businesses identify their strengths and weaknesses and propose suitable improvement strategies.

2 Literature Review

Business performance is a crucial concept in enterprise management, referring to the measurement of efficiency and effectiveness in processes aimed at achieving organizational goals. It involves monitoring and improving key performance indicators (KPIs) such as cost-efficiency, quality, productivity, and customer satisfaction [7]. Performance reflects a company's ability to operate and compete in the market.

Measuring business performance requires aligning performance measurement systems with operational strategies to balance goals such as cost, quality, and delivery [8]. Effective performance improvement programs can significantly boost a company's profitability, making performance measurement essential for designing and implementing functional and business management systems [9]. Recently, the topic has gained increasing academic attention.

A study by Wang et al. used Data Envelopment Analysis (DEA) and Window Analysis to measure performance changes of major container transport companies before and during the COVID-19 period. Input variables included owned and leased fleet capacity, number of employees, energy consumption, and operational costs, while output variables were freight volume and revenue. Results showed that ZIM, Yang Ming, and Hapag-Lloyd achieved the best improvements, while HMM, COSCO, and Wan Hai had the lowest performance [10].

In another study on Vietnamese logistics companies, Lien et al. used three input variables (current assets, non-current assets, owner's equity) and two output variables (net revenue and net profit after tax) to evaluate the performance of nine logistics firms. Findings indicated that four firms maintained high efficiency from 2016–2022, while three showed fluctuating performance due to the COVID-19 pandemic [11].

A study by Wang et al. applied optimization algorithms to assess and forecast performance using input criteria such as total assets, equity, cost of goods sold, and total operating expenses, with sales revenue and net profit as outputs. Among 21 logistics firms analyzed, Gemadept and SAFI were identified as top performers with strong growth potential [6].

However, most prior studies focus solely on financial efficiency and lack a multi-dimensional approach to performance evaluation, which this study aims to address. While DEA and financial indicators have been commonly used, few studies have attempted to incorporate non-financial and service-based criteria using integrated MCDM models.

The Multi-Criteria Decision-Making (MCDM) model is an important technique for selecting optimal alternatives based on multiple criteria or objectives, especially in complex decision-making situations where goals may conflict [12]. MCDM models are applied across various fields, and many MCDM methods have been developed and integrated by researchers worldwide, depending on the level of complexity, weighting methods for criteria, the ability to handle uncertain data, and the type of data aggregation [13].

In the field of business performance measurement and evaluation, MCDM offers greater flexibility and practicality compared to traditional single-criterion methods [14]. Numerous previous studies have demonstrated the effectiveness of MCDM approaches. To provide an overview, Table 1 presents some representative studies and the MCDM methods used in the field of business performance measurement.

Table 1. Overview of research on measuring the performance of logistics enterprises

Author	Year	Method	Research Topic
Çakır et al. [15]	2013	CRITIC, SAW, TOPSIS, VIKOR, Borda	Performance evaluation of logistics companies in Turkey's Fortune 500
Alkhatib et al. [16]	2015	Fuzzy DEMATEL, Fuzzy TOPSIS	Performance evaluation and identification of the best logistics company

(continued)

Table 1. *(continued)*

Author	Year	Method	Research Topic
Gergin, Baki [17]	2015	AHP, TOPSIS	Performance evaluation of logistics companies
Özceylan et al. [18]	2016	AHP, ANP, TOPSIS	Logistics performance evaluation of 81 provinces in Turkey
Agrawal, Singh, Murtaza [19]	2016	Fuzzy TOPSIS	Identification of critical success factors in reverse logistics
Çakır [20]	2017	CRITIC, SAW	Logistics performance evaluation of OECD countries
Li et al. [21]	2018	Cumulative Prospect Theory-Based MCDM	Performance evaluation of third-party reverse logistics companies
Bianchini [22]	2018	AHP, TOPSIS	Performance evaluation of 3PL companies
Riaz, Farid [23]	2022	Fuzzy MCDM	Performance evaluation of 3PL companies
Nguyen, Wang, Dang et al. [24]	2022	Grey AHP, Grey COPRAS	Performance evaluation of cold chain logistics providers
Mešić, Miškić, Stević, Mastilo [25]	2022	CRITIC, MARCOS	Logistics performance evaluation of Western Balkan countries
Boakai, Samanlioglu [26]	2023	Fuzzy BWM	Performance evaluation of 3PL companies
Çalık, Erdebilli, Özdemir [27]	2023	Pythagorean AHP, Fuzzy AHP, AHP, VIKOR, CODAS, TOPSIS	Logistics performance evaluation of countries

3 Methodology

3.1 Determining Criteria Weights Using the CRITIC Method

The CRITIC method, also known as the Criteria Importance Through Intercriteria Correlation method, is used to determine the objective weights of criteria. It was introduced by Diakoulaki et al. [28]. This is a simple approach to calculating the weights of criteria. It combines two key concepts: the standard deviation (σj) and the correlation coefficient, to help better understand the importance of each criterion in the evaluation process [29].

The steps for calculating the weights of criteria using the CRITIC method are presented below [28]. Matrix A is the initial matrix created by the decision-maker. The decision matrix is shown as follows:

$$A = \left[a_{ij}\right]_{m\times n} = \begin{bmatrix} a_{11} & \dots & a_{1j} & \dots & a_{1n} \\ a_{21} & \dots & a_{2j} & \dots & a_{2n} \\ a_{m1} & \dots & a_{mj} & \dots & a_{mn} \end{bmatrix}\# \quad (3.1)$$

with m representing the number of alternatives and n representing the number of criteria considered.

Step 1: Normalize the decision matrix.

Since the criteria may have different scales, the values in the decision matrix must be normalized to a common scale (usually from 0 to 1) [30].

The normalization formulation:

$$r_{ij} = \frac{\left(a_{ij} - a_j^{worst}\right)}{\left(a_j^{best} - a_j^{worst}\right)}\# \quad (3.2)$$

For profit criteria:

$a_j^{best} > a_{ij} > a_j^{worst}$

For cost criteria:

$a_j^{worst} > a_{ij} > a_j^{best}$

Where:

r_{ij} is the normalized value of alternative i with respect to criterion j;
a_{ij} is the actual value of alternative i with respect to criterion j;
a_j^{worst} is the minimum value of criterion j;
a_j^{best} is the maximum value of criterion j.

Then, we obtain the normalized matrix R:

$$R = \left[r_{ij}\right]_{m\times n} = \begin{bmatrix} r_{11} & \dots & r_{1j} & \dots & r_{1n} \\ r_{21} & \dots & r_{2j} & \dots & r_{2n} \\ r_{m1} & \dots & r_{mj} & \dots & r_{mn} \end{bmatrix} \quad (3.3)$$

Step 2: Calculate the standard deviation values of r_j.

The standard deviation of criterion j (s_j) is calculated using Eq. (3.4).

$$s_j = std(v) = \sqrt{\frac{1}{m-1} \times \sum\nolimits_{i=1}^{m} (r_{ij} - r_j)^2}\# \quad (3.4)$$

where: r_j is the mean value of criterion j; m is the number of alternatives.

Step 3: Calculate the correlation coefficient between r_j and r_k The correlation coefficient between two criteria is determined using Eq. (3.5)

$$C_{jk} = Corr(v) = \frac{\sum_{i=1}^{m} (r_{ij} - \overline{r_j})(r_{ik} - \overline{r_k})}{\sqrt{\sum_{i=1}^{m} (r_{ij} - r_i)^2 \times \sum_{j=1}^{m} (r_{ik} - \overline{r_k})^2}}\# \quad (3.5)$$

Calculate the contrast intensity and the weights of the criteria using Eq. (3.6)

$$q_j = s_j \times \sum\nolimits_{k=1}^{n} \left(1 - C_{jk}\right), j = 1, \dots n\# \quad (3.6)$$

where: q_j is the contrast intensity (or information content) of the criteria.

$$w_j = \frac{q_i}{\sum_{k=1}^{n} q_i}\# \quad (3.7)$$

where: w_j is the weight of the criteria.

3.2 Ranking the Performance of Enterprises Using the TOPSIS Method

The TOPSIS method is an MCDM technique developed by Hwang and Yoon to select the best alternative based on the concept of a compromise solution [31]. The fundamental principle of the TOPSIS method is that the chosen alternative should have the shortest Euclidean distance from the positive ideal solution and the farthest Euclidean distance from the negative ideal solution [32]. The positive ideal solution is the one that maximizes the total benefits related to the problem while minimizing the total costs. In contrast, the negative ideal solution is the one that maximizes total costs while minimizing benefits [33]. TOPSIS is one of the most widely used techniques in research over the past three decades due to its rational and intuitive foundation, computational simplicity, and its ability to incorporate weight assessments [34]. The steps of the TOPSIS method are presented below.

Step 1: Construct the Decision Matrix A

The rows and columns of the decision matrix represent the decision alternatives and the evaluation criteria, respectively, which are used for decision-making purposes. Matrix A is the initial matrix created by the decision-maker [28]. The decision matrix is shown as follows:

$$A = \left[x_{ij}\right]_{m\times n} = \begin{bmatrix} x_{11} \dots x_{1j} & \dots x_{1n} \\ x_{21} \dots x_{2j} & \dots x_{2n} \\ x_{m1} \dots x_{mj} & \dots x_{mn} \end{bmatrix} \# \tag{3.8}$$

where:

m: is the number of alternatives and n is the number of criteria.
x_{ij} is the score of alternative i with respect to criterion j
$1 \leq i \leq m$, where m is the number of alternatives;
$1 \leq j \leq n$, where n is the number of criteria.

Step 2: Normalize the Decision Matrix

Construct a normalized decision matrix to ensure that all criteria are on a comparable scale, typically using techniques such as vector normalization.

The elements of the normalized decision matrix are calculated using the following formula:

$$r_{ij} = \frac{x_{ij}}{\sqrt{\sum_{i=1}^{m} x_{ij}^2}} \# \tag{3.9}$$

The normalized matrix R is established as follows:

$$R = \left[r_{ij}\right]_{m\times n} = \begin{bmatrix} r_{11} \dots r_{1j} & \dots r_{1n} \\ r_{21} \dots r_{2j} & \dots r_{2n} \\ r_{m1} \dots r_{mj} & \dots r_{mn} \end{bmatrix} \tag{3.10}$$

Step 3: Multiply the weights w_j with the normalized decision matrix (Matrix R)

Typically, we have a set of weights for each criterion w_j where j is the index of the criteria in the set of n criteria.

Then, the values of the weighted normalized decision matrix V are calculated by multiplying each column of the normalized decision matrix R by its corresponding weight.

$$v_{ij} = w_j \times r_{ij}\# \tag{3.11}$$

The matrix V is represented as follows:

$$V = \left[v_{ij}\right]_{m\times n} = \begin{bmatrix} v_{11} & \ldots & v_{1j} & \ldots & v_{1n} \\ v_{21} & \ldots & v_{2j} & \ldots & v_{2n} \\ v_{m1} & \ldots & v_{mj} & \ldots & v_{mn} \end{bmatrix}\# \tag{3.12}$$

Step 4: Identify the Positive Ideal Solution and the Negative Ideal Solution

The set of positive ideal solutions is represented by the following formula:

$$A^{+} = \left\{v_1^*, \ldots, v_n^*\right\}, withv_j = \left\{\left(v_{ij}\right)ifj \in J; \left(v_{ij}\right)ifj \in J\prime\right\} \tag{3.3}$$

The set of negative ideal solutions is represented by the following formula:

$$A^{-} = \left\{v_1^*, \ldots, v_n^*\right\}, withv_j = \left\{\left(v_{ij}\right)ifj \in J; \left(v_{ij}\right)ifj \in J\prime\right\} \tag{3.14}$$

where:

J is the set of benefit attributes or criteria (more is better);
J' is the set of cost attributes or criteria (less is better).

Step 5: Calculate the Distance of Each Alternative from the Ideal Solutions

The Euclidean distance approach is used in the TOPSIS method to calculate the deviation of each evaluation factor value in relation to the decision point from both the positive and negative ideal solution sets [35]. The deviation values from the decision point calculated in this way are referred to as the Positive Ideal Solution (S_i^*). And the Negative Ideal Solution (S_i^-).

The positive ideal solution is:

$$S_i^* = \sqrt{\sum_{j=1}^{n} (v_{ij} - A^{+})^2}\# \tag{3.15}$$

The negative ideal solution is:

$$S_i^{-} = \sqrt{\sum_{j=1}^{n} (v_{ij} - A^{-})^2}\# \tag{3.16}$$

Step 6: Calculate the Relative Closeness to the Ideal Solution.

The distances to the positive and negative ideal solutions are used to calculate the relative closeness of each decision point to the ideal solution C_i^*. The criterion used here is the proportion of the distance to the negative ideal solution over the total distance. The calculation of the relative closeness to the ideal solution is shown in the following formula:

$$C_i^* = \frac{S_i^{-}}{S_i^{-} + S_i^*}; 0 < C_i^* < 1\# \tag{3.17}$$

Step 7: Rank the Alternatives in Descending Order of C_i^*

4 Case Study

As mentioned in the literature review, previous studies have selected financial and operational indicators to evaluate the performance of logistics enterprises. Commonly used financial indicators include operating costs, owner's equity, total assets, net revenue, revenue growth rate, and pre-tax profit [15]. Operational indicators often include the size of the company's fleet (both vehicles and ships), and the volume of road and sea transport. However, due to limitations in publicly available company data, the author did not include annual freight volume as a criterion. Instead, warehouse area and scope of operation were selected to measure the service capability of the enterprises. After conducting research and reviewing relevant literature, the author developed a structured framework consisting of three hierarchical levels. The top level focuses on measuring the performance of logistics enterprises using a multi-criteria decision-making (MCDM) model. The second level includes three main criteria: economic, service level, and social. The third level comprises 11 sub-criteria categorized under the three main criteria. Under the economic criteria, the five sub-criteria are: revenue, operating costs, inventory turnover, owner's equity, and cost of goods sold. Under the service level criteria, the sub-criteria are: fleet size (vehicles), fleet size (ships), warehouse area, and scope of operation. Finally, the social criterion includes two sub-criteria: number of employees and number of employee training sessions. These main and sub-criteria are presented in Table 2, and the decision tree for the study is illustrated in Fig. 1.

Table 2. Key performance indicators (kpis) for business performance measurement

Main Critera	Sub-Critera	Sub-Criteria Name	Unit	Target
Economic	C1	Revenue	Million VND	Maximum
Economic	C2	Operating Costs	Million VND	Minimum
Economic	C3	Inventory Turnover	Turns	Maximum
Economic	C4	Owner's Equity	Million VND	Maximum
Economic	C5	Cost of Goods Sold	Million VND	Minimum
Service Level	C6	Fleet Size (Ships)	Ships	Maximum
Service Level	C7	Fleet Size (Vehicles)	Vehicles	Maximum
Service Level	C8	Warehouse Area	Square meters	Maximum
Service Level	C9	Scope of Operation	Countries	Maximum
Social	C10	Number of Employees	Employees	Maximum
Social	C11	Number of Employee Training Sessions	Training sessions	Maximum

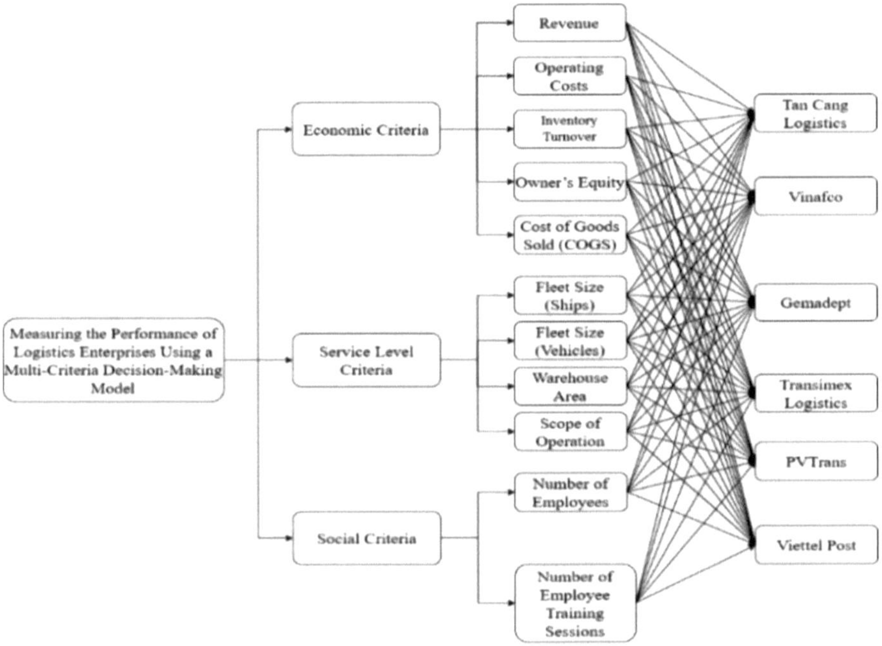

Fig. 1. Decision Tree

5 Results

5.1 Criteria Weight Using CRITIC (Criteria Importance Through Intercriteria Correlation)

In multi-criteria decision-making (MCDM), the initial decision matrix is first constructed. The initial decision matrix of this paper is described as follows in Table 3 (Appendix).

The study applies the CRITIC method to calculate the weights. The author normalizes the matrix and obtains the weight results as shown in Fig. 2.

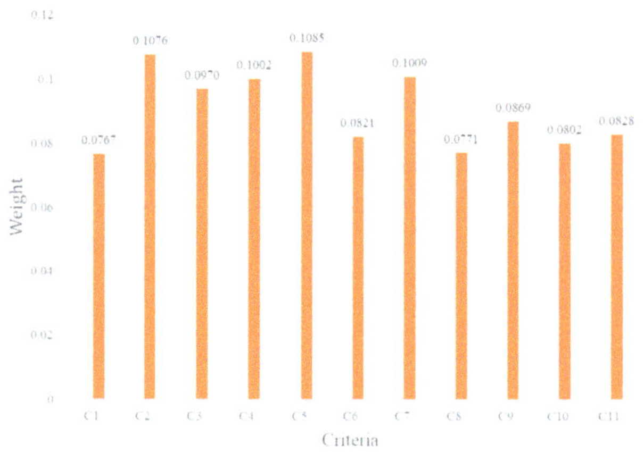

Fig. 2. Chart showing the weights of the criteria using the CRITIC method

Compared to other methods, the CRITIC method can provide a more balanced view of the importance of criteria in the decision-making process, as it does not rely on subjective expert opinions like the AHP or FAHP methods. Therefore, applying this method can help objectively and practically measure and evaluate the performance of enterprises. The weight results of the criteria using the CRITIC method show a reasonable and even distribution, with some criteria standing out and reflecting the actual conditions in Vietnam. The three criteria with the highest weights are C5 (Cost of Goods Sold – COGS) with a weight of 0.1085, C2 (Operating Costs) with a weight of 0.1076, and C7 (Fleet Size – Vehicles) with a weight of 0.1009. This indicates that these criteria play the most significant roles in the evaluation process.

The criterion "Cost of Goods Sold" has the highest weight, highlighting the importance of this factor in evaluating the performance of Vietnamese logistics enterprises in 2023. In the logistics industry, COGS includes direct costs related to the provision of transportation and other logistics services, such as vehicle leasing (trucks, ships, aircraft), fuel expenses, loading and unloading costs, wages of staff directly involved in transport and warehousing, as well as storage and warehousing fees, maintenance, and depreciation of fixed assets. The high weight of this criterion reflects a critical reality in the Vietnamese logistics market, where price competition is intense. To maintain competitive advantage and attract customers, businesses must optimize and tightly control their cost of goods sold. Any inefficiency or increase in COGS components can significantly affect a company's profitability and competitiveness.

5.2 Alternative Ranking Using MARCOS (Measurement of Alternatives and Ranking According to Compromise Solution)

After determining the weights of the criteria, the step of ranking the performance of the enterprises is carried out using the TOPSIS method based on the weighted criteria results. Among the 11 criteria, the negative criteria include C2. Operating Cost and C5. Cost of Goods Sold, while the remaining criteria are benefit criteria. In this ranking step, the initial decision matrix is used for normalization based on the given formula, resulting in a normalized matrix. Then, this normalized matrix is multiplied by the criterion weights obtained through the CRITIC method to form a weighted normalized decision matrix. Next, the positive ideal solution and negative ideal solution are identified. The separation measures are calculated based on Eqs. (3.15) and (3.16) to determine the distance between each alternative and the ideal solutions. Subsequently, the relative closeness is C_i^* obtained by applying Eq. (3.17) with the aid of Excel software. The ranking results of the logistics enterprises are shown in Fig. 3.

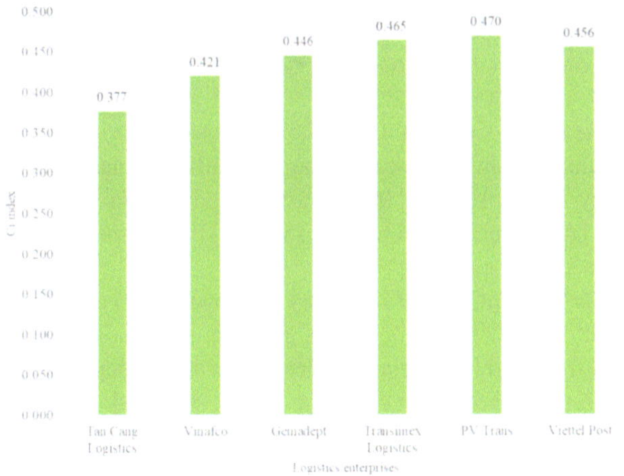

Fig. 3. Performance scores of six logistics enterprise

The results show that PetroVietnam Transportation Corporation (PVTrans) has the highest performance among the enterprises studied. PVTrans is one of Vietnam's leading maritime transport and logistics companies, specializing in the transportation of crude oil, petroleum products, and liquid cargo. It was ranked among the Top 10 most reputable logistics companies in Vietnam in 2022, 2023, and 2024.

Following PVTrans, the company with the second-highest Ci score is Transimex Logistics Joint Stock Company (Transimex Logistics). It is one of the largest third-party logistics (3PL) providers in Vietnam, with strengths in container transport services, heavy-lift cargo transport, and machinery relocation services.

The company with the lowest ranking according to the TOPSIS method in this study is Tan Cang Logistics and Stevedoring Joint Stock Company (TCL). As the first subsidiary of and strongly supported by Saigon Newport Corporation (SNP), Tan Cang Logistics has grown significantly in the fields of port operations, container depot management, stevedoring services, and multimodal transportation.

These results affirm that in the logistics industry—where operating costs, technology, and coordination capacity are critical—high performance is the outcome of a well-aligned combination of long-term development strategy, internal capabilities, and a suitable organizational environment. This also provides a foundation for companies in the industry to review their operational models and develop more effective strategies amid increasing competition and growing pressure for digital transformation.

5.3 Sensitivity Analysis

In multi-criteria decision-making (MCDM) problems, input data is often unstable rather than continuous and consistent. Therefore, sensitivity analysis plays a crucial role in evaluating how changes in criterion weights affect the ranking of alternatives. This study constructed 11 sensitivity scenarios by systematically removing each criterion and recalculating the weights of the remaining ones. Then, performance scores and rankings of six logistics companies were recalculated using the TOPSIS method. The results of performance scores and rankings of the enterprises are presented in Table 4 (Appendix).

The analysis revealed significant variations across scenarios. Tan Cang Logistics consistently maintained a stable ranking throughout all 11 scenarios, indicating minimal dependence on any single criterion. In contrast, companies like Viettel Post, Transimex Logistics, and PVTrans experienced notable ranking shifts, demonstrating their reliance on specific criteria.

Notably, Scenario 3 (removal of Inventory Turnover – C3) and Scenario 9 (removal of Scope of Operational – C9) had the most significant impact. In Scenario 3, Transimex Logistics dropped from 2nd to 5th place, reflecting its strong dependence on high inventory turnover—a key strength of the company, which achieved the highest turnover rate in 2023 with 573.04 turns/year. This showcases its efficient logistics cycle, supported by advanced transport coordination technology.

In Scenario 9, PVTrans fell from 1st to 5th, underscoring the critical role of international operational reach. With over 85% of its fleet operating on global routes across 80 + countries, international presence is a cornerstone of PVTrans's long-term strategy and a major contributor to its overall performance.

Figure 4 clearly illustrates the ranking fluctuations of logistics companies across different sensitivity analysis scenarios are most critical to ensuring a reliable and effective 3PLs selection.

Fig. 4. Final rankings of companies for each scenario

6 Conclusion

This study successfully achieved its objective of measuring and ranking the year of 2023 performance of Vietnamese logistics companies using a set of criteria based on a multi-criteria decision-making (MCDM) model, combining the CRITIC and TOPSIS methods. The evaluation framework included 11 criteria such as revenue, operating costs, cost of goods sold, fleet size, inventory turnover, and scope of operation. Initially intended to analyze the top 10 logistics firms in Vietnam, data limitations reduced the final sample to six companies. With actual company data, the study enabled objective performance assessments and provided a useful reference for managers to benchmark and enhance their competitive positioning. Results showed that PVTrans and Transimex Logistics had the highest performance scores, while Tan Cang Logistics ranked lowest. Cost-related and transport capacity criteria had the highest weights and strongest influence on overall performance.

Despite its findings, the study faced certain limitations, including a small sample size and the absence of environmental criteria due to insufficient data disclosure. The author recommends future studies expand the scope to include foreign and small-to-medium logistics firms, categorize companies by size, and enrich the evaluation framework by incorporating environmental and qualitative criteria. Furthermore, logistics companies should focus more on controlling cost of goods sold and operating expenses, as these heavily impact overall efficiency. Applying quantitative performance evaluation models such as CRITIC–TOPSIS can support objective, transparent monitoring and inform strategic decision-making processes.

Acknowledgement. The authors appreciate the support from the Hong Bang International University and the Industrial University of Ho Chi Minh City, Vietnam.

Appendix

Table 3. The decision matrix consists of the collected data

	C1	C2	C3	C4	C5	C6	C7	C8	C9	C10	C11
Tan Cang Logistics	1,525,530	1,395,628	115.89	550,929	1,258,007	5	26	67,000	1	295	439
Vinafco	1,272,366	1,244,229	56.09	722,989	1,179,963	3	1,005	230,000	4	721	1,200
Gemadept	3,845,826	3,302,921	27.44	9,732,374	2,067,811	21	330	450,000	6	1,498	1,561
Transimex Logistics	248,429	218,724	571.04	90,458	194,550	13	160	330,000	3	287	563
PVTrans	9,555,979	8,146,980	37.47	9,030,395	7,717,484	51	6	7,413	83	2341	4,242
Viettel Post	19,587,522	19,183,269	50.6	1,581,216	18,706,908	0	1,100	740,000	3	15,389	51,260

Table 4. The performance scores of the model with different coefficient values

Criteria	Scenario 0	Scenario 1	Scenario 2	Scenario 3	Scenario 4	Scenario 5	Scenario 6	Scenario 7	Scenario 8	Scenario 9	Scenario 10	Scenario 11
Tan Cang Logistics	0.377	0.387	0.304	0.391	0.389	0.299	0.389	0.390	0.384	0.397	0.393	0.395
Vinafco	0.421	0.433	0.363	0.444	0.435	0.360	0.436	0.394	0.424	0.442	0.439	0.442
Gemadept	0.446	0.456	0.404	0.479	0.413	0.393	0.449	0.453	0.441	0.472	0.466	0.472
Transimex Logistics	0.465	0.480	0.415	0.423	0.483	0.412	0.474	0.478	0.465	0.490	0.486	0.489
PVTrans	0.4695	0.4690	0.4590	0.5052	0.4444	0.457	0.442	0.492	0.484	0.425	0.488	0.495
Viettel post	0.4558	0.4325	0.4918	0.4833	0.4683	0.494	0.456	0.428	0.438	0.482	0.423	0.419

References

1. General Statistics Office. Vietnam's Import and Export Picture in 2024 – Recovery, Development, and New Records. Department of Statistics – Ministry of Finance, Ha Noi (2025)
2. World Trade Organization. Global Trade Outlook and Statistics. World Trade Organization (2024)
3. iTS Global. Overview of the Logistics Sector in 2024 and Development Trends for 2025 in the Vietnamese Market. iTS Global (2025)
4. Ministry of Industry and Trade. Vietnam Logistics Report 2024. Industry and Trade Publishing House (2024)
5. Hudson, M., Lean, J., Smart, P.: Improving control through effective performance measurement in SMEs. Prod. Plan. Control **12**, 804–813 (2001)
6. Le, T.M., Wang, C.N., Nguyen, H.K.: Using the optimization algorithm to evaluate and predict the business performance of logistics companies–a case study in Vietnam. Appl. Econ. **52**(38), 4196–4212 (2020)
7. Punnavanam, N., Rinju, P.N.: Investment decisions among the stock market investors and awareness on operational performance of privatized companies. Int. J. Res. Commer. Manag. Stud. **6**(3), 1–7 (2024)
8. Neely, A.: Measuring performance: the operations management perspective. In: Business Performance Measurement Unifying Theory and Integrating Practice, pp. 64–81. Cambridge University Press (2009)
9. de Lima, E.P., da Costa, S.E.G., Ferreira, P.S., Angelis, J.J.: Operations strategy and performance measurement roles. Business (2010)
10. Wang, C.N., Quang, B.X., Dang, T.T.: Performance measurement of international shipping companies before and during COVID-19: a DEA Malmquist index and window analysis approach. Transport. J. **63**(3), 207–221 (2024)
11. Nguyen, T.K.L., Nguyen, T.L.H., Ngo, T.L., Hoang, B.A., Le, H.H., Tran, T.T.H.: An integrated approach of fuzzy analytic hierarchy process and super slack-based measure for the logistics industry in Vietnam. Sustainability **15**(16), 12654 (2023)
12. Majumder, M., Saha, A.K.: Multi criteria decision making. In: Feasibility Model of Solar Energy Plants by ANN and MCDM Techniques, pp. 9–12. Springer, Cham (2016)
13. Bączkiewicz, A., Wątróbski, J., Kizielewicz, B., Sałabun, W.: Towards objectification of multi-criteria assessments: a comparative study on MCDA methods. In: 16th Conference on Computer Science and Intelligence Systems (2021)
14. Iazzolino, G., Laise, D., Marraro, L.: Business multicriteria performance analysis: a tutorial. Benchmark. Int. J. **19**(3), 395–411 (2012)
15. Çakır, S., Perçin, S.: Performance measurement of logistics firms with multi-criteria decision making methods. Ege Acad. Rev. **13**(4), 449–460 (2013)

16. Alkhatib, S.F., Darlington, R., Yang, Z., Nguyen, T.T.: A novel technique for evaluating and selecting logistics service providers based on the logistics resource view. Expert Syst. Appl. **42**(20), 6976–6989 (2015)
17. Gergin, R.E., Baki, B.: Evaluation by integrated AHP and TOPSIS method of logistics performance in turkey's regions. Bus. Econ. Res. J. **6**(4), 115–135 (2015)
18. Özceylan, E., Çetinkaya, C., Erbaş, M., Kabak, M.: Logistic performance evaluation of provinces in Turkey: a GIS-based multi-criteria decision analysis. Transport. Res. Part A: Policy Pract. **94**, 323–337 (2019)
19. Agrawal, S., Singh, R.K., Murtaza, Q.: Prioritizing critical success factors for reverse logistics implementation using fuzzy-TOPSIS methodology. J. Ind. Eng. Int. **12**, 15–27 (2016)
20. Çakır, S.: Measuring logistics performance of OECD countries via fuzzy linear regression. J. Multi-Criteria Decis. Anal. **24**(3–4), 163–177 (2014)
21. Li, Y.L., Ying, C.S., Chin, K.S., Yang, H.T., Xu, J.: Third-party reverse logistics provider selection approach based on hybrid-information MCDM and cumulative prospect theory. J. Clean. Prod. **195**, 573–584 (2018)
22. Bianchini, A.: 3PL provider selection by AHP and TOPSIS methodology. Benchmark. Int. J. **25**(1), 235–252 (2018)
23. Riaz, M., Farid, H.M.A.: Picture fuzzy aggregation approach with application to third-party logistic provider selection process. Rep. Mech. Eng. **3**(1), 227–236 (2022)
24. Nguyen, N.-A.-T., Wang, C.-N., Dang, L.-T.-H., Dang, L.-T.-T., Dang, T.-T.: Selection of cold chain logistics service providers based on a grey AHP and grey COPRAS framework: a case study in Vietnam. Axioms **11**(4), 154 (2022)
25. Mešić, A., Miškić, S., Stević, Ž, Mastilo, Z.: Hybrid MCDM solutions for evaluation of the logistics performance index of the Western Balkan countries. ECONOMICS **10**(1), 13–34 (2022)
26. Boakai, S., Samanlioglu, F.: An MCDM approach to third party logistics provider selection. Int. J. Logist. Syst. Manag. **44**(3), 283–299 (2023)
27. Çalık, A., Erdebilli, B., Özdemir, Y.S.: Novel integrated hybrid multi-criteria decision-making approach for logistics performance index. Transport. Res. Rec. **2677**(2), 1392–1400 (2023)
28. Diakoulaki, D., Mavrotas, G., Papayannakis, L.: Determining objective weights in multiple criteria problems: the critic method. Comput. Oper. Res. **22**(7), 763–770 (1995)
29. Fontela, E., Gabus, A.: World Problems an Invitation to Further Thought within the Framework of DEMATEL (1972)
30. Gunawan, R.D.: Combination of SMART and CRITIC methods in decision support systems for determination of superior products. J. Inf. Technol. Softw. Eng. Comput. Sci. (ITSECS) **2**(4), 160–170 (2024)
31. Hwang, C.L., Yoon, K.: Multiple attribute decision making methods and applocations. In: Multiple Attribute Decision Making. Springer, Heidelberg (1981)
32. Opricovic, S., Tzeng, G.-H.: Defuzzification within a multicriteria decision model. Int. J. Uncertain. Fuzz. Knowl.-Based Syst. **11**(5), 635–652 (2023)
33. Yousefi, A., Hadi-Vencheh, A.: An integrated group decision making model and its evaluation by DEA for automobile industry. Expert Syst. Appl. **37**(12), 8543–8556 (2010)
34. Deng, H., Yeh, C.-H., Willis, R.J.: Inter-company comparison using modified TOPSIS with objective weights. Comput. Oper. Res. **27**(10), 963–973 (2000)
35. Kazan, H., Ozdemir, O.: Financial performance assesment of large scale conglomerates via topsis and critic methods. Int. J. Manag. Sustainabil. **3**(4), 203–224 (2014)

Optimizing E-commerce Warehouse Operations: Leveraging a Star and Dijkstra's Algorithms for Efficient Picking Routes

Vo Thi Hong Hanh(✉), Dinh Cao Nguyen, and Ho Thanh Phong

Hong Bang International University, Ho Chi Minh City, Vietnam
hanh.ise.bku@gmail.com

Abstract. The aim of this study included research and application of optimization order picking process in warehouse E-commerce to reduce the route and time of travel. A Top-Down approach methodology was adopted, started with the comprehensive analysis of the picking process, followed by the design of a general management system architecture, and then the detailed development of functions based on this architecture. To solve the route optimization problem, two well-established algorithms, A* and Dijkstra's, were selected due to their efficiency in solving shortest path problems. Supporting software such as Python and SPSS were employed to develop the system and validate the software. Data were collected from the operational areas of a leading digital marketplace platform's warehouse facility in Ho Chi Minh City. The results showed a 36.5% reduction in picking time, a 28.5% reduction in travel distance, and a 32.55% increase in picker efficiency. These findings demonstrate that the A* algorithm is more effective in environments requiring rapid and accurate path calculations. The proposed framework can be implemented to various picking policies, independent of the specific warehouse layout, enhancing the system's scalability and efficiency in today's competitive online retail market.

Keywords: E-commerce warehouses · Picking route optimization · Dijkstra's algorithm · A* algorithm

1 Introduction

Warehouses constitute a critical component of logistics systems that accounts for approximately 20% of the logistics costs of the surveyed companies in 2003, as reported by ELA/AT Kearney [1]. As e-business continues to grow, optimizing warehouse operations is key to reducing costs and improving productivity. Order picking in storage place is a critical and labor-intensive process [2, 3] that significantly impacts customer service and operational efficiency. However, many warehouses still rely on the experience of workers to manage the picking routes, leading to time wastage, unnecessary travel, and congestion within the warehouse. Optimizing automated picking routes by using robotics, sensors and mobile devices in many large enterprises remains a challenge due to frequent layout changes, fast-moving inventory, and large order volumes [4, 5].

M. Li et al. (Eds.): ICLS 2025, *Proceeding of the 19th International Congress on Logistics and Supply Chain Management Systems*, pp. 104–120, 2026.
https://doi.org/10.1007/978-981-95-7700-2_9

Recent research has focused on optimizing picking strategies, including storage assignment, order batching, and integrating multiple approaches [6–10]. Additionally, the use of mathematical models and heuristic algorithms can optimize the allocation of picking routes and products, along with the navigation of automated picking machines, thereby improving both the energy consumption and time efficiency during the picking process [11–14]. Other advancements have incorporated machine learning techniques, such as deep learning, alongside traditional optimization models to improve route forecasting and save both time and costs [15, 16].

Among pathfinding algorithms, Dijkstra's algorithm and the A* algorithm has been widely used for shortest path problems in warehouse route optimization [17–19]. A research by Leni Marlina et al. demonstrates the effectiveness of the A* algorithm in optimizing picking routes by integrating detailed warehouse layouts and heuristic functions, allowing for real-time path adjustments [20]. Yumeng Yan' work further highlights A*'s ability to reduce computation time while maintaining accuracy through heuristics [21]. Practical applications of Dijkstra's algorithm, including logistics and healthcare routing scenarios, have shown its utility beyond warehouse [22–24].

The goal of this research is to develop and implement an automated solution for optimizing the picking process in warehouses to enhance operational efficiency in the competitive online shopping environment. It focuses on reducing travel distance, cutting picking time, lowering labor costs, enhancing order accuracy, and optimizing resource allocation. The solution employs optimization algorithms, notably A* and Dijkstra's, which are effective for pathfinding.

The remainder of this paper is organized as follows: Sect. 2 lays the theoretical groundwork, discussing algorithms like A* and Dijkstra. Section 3 presents the detailed methodology used in this study, including data collection, system design, and the application of algorithms for route optimization. In Sect. 4 a case-study background is presented. Finally, Sect. 5 concludes with an evaluation of the results while Sect. 6 presents the conclusion of the study, limitation as well as suggests directions for future research.

2 Literature Review

2.1 E-commerce Warehouse and Order Picking Activities

E-commerce warehouses apparently form an important part in managing inventory, processing orders, and fulfilling customer expectations in the online retail industry [25]. Strategies for improving online marketplace's warehouse operations include effective stock arrangement, order picking and packing, and transportation optimization, that help address challenges such as demand forecasting, inventory management, and order processing efficiency [26, 27]. The main methods for order picking in-clude order picking, batch picking and zone picking, in which the former focuses on collecting items for a single order at a time, particularly suitable for warehouses that has a low order volume and a diverse range of products. The goal of order picking is to optimize the process to ensure orders are fulfilled quickly and accurately. Being the most labor-intensive and expensive operation within the warehouse, it has a direct impact on the quality of downstream customer service.

2.2 Routing Method and Optimization Routing

A study by Đukić & Oluić calculated that an operator spends 50% of the total order picking time traveling through the warehouse to locate and retrieve the correct items [28], underscoring the requirement for changes in organizational processes alongside the use of various picking methods to shorten travel paths. Other time components, such as picking, searching, administrative tasks, and waiting, although smaller, can be significantly improved using technology like automated warehouse management systems, digitalizing administrative procedures, and optimizing management workflows [29, 30]. In warehouse operations, routing involves finding the most efficient path for order picking from a starting point to a destination, with the goal is to minimize overall costs such as time, distance, or other resources. In logistics and traffic management, routing aims to find the shortest or most efficient paths, reducing time and transportation costs. Various heuristic methods, such as S-shape, backtracking, and max distance first, are applied to further optimize warehouse operations by improving travel efficiency and reducing unnecessary backtracking.

2.3 Dijsktra Algorithm and A* Algorithm

Dijkstra's Algorithm focuses on finding the shortest path in a graph with non-negative weights. It systematically explores all possible paths from a source node and iteratively updates the shortest path until it reaches the target node. Dijkstra's method, while effective in static environments, may struggle in dynamic scenarios where warehouse layouts frequently change or inventory positions fluctuate [31]. However, it remains a fundamental algorithm for optimizing routing in scenarios where the warehouse design is relatively stable, and is commonly used in systems for static warehouse layouts or short-term planning.

While Dijkstra's algorithm is effective in stable environments, the A* algorithm excels in dynamic settings due to its adaptability to real-time changes. The A* algorithm combines greedy best-first search and breadth-first search, making it an ideal candidate for real-time route optimization in dynamic environments [21]. It combines the real cost incurred to arrive at a given node with an estimated cost from that node to the target, employing a heuristic-based strategy to optimize both travel time and overall path length. This combination ensures that the algorithm not only finds the shortest route but also adapts efficiently to changes in the environment, such as altering layouts and real-time traffic conditions in the warehouse. The flexibility of A* allows its integration with complex, real-time systems for automated warehouse operations, improving both speed and accuracy in picking tasks.

2.4 Application of System Engineering for Optimizing Warehouse Operations

Systems engineering is an interdisciplinary approach for analyzing, designing, and managing complex systems, focusing on the whole system rather than individual components, addressing the challenge of understanding emergent behaviors in complex systems [32]. This study employed a top-down approach to problem-solving, define customer needs and required functionality early in designing solutions for warehouse operations.

Pareto charts, Ishikawa diagrams, and the 5 Whys method are highlighted as effective analytical tools that help identify inefficiencies, prioritize issues, determine root causes, and develop improvement strategies [33, 34].

3 Methodology

3.1 Research Content

The paper presents a research framework aimed at optimizing the picking process at a digital warehouse operations, which includes several key steps such as requirement analysis, system design, and performance evaluation. The process begins with defining requirements and goals, such as picking time, accuracy, and cost, to guide system development. Process optimization follows, using strategies like wave picking and algorithms like A* and Dijkstra to improve travel time and efficiency. The final step is monitoring and continuous improvement, using feedback and performance data to identify bottlenecks and refine the system.

The research procedure is shown in Fig. 1 below and includes eight main steps.

- Step 1: Define research objectives and solution scope.
- Step 2: Investigate the company and current warehouse processes; analyze challenges and strengths.
- Step 3: Review relevant research and models in warehouse management and picking optimization.
- Step 4: Analyze warehouse data focusing on picking efficiency factors.
- Step 5: Identify key issues in picking route management to improve efficiency.
- Step 6: Design and develop a system with route optimization, order management, and inventory tracking.
- Step 7: Test and evaluate system feasibility and effectiveness; implement if successful or refine as needed.
- Step 8: Summarize the research and suggest future improvements.

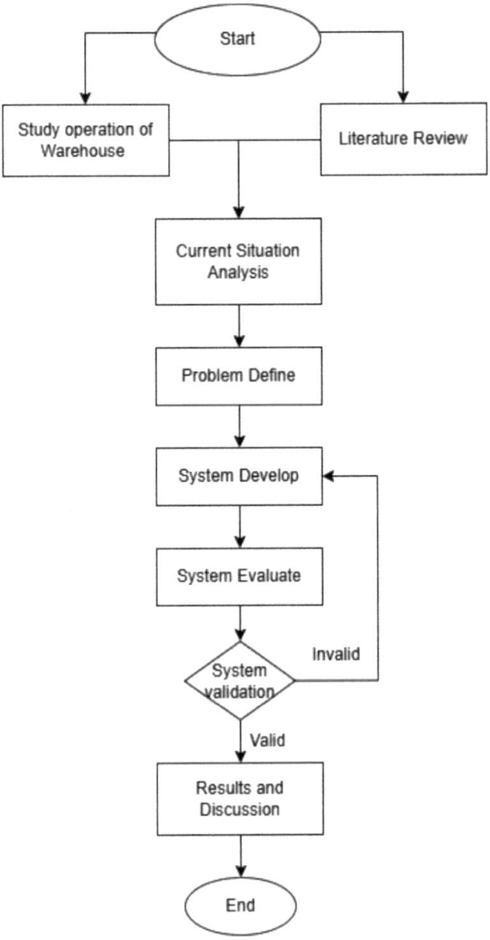

Fig. 1. Research Implementation Flowchart

3.2 Data Collection Methods

Data collection is critical for accurately modeling the warehouse layout and understanding the operational constraints. Key data gathered include warehouse layout, real-time product locations, order frequency, picking patterns, picking times, travel distances, picker efficiency, and error rates. Data were obtained via observations, employee interviews, and WMS reports over two consecutive weeks (Monday to Saturday), each week focusing on a different group of pickers. This schedule ensures comprehensive data capturing and minimizes bias that could result from collecting data on limited days.

3.3 Route Optimization Model Design

The route optimization model design for warehouse operations is structured through the following key steps:

- Step 1: Needs analysis: the process begins by thoroughly analyzing operational requirements employing techniques such as Pareto charts, Ishikawa diagrams, and the 5 Whys method to identify key factors impacting picking efficiency.
- Step 2: Problem Modeling: Drawing from the needs analysis, a clear problem model is developed defining the objectives of reducing travel time and costs while improving overall warehouse management.
- Step 3: The mathematical model is subsequently formulated as a binary integer programming problem with clearly stated assumptions.

• Hypotheses: Assumptions include fixed picking times per location, average travel speed, and constraints on route feasibility.
• Decision variables: variables represent whether travel occurs between storage locations i and j
• Parameters: distance $d$ij, picking time th and travel time $t$ij based on distance and average speed are defined.
• Objective function and constraints: minimize total travel and picking time while ensuring all necessary locations are visited exactly once, and time limits are respected.

- Step 4: A detailed distance matrix representing all storage locations within the warehouse is created
- Step 5: Implementing the A* Algorithm
- Step 6: Implementing the Dijkstra Algorithm
- Step 7: Model validation and software verification: The implemented model and software undergo rigorous validation by comparing computed routes with real-world measurements. Statistical test (e.g., independent samples t-test) is used to confirm the reliability of the model.
- Step 8: Constructing the time matrix based on the distance matrix and average travel speed.
- Step 9: Algorithm flow and system integration: the entire route optimization process is encapsulated in a programmatic flow chart. Python programming language is used for its robust data handling and optimization capabilities.
- Step 10: Finally, the optimized route model is embedded into daily warehouse operations.

3.4 Research Methods

Application of the A* Algorithm for Warehouse Route Optimization

The A* algorithm is applied to the warehouse picking route problem through the following steps:

- Initialize the start node as the starting point and set the goal node as the final destination. Create an open set containing only the start node.
- Calculate the evaluation function f(n) = g(n) + h(n) for the start node. Move the start node to the closed set, which tracks visited nodes. Here, g(n) represents the actual cost from the start node to node n while h(n) d estimates the cost from node n to the goal.

- Expand nodes by selecting the node with the smallest f(n) value from the open set. For each neighboring node, calculate their f(n) values. Update the open set with these neighbors, and move nodes to the closed set as they are visited.
- The algorithm terminates once the goal node is included in the closed set. From the goal node, trace back through the parent nodes to construct the complete optimal path from start to goal.

Application of the Dijsktra Algorithm for Warehouse Route Optimization
Dijkstra's algorithm is employed to the warehouse picking route problem through the following steps:

- Set the start node with a label of zero and create an open set containing only the start node.
- For each neighboring node, calculate its tentative distance and update its label.
- Select the node with the smallest tentative distance from the open set and transfer it to the closed set.
- For the selected node, calculate the distances to its neighbors and update the open set.
- Continue until the goal node is reached.
- Once the goal is reached, trace back through parent nodes to find the shortest path.

Validation and Results Analysis
The Independent Samples T-test is a statistical technique that applied to compare the mean values of two distinct groups from separate populations, aiming to define whether a statistically significant difference exists between them. The hypotheses for the test are formulated as follows:

- Null hypothesis (H_0): posits that the means of the two populations are equal, indicating no significant difference.
- Alternative hypothesis (H_1): asserts that the means differ significantly.

The test statistic t is calculated using the formula:

$$t = \frac{\overline{X}_1 - \overline{X}_2}{\sqrt{\frac{s_1^2}{n_1} + \frac{s_2^2}{n_2}}} \tag{1}$$

where $\overline{X}_1$, $\overline{X}_2$ denote the sample means, and s_1^2, s_2^2 are the sample variances, and n_1, n_2 represent the respective sample sizes of the two groups.

The degrees of freedom (*df*) for the test are computed as:

$$\mathrm{df} = \frac{\left(\frac{s_1^2}{n_1} + \frac{s_2^2}{n_2}\right)^2}{\frac{\left(\frac{s_1^2}{n_1}\right)^2}{n_1 - 1} + \frac{\left(\frac{s_2^2}{n_2}\right)^2}{n_2 - 1}} \tag{2}$$

The calculated t-value is then compared against the critical value from the Student's t-distribution table at a predefined significance level (commonly $\alpha = 0.05$). If t exceeds the critical value, H0 is rejected, indicating a significant difference between groups.

4 Case Study

The pilot test was conducted over a four-month period at a leading e-commerce platform's warehouse in Ho Chi Minh City. Based on survey results and analysis from the area management team, employees were divided into two main groups according to their level of work experience. Group 1 includes employees with over one month of experience, familiar with warehouse operations; Group 2 comprises new employees with less than one month, still adapting to procedures. Data collection and observation revealed an 18% delay rate in order handovers to transportation, adversely impacting service quality. A Pareto chart was employed to analyze the causes contributing to the failure in meeting the target, as illustrated in Fig. 2. Root cause analysis using Ishikawa and 5 Whys identified insufficient investment in upgrading the automated picking system due to budget limits as the primary cause. Key issues include incomplete or inaccurate order information, prolonged processing time due to unoptimized workflows and unclear staff roles, software incompatibility causing tracking errors, poor coordination among warehouse, delivery, and customer service departments, and employees' lack of skills in accurate order picking.

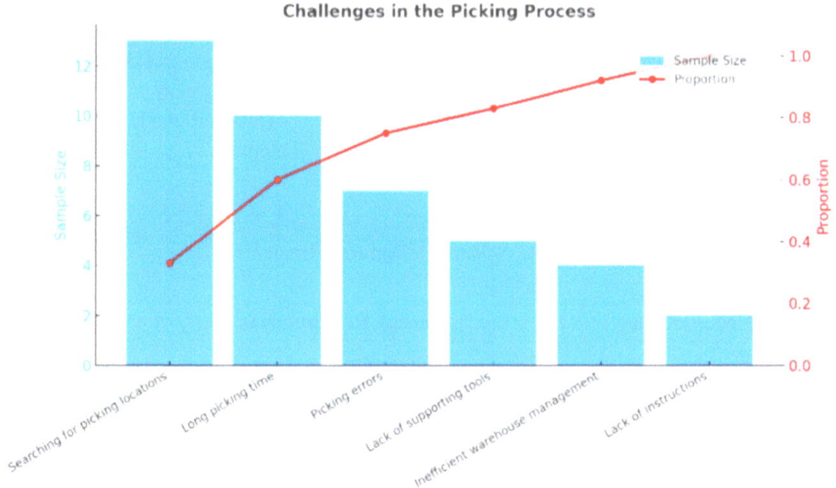

Fig. 2. Pareto Chart

Employee performance evaluation of 30 samples showed Group 1's efficiency at 16.4% compared to Group 2's 13.6%, with an overall low efficiency of 15%. Both groups traveled an average of 600.2 m per picking route, indicating suboptimal warehouse layout. Fast-moving items cause congestion without proper solutions, highlighting the need for a picking route support system to reduce travel distance, optimize layout, speed up picking, and improve productivity, especially for less experienced staff.

To address these challenges, Table 1 outlines stakeholder needs, and Table 2 presents system design requirements for the order picking route management system.

Table 1. Stakeholder needs and system requirements

Stakeholders	Stakeholder Needs	System Requirements
Management	- Shorten picking time - Efficient inventory management - High employee operational efficiency - Accurate item picking	- Apply optimization algorithms to determine optimal picking routes - Use data analysis tools and visual charts - Detect data entry errors
Order Processing Staff	- Efficient order management - Timely order status updates	- User-friendly and intuitive interface - Integrated order management with tracking support - Quick solution determination
Pickers	- Accurate and fast picking guidance - Easy access to product and storage location information - Optimized picking routes	- Provide accurate and fast picking guidance - Easy access to product and storage location information - Optimize picking routes
3PL Providers	- Receive more orders - Synchronize transportation info with warehouse system - Ensure safety and security of goods during transportation	- Quick solution determination - Real-time tracking and status update system - Data and goods security methods

Table 2. System Design Requirements

Functional Requirements	Design Requirements
Process 4000 orders per day	Support tools: -Workforce: 7 staff -Equipment: 5 laptops, 3 printers, 4 barcode scanners, 5 forklifts -The system must be structurally optimized, using algorithms and distributed architecture to allocate and process orders efficiently
Picking time per item not exceeding 2 min	The system design must integrate automation technologies and optimization algorithms to ensure efficient searching, selection, and movement of goods
Continuous operation capability	Hardware and software design must ensure flexibility and scalability to accommodate changing needs over time without impacting performance

(*continued*)

Table 2. *(continued)*

Functional Requirements	Design Requirements
User-friendly and intuitive interface	Important information such as order status, route progress, and product location must be clearly displayed and quickly accessible
Compatibility and customizability	The system must be highly compatible with existing warehouse software and systems such as WMS, ERP software, and terminal devices including barcode scanners, mobile devices, and other supporting tools

The solution requirements for optimizing the picking route in the warehouse focus on several key aspects. Firstly, it is essential to minimize the travel time of employees or robots. The solution requirements for optimizing the picking route in the warehouse focus on several key aspects. Firstly, it is essential to minimize the travel time of employees or robots between picking locations while reducing operational costs and efficiently utilizing labor. The allocation of goods within the warehouse must be arranged to maximize storage space and shorten product search times. Warehouse design should aim to reduce congestion and bottlenecks during movement, while improving accessibility to picking areas to enhance efficiency. Regarding order volume and priority, the solution must accelerate the processing of urgent orders and ensure timely delivery. Finally, constraints related to resources such as labor and equipment must be carefully managed to ensure proper allocation and optimization, thereby minimizing resource wastage during warehouse operations.

The solution model was selected by reviewing relevant literature and analyzing its alignment with the specified requirements, thereby determining the appropriate model and supporting tools. The key factors in the selection process include:

- A binary integer programming model.
- The branch and bound algorithm.
- Python programming software for implementation.
- The use of the Vietnamese language for interface and documentation.

Now key factors such as working time, costs, and operational parameters must be clearly defined. The goal is to optimize the movement of warehouse staff or vehicles to minimize time and costs. Factors considered include travel distance, order processing time, product location distribution, and random events like congestion or unexpected disruptions. It is assumed that applying optimization algorithms such as A* and Dijkstra can compute optimal routes effectively, improving both speed and accuracy. *Tij* denotes travel time from i to j, calculated by dividing distance by average walking speed v. Based on data analysis, $v = 1.25\ m/s$. Thus,

$$t = \frac{d_{ij}}{1.25} \tag{3}$$

Assuming that our model has n storage locations and m is the number of orders to be picked during a work shift, the objective function can be expressed as follows:

$$MaxZ = \frac{30\sum_{i=1}^{n} m}{(30\sum_{i=1}^{n} m + \sum_{i=0}^{n}\sum_{j=0}^{n} t_{ij} * x_{ij}) * \frac{100}{65}} \quad (4)$$

where Z represents the maximum operational efficiency of the employee.

A fundamental constraint is the determination of feasible paths between storage locations in the warehouse. If no direct path exists between two locations, the distance Dij is considered infinite ($Dij = +\infty$), and the decision variable xij must be zero, ensuring $xij \leq Cij$, where Cij limits allowed movements. The binary decision variable $xij \in \{0,1\}$ indicates whether the route includes movement from location i to j.

Key constraints of the model include:

- The total visits to storage locations must equal the required number of picks m:

$$\sum_{i=1}^{n} x_{ij} = m \quad (5)$$

- Each storage location must be entered exactly once:

$$\sum_{i=0}^{n} x_{ij} = 1 \quad (6)$$

- Each storage location must be exited exactly once:

$$\sum_{j=0}^{n} x_{ij} = 1 \quad (7)$$

- Time constraints ensure the total picking route duration does not exceed 20 min (1200 s), formulated as:

$$(30\sum_{i=1}^{n} m + \sum_{i=0}^{n}\sum_{j=0}^{n} t_{ij} * x_{ij} * \frac{100}{65}) \leq 1200 \quad (8)$$

where t_{ij} is the travel time from location i to j based on distance and average speed.

Next, the optimization model was developed by integrating the A* and Dijkstra algorithms into a hybrid system that can handle both static and dynamic route optimization within the warehouse. Distance Matrix (Dij) was constructed based on the layout data, representing the distances between key locations (e.g., shelves, packing stations). The matrix is a square matrix structured, where the first column contains the names of the starting positions and the first row contains the names of the destination positions, while the cells along the diagonal have values equal to 0.

Due to the large number of destination points (180 points), calculating this matrix manually would be time-consuming and prone to errors. To overcome this issue, it is necessary to develop software that automatically computes the distance matrix. Based on its popularity, ease of use, and data processing capabilities, Python was chosen as the programming language to apply the A* algorithm and Dijsktra algorithm to determine the shortest path between points within the warehouse.

The results obtained from the software were analyzed and compared with actual system measurements to evaluate the reliability of the developed model. The route length and travel sequence were used as validation criteria. After randomly selecting start and end point pairs using the Random function in Microsoft Excel, actual measurements were conducted Using SPSS, an independent samples t-test compared the software results with real measurements across 20 samples at a 95% confidence level. Statistical testing resulted in Sig. (2-tailed) = 0.987 > 0.05, indicating no significant difference between software predictions and observed measurements. Thus, the software results are confirmed accurate and reliable.

Next, the Time Matrix (Tij) capturing the time required to move between locations is calculated using formula (3), which is presented in Table 3.

Table 3. The result of the Tij matrix

Dij (m)	A1–1	A1–2	A1–3	A1–4	…
A1-1	0	1	2	3	…
A1-2	1	0	1	2	…
A1-3	2	1	0	1	…
A1-4	3	2	1	0	…
…	…	…	…	…	…

Upon completion of the distance matrix (Dij) and the time matrix (Tij), the study advanced by evaluating criteria such as programming language prevalence, usability, and data processing efficiency. The analysis demonstrated that Python most effectively satisfied the research requirements. To ensure the implementation's efficacy and alignment with the study objectives, it is necessary to develop modular, independent components that can be integrated for simultaneous operation. It verifies execution time (max 20 min), outputs the route if valid, else prompts adjustments, and ends after completing these steps.

5 Results

5.1 Calculation Using Shortest Travel Distance

After data collection from two groups of pickers in the fast-moving area, the total travel time and distance for each employee are calculated and compared with the optimized routes generated by the software. The reductions are summarized in Table 4.

Table 4. The reduction rates of picking distance and time when applying the shortest path problem.

Group	Distance Reduction (%)	Time Reduction (%)	Employee Efficiency (%)
1	8.8	5.4	20.9
2	11	17.5	18.6
Average	9.9	11.45	19.75

Implementation of the shortest path model via programming reduced average travel distance by 9.9% and travel time by 11.45%, significantly optimizing operations and improving employee efficiency. Notably, Group 1 achieved an 8.8% distance reduction, reflecting their familiarity with warehouse layout, enabling automated route selection without detailed guidance—only order sequence is necessary. Group 2 achieved an 11% distance reduction but requires training to better understand warehouse layout and improve route planning and performance. These findings suggest tailored training programs are essential for less experienced staff to enhance overall efficiency.

5.2 Calculation Using Order Picking Sequence Scheduling

Through experimental calculations of completed picking routes, the average time to complete one order picking sequence scheduling process per route is approximately 40 s. This duration is relatively short and feasible for practical application. The reduction rates of distance, time, and employee efficiency calculated using the A* algorithm and Dijsktra algorithm in the programming software for each group of operator is then calculated. The entire detailed analysis results are presented in Table 5.

A* demonstrates superiority in both optimization and processing speed compared to Dijkstra's algorithm, with a time savings rate of up to 36.5% and employee efficiency reaching 32.55%. These findings suggest that applying the A* algorithm yields higher effectiveness in systems requiring shortest path computations, especially in operational scenarios demanding fast and accurate data processing.

Table 5. Summary of Reduction rates of Distance, Time, and Employee efficiency

Tool / Method	Distance reduction rate	Time reduction Rate	Employee efficiency
Shortest Path Algorithm	9.9%	11.45%	19.75%
Order Picking Sequencing Using A*	28.5%	36.5%	32.55%
Order Picking Sequencing Using Dijkstra	25.21%	32.85%	29.55%

5.3 Developing the Operational Workflow for the Application of the Programming System

The system's operational process was thoroughly updated with clear steps, from order receipt and categorizing goods by area to transporting items to the packing zone. Compared to the initial flowchart, the proposed version provides additional detailed steps, such as task assignment to specific departments and precise instructions for order picking. It also includes multiple verification points, allowing for error correction by returning items to their original positions and recording discrepancies.

6 Conclusion

In conclusion, this research successfully provided a solid foundation for future advancements in warehouse route optimization, demonstrating the potential of algorithmic solutions to transform the way online businesses manage their warehouse operations. In particular, this study presented a novel approach to optimizing picking routes in e-commerce warehouses, leveraging A* and Dijkstra algorithms to reduce travel time, minimize costs, and improve picker efficiency. The feasibility and flexibility of the solution system designed in this research have been proven effective at an actual company's warehouse in Ho Chi Minh City. The results from the pilot test demonstrate that the proposed solution can lead to significant improvements in warehouse operations, including a 36.5% reduction in picking time, a 28.5% reduction in travel distance, and a 32.55% increase in picker efficiency. Implementation within the Python environment enabled optimal route simulation, while statistical verification using SPSS confirmed the significance of these improvements. The scalability and adaptability of the system make it a viable solution for digital businesses looking to optimize their warehouse operations. By reducing labor costs, increasing efficiency, and improving order accuracy, the solution directly contributes to enhancing operational performance and maintaining competitiveness in the rapidly evolving online retail landscape.

While the system proved effective, there are opportunities for further improvement. First of all, there is a need to expand its applicability to warehouses at other locations with different scales and layouts to maximize its application across the business entire network. Future studies could focus on expanding the proposed system to other stages of the warehouse process and integrate customer feedback, that could provide valuable insights into enhancing customer satisfaction, into the optimization process. The author also recommends future studies extend the scope to integrate advanced machine learning techniques and refining the system's adaptability to dynamic warehouse environments as e-commerce continues to grow.

Acknowledgment. We would like to thank Hong Bang International University for supporting this research. Sincere thanks are also extended to the lecturers of the Logistics and Supply Chain Management program for their valuable support and guidance, which were essential to the successful completion of this study.

References

1. Kearney, A.T.: Excellence in Logistics. Kearney Chic. (2009)
2. Goetschalckx, M., Donald Ratliff, H.: Order picking in an aisle. IIE Trans. **20**(1), 53–62 (1988). https://doi.org/10.1080/07408178808966150
3. Tompkins, J.A., White, J.A., Bozer, Y.A., Tanchoco, J.M.A.: Facilities Planning, 4th edn. John Wiley & Sons, Hoboken, NJ (2010). ISBN: 978-0-470-44404-7
4. Bormann, R., De Brito, B.F., Lindermayr, J., Omainska, M., Patel, M.: Towards automated order picking robots for warehouses and retail. In: Tzovaras, D., Giakoumis, D., Vincze, M., Argyros, A. (eds.) Computer Vision Systems, Lecture Notes in Computer Science, vol. 11754, pp. 185–198. Springer International Publishing, Cham (2019). https://doi.org/10.1007/978-3-030-34995-0_18
5. Azadeh, K., De Koster, R., Roy, D.: Robotized and automated warehouse systems: review and recent developments. Transp. Sci. **53**(4), 917–945 (2019). https://doi.org/10.1287/trsc.2018.0873
6. Li, Y., Zhang, R., Jiang, D.: Order-picking efficiency in e-commerce warehouses: a literature review. J. Theor. Appl. Electron. Commer. Res. **17**(4), 4 (2022). https://doi.org/10.3390/jtaer17040091
7. de Koster, R., Le-Duc, T., Roodbergen, K.J.: Design and control of warehouse order picking: a literature review. Eur. J. Oper. Res. **182**(2), 481–501 (2007). https://doi.org/10.1016/j.ejor.2006.07.009
8. Dekker, R., De Koster, M.B.M., Roodbergen, K.J., Van Kalleveen, H.: Improving order-picking response time at Ankor's warehouse. Interfaces **34**(4), 303–313 (2004). https://doi.org/10.1287/inte.1040.0083
9. Chan, F.T.S., Chan, H.K.: Improving the productivity of order picking of a manual-pick and multi-level rack distribution warehouse through the implementation of class-based storage. Expert Syst. Appl. **38**(3), 2686–2700 (2011). https://doi.org/10.1016/j.eswa.2010.08.058
10. Sarker, B.R., Babu, P.S.: Travel time models in automated storage/retrieval systems: a critical review. Int. J. Prod. Econ. **40**(2), 173–184 (1995). https://doi.org/10.1016/0925-5273(95)00075-2
11. Agardi, A., Kovacs, L., Banyai, T.: Optimization of automatized picking process. In: 2019 IEEE 13th International Symposium on Applied Computational Intelligence and Informatics (SACI), pp. 364–369. IEEE, Timisoara, Romania (2019). https://doi.org/10.1109/SACI46893.2019.9111597
12. Applegate, D.L., Bixby, R.E., Chvátal, V., Cook, W.J.: The traveling salesman problem: a computational study. Princeton University Press, Princeton (2007)
13. Ting, C.-K., Liao, X.-L., Huang, Y.-H., Liaw, R.-T.: Multi-vehicle selective pickup and delivery using metaheuristic algorithms. Inf. Sci. **406–407**, 146–169 (2017). https://doi.org/10.1016/j.ins.2017.04.001
14. Damayanti, D.D., Novitasari, N., Setyawan, E.B., Muttaqin, P.S.: Intelligent warehouse picking improvement model for e-logistics warehouse using single picker routing problem and wave picking. JOIV Int. J. Inform. Vis. **6**(2), 418–426 (2022). https://www.joiv.org/index.php/joiv/article/view/1006. Accessed 14 May 2025
15. Belter, J., Hering, M., Weichbroth, P.: Motion trajectory prediction in warehouse management systems: a systematic literature review. Appl. Sci. **13**(17), 9780 (2023). https://doi.org/10.3390/app13179780
16. Wang, D., Jiang, J., Ma, R., Shen, G.: Research on hybrid real-time picking routing optimization based on multiple picking stations. Math. Probl. Eng. **2022**, 1–15 (2022). https://doi.org/10.1155/2022/5510749

17. Dobrilovic, D., Jevtic, V., Beker, I., Stojanov, Z.: Shortest-path based model for warehouse inner transportation optimization. In: 2012 7th IEEE International Symposium on Applied Computational Intelligence and Informatics (SACI), pp. 63–68. IEEE, Timisoara, Romania (2012). https://doi.org/10.1109/SACI.2012.6249977
18. Zhang, X., Chen, Y., Li, T.: Optimization of logistics route based on Dijkstra. In: 2015 6th IEEE International Conference on Software Engineering and Service Science (ICSESS), pp. 313–316. IEEE, Beijing, China (2015). https://doi.org/10.1109/ICSESS.2015.7339063
19. Universitas Logistik dan Bisnis Internasional, C. Prianto, and N. T. R. Adiningrum, "Effectiveness of Pickup and Delivery Services in Logistics Companies with Route Optimization using the A* Algorithm," Telematika, vol. 17, no. 2, pp. 95–111 (2024). https://doi.org/10.35671/telematika.v17i2.2860
20. Marlina, L., Gunawan, D.: Implementation of the a star heuristic search algorithm in determining the shortest path. Int. J. Comput. Sci. Math. Eng. **2**(1), 28–35 (2023). https://ijecom.org/index.php/IJECOM/article/view/20. Accessed 14 May 2025
21. Yan, Y.: Research on the a star algorithm for finding shortest path. Highlights Sci. Eng. Technol. **46**, 154–161 (2023). https://doi.org/10.54097/hset.v46i.7697
22. Javaid, M.A.: Understanding Dijkstra's Algorithm (2013). SSRN: https://ssrn.com/abstract=2340905, http://dx.doi.org/10.2139/ssrn.2340905
23. Siever, M., Valentino, A., Suryaningrum, K.M., Yunanda, R.: Dijkstra's algorithm to find the nearest vaccine location. Procedia Comput. Sci. **216**, 5–12 (2023). https://www.sciencedirect.com/science/article/pii/S1877050922021834. Accessed 14 May 2025
24. Rosita, Y.D., Rosyida, E.E., Rudiyanto, M.A.: Implementation of Dijkstra algorithm and multi-criteria decision-making for optimal route distribution. Procedia Comput. Sci. **161**, 378–385 (2019). https://www.sciencedirect.com/science/article/pii/S1877050919318460. Accessed 14 May 2025
25. Boysen, N., de Koster, R., Weidinger, F.: Warehousing in the e-commerce era: A survey. Eur. J. Oper. Res. *277*(2), 396-411 (2019). https://doi.org/10.1016/j.ejor.2018.08.023
26. Dr. E. P, B. S, and PG Scholar, Department of Management Studies, Vel Tech Rangarajan Dr. Sagunthala R&D Institute of Science and Technology, Avadi, Tamil Nadu, INDIA, "A Study on Optimizing E-Commerce Warehousing: Strategies for Efficient Operations," Int. J. Innov. Res. Inf. Secur. **10**(03), 126–130 (2024). https://doi.org/10.26562/ijiris.2024.v1003.02
27. Mulla, F.M.: Optimizing E-commerce fulfillment: the strategic role of warehouse management systems (WMS). Int. J. Sci. Res. Eng. Manag. **08**(11), 1–7 (2024). https://doi.org/10.55041/IJSREM26799
28. Dukic, G., Oluic, C.: Order-picking methods: improving order-picking efficiency. Int. J. Logist. Syst. Manag. **3**(4), 451 (2007). https://doi.org/10.1504/IJLSM.2007.013214
29. Pereira, M.T., Sousa, J.M.C., Ferreira, L.P., Sá, J.C., Silva, F.J.G.: Localization system for optimization of picking in a manual warehouse. Procedia Manuf. **38**, 1220–1227 (2019). https://doi.org/10.1016/j.promfg.2020.01.213
30. Alherimi, N., Saihi, A., Ben-Daya, M.: A systematic review of optimization approaches employed in digital warehousing transformation. IEEE Access **12**, 145809–145831 (2024). https://doi.org/10.1109/ACCESS.2024.3463531
31. Qiu, L., Hsu, W.-J., Huang, S.-Y., Wang, H.: Scheduling and routing algorithms for AGVs: A survey. Int. J. Prod. Res. 40(3), 745-760 (2002). https://doi.org/10.1080/00207540110091712
32. Bahill, A.T., Dean, F.F.: WHAT is systems engineering? A consensus of senior systems engineers1. INCOSE Int. Symp. **6**(1), 500–505 (1996). https://doi.org/10.1002/j.2334-5837.1996.tb02045.x

33. Żabińska, I., Piller, A.: Possibilities of improving the process of picking warehouse orders on a selected example. Sci. Pap. Silesian Univ. Technol. Organ. Manag. Ser. **2020**, 144 (2020). https://doi.org/10.29119/1641-3466.2020.142.9
34. Knop, K.: Use of selected tools of quality improvement in a company producing parts for the automotive industry – case study. Qual. Prod. Improv. Syst. Saf., 344–353 (2023). https://doi.org/10.21741/9781644902691-40

Building Customer Satisfaction in Last-Mile Deliveries in e-commerce – Pilot Study

Thi Bao Chau Huynh and Paulina Golinska-Dawson(✉)

Institute of Logistics, Poznan University of Technology, 2 J. Rychlewskiego Str., 60-965 Poznan, Poland
thibaochau.huynh@doctorate.put.poznan.pl,
paulina.golinska@put.poznan.pl

Abstract. The swift growth of e-commerce, particularly following the COVID-19 epidemic, has made last-mile delivery services an essential link between retailers and users. Nevertheless, the current research frequently lacks a comprehensive analysis of the user experience in this setting. This study seeks to address this deficiency by determining the principal elements that affect user satisfaction with last-mile delivery services.

The research uses a quantitative research method approach, incorporating online surveys to investigate consumer expectations, challenges, and preferences. The results identify six key criteria that substantially influence the user experience: timely delivery, economical delivery fees, secure management of personal and financial data, trustworthy tracking systems, well-preserved packaging, and reliable delivery.

This research is provides practical insights that can assist firms in securing a competitive edge in the swiftly changing e-commerce landscape.

Keywords: Last-mile delivery · user satisfaction · user expectations · customer loyalty · E-commerce · operational logistics service quality · logistics service quality

1 Introduction

E-commerce has undergone swift expansion globally, propelled by changes in consumer behavior post-COVID-19 pandemic (Dumanska et al., 2021) and the ambition of enterprises to broaden their market (Kraemer et al., 2006). The e-commerce growth rates in 2019 for the UK (7.5%), Germany (7.7%), France (10.6%), Spain (10.7%), and Italy (8.4%) underscore this expansion, significantly affecting delivery services (Viu-Roig & Eduard J. Alvarez-Palau, 2020). Last-mile delivery is a pivotal growth sector, significantly influencing e-commerce through its direct effect on consumer happiness and overall business efficacy (Gevaers et al., 2011; Prayogo et al., 2024).

Businesses are focusing on enhancing delivery services by offering adaptable delivery options, including home delivery, in-store pickup, and alternative pickup locations

M. Li et al. (Eds.): ICLS 2025, *Proceeding of the 19th International Congress on Logistics and Supply Chain Management Systems*, pp. 121–135, 2026.
https://doi.org/10.1007/978-981-95-7700-2_10

(Viu-Roig & Eduard J. Alvarez-Palau, 2020). However, last-mile delivery continues to be costly and complex, significantly impacting overall e-commerce costs (Kämäräinen et al., 2001), especially due to customer expectations, environmental concerns, and urban congestion (Olsson et al., 2022).

Omnichannel shopping is associated with customer satisfaction, with last-mile delivery playing a key role in assessing the quality of online experiences (Xiao et al., 2017). Studies also highlight the central role of customer experience in retail and supply chains, especially expectations about last-mile delivery (Grewal & Roggeveen, 2020); (Esper et al., 2020).

Given the above challenges, improving last-mile delivery is critical for companies that expect to meet consumer expectations and remain competitive (Buldeo Rai et al., 2021). Since consumers often rely on delivery performance to determine their loyalty (Vrhovac et al., 2023), understanding the specific factors that shape customer satisfaction is essential. Technological solutions—such as real-time tracking and route optimization—offer potential improvements (Zhou et al., 2020).

This study aims to identify the key factors that consumers prioritize when evaluating last-mile delivery services. We apply an online survey with a minimum sample size of 50 participants. The results provides insights for retailers and logistics companies to improve their delivery services, ensure alignment with consumer expectations and optimize logistics processes.

2 Theoretical Background

2.1 Last-Mile Delivery in E-commerce

E-commerce is a term that describes the use of the internet and electronic means to trade products and services (Jain et al., 2021). This business model has grown rapidly due to the widespread adoption of digital technology and online shopping (Fauska et al., 2013). The COVID-19 pandemic further accelerated this trend, with more consumers preferring online purchases and home delivery (Vrhovac et al., 2023).

As e-commerce expands, last-mile delivery has become a critical component, ensuring goods reach consumers efficiently (Buldeo Rai et al., 2021). It includes all logistics operations related to delivering products from distribution centers to customers in urban areas (Boysen et al., 2021). (Junnarkar et al., 2023) define last-mile delivery as the process where retailers or distributors directly transport goods to consumers, rather than relying on traditional carriers. Despite its importance, last-mile delivery is often underestimated, though it accounts for up to 28% of total shipping costs (Sarder, 2020).

2.2 User Satisfaction in E-commerce

The development of e-commerce and the concept of "last mile delivery" as mentioned above are inseparable, the final step contributing to the completeness and success of the distribution chain. Realizing this, retail businesses focus on building a last-mile delivery system that is closely linked with the rest of the distribution chain, helping to bring a good shopping experience into the users' minds with their products and services.

(Wijaya et al., 2019) found that e-commerce customer satisfaction is established when the customer interacts with the seller online, such as viewing the website, making a purchase, or contacting technical support and delivery. Moreover, it also demonstrates the appropriateness of the products and services offered based on client preferences and requirements (Ilieva et al., 2022). Assessing consumer perceived value is crucial in the field of e-commerce as it allows for the evaluation of customer satisfaction (Chi Lin, 2003).

Customer trust and retailer service excellence have a mutually influential relationship. To increase customer confidence in a product or service, the supplier should put effort into minimizing the uncertainty and risk that the customer may face. On the other hand, if the customer trusts the retailer's solution, their evaluation and satisfaction of the products and services will improve (Ejdys & Gulc, 2020). Hence, if logistics service providers are unable to meet client expectations and fulfill them, they will lose their position to competitors who excel in this aspect (Meidutė-Kavaliauskienė et al., 2014).

The findings of (Vakulenko et al., 2019) suggest that the last-mile delivery experience plays a role in connecting customer perceptions of online purchasing experiences with customer happiness. The results of delivery services can have an impact on consumers' connections with e-retailers based on their experiences with the service they receive (Fisher et al., 2017). Therefore, logistics services have received increased focus as a crucial marketing element for fostering customer loyalty and satisfaction (Rajendran et al., 2018).

2.3 Key Factors Influencing Users' Experience in Last-Mile Delivery

The interplay between logistics interaction and operational excellence has a direct impact on customer satisfaction with third-party logistics service providers, which in turn influences consumer happiness with the overall business (Zuoliang et al., 2011). Customer service plays a crucial role in enhancing customer satisfaction levels. (D. Zhang et al., 2016) state that the final leg of transportation is responsible for the largest portion of time and expenses in the whole logistics process. This aspect has emerged as the primary concern impacting the effectiveness of logistics services.

Essential Factors Shaping Last-Mile Delivery Experience.
Research conducted by (Vrhovac et al., 2023) has identified six characteristics that influence the consumer experience in last-mile logistics: delivery efficiency, order tracking, smooth delivery processes, brand identity through packaging, convenience, and the excitement of receiving goods. (Liu et al., 2019) found that customer satisfaction is influenced by the capacity to monitor the time and location of goods to be proactive in obtaining information about them. Moreover, perceptual disagreement resulting from delayed delivery hurts customers' assessment of the online shopping experience (Liao & Keng, 2013).

With the rapid expansion of e-commerce, shops are increasingly offering home delivery services. While, IKEA imposes a substantial fee for home delivery of their products, yet the buyer willingly opts to bear the cost of this service as per Yu et al., 2016, online supermarket Ulabox does not charge any last-mile delivery fees to ensure customer satisfaction (García et al., 2019). According to Escursell et al., 2021, companies should enhance the consumer experience by improving the practical and aesthetic appearance of their packaging to ensure their brand image is maintained. Additionally, businesses offer same-day and immediate shipping to enhance customer convenience. Studies show that consumers perceive speedier delivery as a value-added service and are willing to pay an additional cost for it (P. Zhang & Li, 2018), (Capgemini Research Institute, 2019).

Enhancing Last-Mile Communication and Service Quality.
Efficient communication between shipping units, retailers, and customers enhances trust and minimizes delivery-related uncertainties (Sorted, 2024). Delivery status updates, receipt convenience, reception experience, and return convenience. Additionally, it was established that customer loyalty has a good effect on online merchants' performance and that customer satisfaction has a favorable effect on customer loyalty (Kawa & Zdrenka, 2023).

In conclusion, cost, speed, tracking, packaging, and communication are key determinants of last-mile delivery experience. Businesses must continuously optimize these elements to enhance user satisfaction, foster brand loyalty, and maintain a competitive edge in e-commerce logistics.

2.4 Technological Implementations in Last-Mile Delivery

Modern technology plays a key role in improving the quality of last-mile delivery by shortening delivery times, reducing costs, and improving customer satisfaction. Advanced tracking systems enable precise tracking of shipments, although their impact on customer experience has yet to be fully explored (Akturk et al., 2022). Delivery robots and drones: Automate the delivery process, minimize labor expenses, and enhance precision (Suguna et al., 2022). Smart lockers provide cost-effective, low-emission solutions for non-urgent deliveries (Mohammad et al., 2023). Additionally, blockchain enhances transparency, accountability, and security in logistics, addressing inefficiencies in supply chain integration (Zou et al., 2020); (Kshetri, 2018); (Biswas et al., 2017); (Kawa & Golinska, 2010).

2.5 The Challenges of Last-Mile Delivery in Conquering and Satisfying Customers

Last-mile delivery accounts for 41% of total supply chain costs, surpassing warehousing and packaging (Patel & Parmar, 2020).

Core obstacles include rising freight volumes (Visser et al., 2014), sustainability concerns (Golinska-Dawson & Sethanan, 2023), high operational costs (Patel & Parmar, 2020), constrained delivery times (Bopage et al., 2019; Golinska & Hajdul, 2011), and workforce aging (Otto et al., 2017). Despite technological advancements, issues such as emissions and delivery inefficiencies persist. Enhancing service quality and relationship management significantly improves customer loyalty (Sann et al., 2024); (Huma et al., 2019). Continuous innovation remains essential to adapt to changing consumer expectations and maintain competitiveness.

3 Methodology

The study has two main objectives:

1. Objective 1 - To identify and evaluate key factors that influence the user experience of last-mile delivery services.
2. Objective 2 - To propose specific and practical improvements that help businesses enhance the user experience on e-commerce platforms, thereby increasing loyalty and creating a competitive advantage.

Data were collected through semi-structured interviews (minimum 10 people) and online surveys using Google Forms (minimum 50 people), as recommended by (Bernard, 2013). The survey focused on factors affecting user experience with last-mile delivery services. According to (Ipsos Insights, No date (n.d.)), a mixed method of online survey and face-to-face interviews was used to increase representativeness and response rate. However, in this pilot study, the author only applied a quantitative research method through online interviews by Google form questionnaires, employing the 5-level Likert scale with an expected minimum of 50 participants. According to (Hox & Boeije, 2005), data collection includes both primary and secondary data. Primary data is collected through online surveys, while secondary data comes from published research. This study combines both: online surveys on user experience and secondary data to update market trends (see Fig. 1).

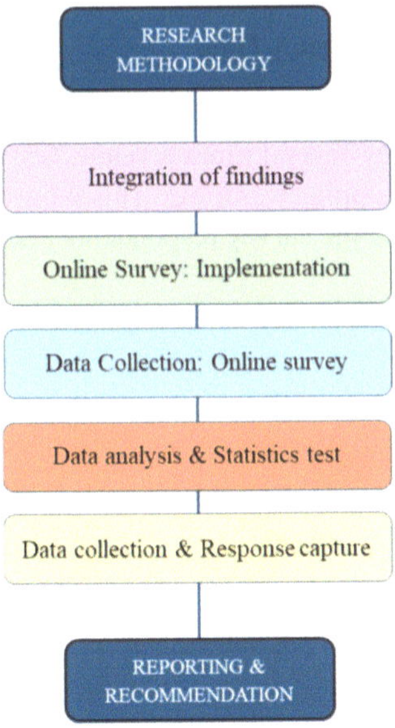

Fig. 1. Graphical Diagram of Research Data Collection (Source: own elaboration)

4 Results of Online Survey Collection Data

4.1 Demographic Data

The study collected data from 64 people, 7 samples were excluded, leaving 57 people. Demographically result as Table 1: 61.4% were female (35), 38.6% were male (22). Age: under 20 (7%), 21–30 (52.6%), 31–40 (31.6%), over 40 (8.8%).

Table 1. Demographic of the survey's sample. (Source: Own elaboration)

Question	Content	Sample	Percentage
Gender	*Male*	22	38.6%
	Female	35	61.4%
Total		57	100.0%
Age group	*< 20 years old*	4	7.0%
	From 21–30 years old	30	52.6%
	From 31–40 years old	18	31.6%
	> 40 years old	5	8.8%
Total		57	100.0%

4.2 E-commerce Using Frequency Data

The survey results showed that the most common frequency of online shopping was monthly (45.6%), followed by several times a year (26.3%). The percentage of weekly (17.5%) and daily (10.5%) shopping was lower. This shows that monthly online shopping was the most common among the survey respondents (Table 2).

Table 2. The online shopping frequency of participants in the online survey. (Source: Own elaboration).

Question	Content	Sample	Percentage
Online shopping frequency	*Daily*	6	10.5%
	Weekly	10	17.5%
	Monthly	26	45.6%
	A few times a year	15	26.3%
Total		57	100.0%

4.3 Favorite Place to Receive Delivered Goods

Respondents preferred home delivery via courier (42.1%). Workplace delivery was also popular (21.1%). Pick-up at a delivery point (19.3%) and parcel locker (17.5%) were similar. Businesses can offer a variety of delivery location options to meet the diverse needs of customers (Table 3).

Table 3. The favorite places to pick up goods of participants in the online survey. Source: Own elaboration.

Question	Content	Sample	Percentage
Place to pick up goods	*At delivery points*	11	19.3%
	At home by couriers	24	42.1%
	At workplaces	12	21.1%
	At parcel lockers	10	17.5%
Total		57	100.0%

4.4 Key Factors of Last-Mile Delivery that Influence Users' Experience

Several significant elements assessed influence the user experience with last-mile delivery services. The factors can be categorized as follows:

- Delivery speed: Factors such as rapid delivery (50.9%) and delivery within 24 h (38.6%) are deemed highly significant, although a willingness to pay additional fees for expedited delivery is not widely endorsed (only 30% regard it as crucial).
- Delivery flexibility: Aspects like convenient cancelation (65%) and the ability to modify delivery location (54%) are greatly esteemed. Despite the perception that delivery outside of business hours (evenings/weekends) is of lesser importance, a notable proportion of users (37%) still want this service.
- Delivery reliability: Timely and accurate delivery is the paramount factor (82%) and is regarded as the essence of the service.
- Shipping expenses: Reasonable shipping expenses received a high rating of 84%, signifying that this is a significant factor in customer satisfaction.
- Security and safety: A significant majority of users prioritize the protection of personal and financial information (75%) and the proper packaging of items (72%).
- Customer service: Pre-delivery alerts via phone or text message (65%) and assistance from delivery personnel (61%) are significant elements in improving the user experience.

The results summarize the factors that influence user experience for last-mile delivery services, shown in the Table 4:

Table 4. Factors Affecting the User Experience in Last-Mile Delivery. (Source: Own elaboration)

Factor	Description	Percentage of users rating important (%)
Delivery speed	Rapid delivery (50.9%) and delivery within 24 h (38.6%) are highly significant. However, few users are willing to pay extra for expedited delivery (only 28.1%)	- Rapid delivery: 50.9% - Delivery within 24 hs: 38.6% - Willingness to pay extra for expedited delivery: 28.1%
Delivery Flexibility	Aspects like convenient order cancellation (65%) and the ability to change delivery location (54%) are highly valued. Although delivery outside business hours (evenings/weekends) is less important to some, a significant proportion (37%) still desires this service	- Order cancellation: 65% - Change delivery location: 54% - Delivery outside business hours: 37%
Delivery Reliability	Timely and accurate delivery is the most important factor (82%) for users	Timely and accurate delivery: 82%
Shipping Costs	Reasonable shipping costs are highly rated (84%) and have a significant impact on customer satisfaction	Reasonable shipping costs: 84%
Security and Safety	A majority of users prioritize the protection of personal and financial information (75%) and proper packaging of products (72%)	- Protection of personal and financial information: 75% - Proper product packaging: 72%
Customer Service	Pre-delivery alerts via phone or text (65%) and assistance from delivery personnel (61%) are important factors in improving the user experience	- Pre-delivery alerts: 65% - Assistance from delivery personnel: 61%

4.5 User Satisfaction with the Current Last-Mile Delivery Service

The survey results show in Fig. 2 that 50.9% of respondents rated the last mile delivery service as satisfactory to very satisfactory, indicating that half of users are quite satisfied with the current service. However, a large proportion of respondents (36.5%) were unclear about their level of satisfaction, indicating that there may be room for improvement. Only a small proportion (12.3%) were dissatisfied, but they are still a group that can influence purchasing decisions and service revenue. Service providers need to carefully consider the factors that customers are dissatisfied with in order to improve service quality.

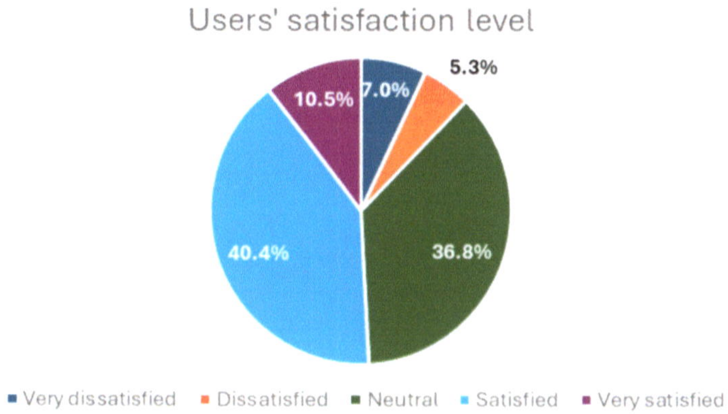

Fig. 2. The survey results of Users' satisfaction with last-mile delivery service

4.6 User Expectation on the Improvement of Last-Mile Delivery Factors

The final question in the online survey was to survey users' expectations for factors that would be improved in the future. These factors included: Order tracking, Delivery staff support, Customer support, Call/text before delivery, Safe and secure delivery, Reasonable cost, On-time and accurate address, Easy cancellation, Flexible delivery location change, and Fast delivery.

The survey results showed that the factor that users expected to improve the most was Fast delivery with a rate of 52.6%, followed by Reasonable cost with 50.9%. These factors show that users are particularly concerned about delivery speed and reasonable cost. The next important factors were Safe and secure delivery (40.4%) and Order tracking (31.6%), showing that users also pay attention to protecting customer information, safety during delivery, and the ability to track order status. Factors such as Call/Text Before Delivery, Customer Service and Delivery Person Support have low improvement expectation rates, indicating that the majority of users are already satisfied with these factors (Table 5).

Table 5. The collected survey data on user's expectations for last-mile delivery factor improvement. *Source: Own elaboration*

Last-mile delivery factors	Sample (57)	Percentage
Fast Delivery	30	52.6%
Flexible change delivery location	12	21.1%
Easy cancelation	17	29.8%
On time and correct address	16	28.1%
Reasonable cost	29	50.9%
Secure and safe delivery	23	40.4%

(continued)

Table 5. (*continued*)

Last-mile delivery factors	Sample (57)	Percentage
Call/message before Delivery	14	24.6%
Supportive customer service	10	17.5%
Supportive delivery staff	9	15.8%
Order tracking	18	31.6%

5 Discussion and Recommendations

5.1 Summary of Key Findings

Based on the findings from the online survey, the author identified six key factors that received the highest ratings from users. These factors were selected for further analysis to improve the current last-mile logistics service and provide a better user experience (Table 6).

Table 6. Ranking of last-mile delivery key factors that influence users' experience in E-commerce. Source: Own elaboration

Ranking	Important Last-mile delivery factors	Online survey rating
1	Fast delivery	77%
2	Reasonable Cost of Delivery	84%
3	Secure personal and payment information	75%
4	Good condition of packing	72%
5	Order tracking system	56%
6	Reliability: On time, right location	82%

The satisfaction rate of users with the current last-mile service is summarized in the Table 7.

Table 7. Summary of user satisfaction rates with the current last-mile service. Source: Own elaboration

User satisfaction level	Online survey rating
Satisfied	50.9%
Neutral	36.8%
Unsatisfied	12.3%
Total	100.0%

5.2 Improvement Suggestion

Fast Delivery Factor: Delivery companies should invest in smart routing technology to optimize delivery routes, avoiding traffic congestion and accidents. It is necessary to use weather forecast resources to adjust shipping schedules and organize regular vehicle maintenance to ensure safety during transportation.

Reasonable delivery costs: To optimize costs, companies should use fuel-efficient vehicles such as electric vehicles and apply automation systems in warehouses and transportation. In addition, regular vehicle maintenance and employee training will help improve work efficiency.

Personal information and payment security: It is necessary to prioritize protecting user information by applying security measures such as anti-virus software, SSL/TLS data encryption and multi-factor authentication (MFA) to ensure the safety of customer payment data and accounts.

Ensure quality packaging and safe delivery: Using quality, environmentally friendly packaging materials and training employees on proper packaging procedures are essential to ensure that products are not damaged during transportation.

Order tracking system: Improve IT infrastructure and deploy modern order tracking software such as GPS, IoT and RFID to provide updates on order status and location, ensuring accurate and continuous tracking.

Reliability (Deliver on time, to the right place): Develop flexible shipping plans to cope with traffic congestion and bad weather. Use applications such as Google Maps, Waze to monitor traffic conditions and weather forecasts, and improve warehouse management and order processing for fast and accurate deliveries.

Ensure quality packaging and safe delivery: Using quality, environmentally friendly packaging materials and training employees on proper packaging procedures are essential to ensure that products are not damaged during transportation.

Order tracking system: Improve IT infrastructure and deploy modern order tracking software such as GPS, IoT and RFID to provide updates on order status and location, ensuring accurate and continuous tracking.

Reliability (Deliver on time, to the right place): Develop flexible shipping plans to cope with traffic congestion and bad weather. Use applications such as Google Maps, Waze to monitor traffic conditions and weather forecasts, and improve warehouse management and order processing for fast and accurate deliveries.

6 Conclusion

The author accomplished the initial research objectives by employing quantitative research methods, analyzing data obtained via online surveys.

- The objective 1 - To identify important factors that affect user experience with the final delivery service. The six important factors were fast delivery, reasonable cost, data security, good packaging, effective tracking system, and reliability. The results showed that 50.5% of users were satisfied, while 33.4% were neutral and 16.2% were dissatisfied.

- The objective 2 - To introduce improvements such as optimizing shipping routes, investing in new technology, and improving packaging processes, to enhance user experience and increase satisfaction, helping businesses compete better in the market.

Research limitations: This study was carried out in Poznan, Poland over a two-month period with time, scope, and sample size restrictions, hence perhaps not providing a totally representative sample of the target population. Notwithstanding time and sample restrictions, the study gave top priority to choosing premium samples—including actual users who knew about online buying and last-mile delivery systems. These individuals were willing to share their experiences and were eager to improve, ensuring the reliability of the results.

Suggestion for future research: As sustainability in Logistics and Supply Chains becomes more important than ever, the author will continue to research on building a Sustainable Supply Chain Network, especially Green Logistics, to protect the environment and reduce CO_2 emissions. The research will also explore the relationship between consumers' satisfaction with last-mile delivery services and their support for sustainable development goals.

References

MS Akturk R Mallipeddi X Jia 2022 Estimating impacts of logistics processes on online customer ratings: Consequences of providing technology-enabled order tracking data to customers J. Oper. Manag. 68 775 811 https://doi.org/10.1002/joom.1204

Bernard, H.R.: Social Research Methods: Qualitative and Quantitative Approaches (2nd edn.). SAGE Publications, Inc. (2013)

Biswas, K., Muthukkumarasamy, V., Tan, W.L.: Blockchain based Wine Supply Chain Traceability System (2017)

Bopage, G., Nanayakkara, J., Vidanagamachchi, K.: A Strategic Model to Improve the Last Mile Delivery Performance in E-commerce Parcel Delivery (2019)

N Boysen S Fedtke S Schwerdfeger 2021 Last-mile delivery concepts: A survey from an operational research perspective OR Spectrum 43 1 1 58 https://doi.org/10.1007/s00291-020-00607-8

H Buldeo Rai C Broekaert S Verlinde C Macharis 2021 Sharing is caring: How non-financial incentives drive sustainable e-commerce delivery Transp. Res. Part D: Transp. Environ. 93 102794https://doi.org/10.1016/j.trd.2021.102794

Capgemini Research Institute.: The Last-Mile Delivery Challenge. Capgemini (2019). https://www.capgemini.com/wp-content/uploads/2019/01/Report-Digital-%E2%80%93-Last-Mile-Delivery-Challenge1.pdf?utm_source=chatgpt.com

C Chi Lin 2003 A critical appraisal of customer satisfaction and e-commerce Manag. Auditing J. 18 3 202 212 https://doi.org/10.1108/02686900310469952

Dumanska, I., Hrytsyna, L., Kharun, O., Matviiets, O.: E-commerce and M-commerce as Global Trends of International Trade Caused by the Covid-19 Pandemic. Wseas Trans. Environ. Develop. **17**, 386–397 (2021). https://doi.org/10.37394/232015.2021.17.38

J Ejdys A Gulc 2020 Trust in courier services and its antecedents as a determinant of perceived service quality and future intention to use courier service Sustainability 12 21 9088 https://doi.org/10.3390/su12219088

S Escursell P Llorach-Massana MB Roncero 2021 Sustainability in e-commerce packaging: A review J. Cleaner Prod. 280 124314https://doi.org/10.1016/j.jclepro.2020.124314

Esper, T., et al.: Everything old is new again: the age of consumer-centric supply chain management. J. Bus. Logist.**41**, 286–293 (2020)https://doi.org/10.1111/jbl.12267

P Fauska N Kryvinska C Strauss 2013 The role of e-commerce in B2B markets of goods and services Int. J. Ser. Econ. Manag. 5 41 47 https://doi.org/10.1504/IJSEM.2013.051872

Fisher, M., Gallino, S., Xu, J.: The Value of Rapid Delivery in Online Retailing (2017). https://doi.org/10.13140/RG.2.2.17868.62080

García, M., Torres, L., Pérez, D., Bergillos, A., Dios, E.: E-commerce Packaging (Patent No. US20190367210A1) (2019). https://patentimages.storage.googleapis.com/0d/14/22/fe57c1c84aa56a/US20190367210A1.pdf

Gevaers, R., De, E., Vanelslander, T.: A quantitative assessment of last-mile characteristics in B2C supply chains and urban distribution (2011).

P Golinska-Dawson K Sethanan 2023 Sustainable urban freight for energy-efficient smart cities—systematic literature review Energies 16 6 2617 https://doi.org/10.3390/en16062617

Golinska, P., Hajdul, M.: Multi-agent coordination mechanism of virtual supply chain. In KES International Symposium on Agent and Multi-Agent Systems: Technologies and Applications, pp. 620–629. Berlin, Heidelberg: Springer, Cham (2011). https://doi.org/10.1007/978-3-642-22000-5_64

D Grewal AL Roggeveen 2020 Understanding retail experiences and customer journey management J. Retail. 96 1 3 8 https://doi.org/10.1016/j.jretai.2020.02.002

J Hox H Boeije 2005 Data collection, primary versus secondary Encycl. Soc. Meas. 1 593 599 https://doi.org/10.1016/B0-12-369398-5/00041-4

S Huma W Ahmed M Ikram MI Khawaja 2019 The effect of logistics service quality on customer loyalty: case of logistics service industry South Asian J. Bus. Stud. 9 1 43 61 https://doi.org/10.1108/SAJBS-10-2018-0114

G Ilieva T Yankova S Klisarova Y Dzhabarova 2022 Customer Satisfaction in e-Commerce during the COVID-19 Pandemic Systems 10 6 213 https://doi.org/10.3390/systems10060213

Ipsos Insights. (No date (n.d.)). Mixed Mode Surveys: Enhancing quality using online and face-to-face | Ipsos iris. https://iris.ipsos.com/mixed-mode-surveys-enhancing-quality-using-online-and-face-to-face/

Jain, V., Malviya, B., Arya, S.: An Overview of Electronic Commerce (e-Commerce). J. Contemp. Issues Bus. Govern. **27**, 665–670 (2021). https://doi.org/10.47750/cibg.2021.27.03.090

Junnarkar, N., Muralidharan, M., Muralidharan, P.: Supply Chain Management. Archers & Elevators Publishing House (2023).

V Kämäräinen J Saranen J Holmström 2001 The reception box impact on home delivery efficiency in the e-grocery business Int. J. Phys. Distrib. & Logis. Manag. 31 414 426 https://doi.org/10.1108/09600030110399414

A Kawa W Zdrenka 2023 Logistics value in e-commerce and its impact on customer satisfaction, loyalty and online retailers' performance Int. J. Logis. Manag. 35 2 577 600 https://doi.org/10.1108/IJLM-02-2023-0078

Kawa, A., Golinska, P.: Supply chain arrangements in recovery network. In KES International Symposium on Agent and Multi-Agent Systems: Technologies and Applications, pp. 292–301. Berlin, Heidelberg: Springer, Cham (2010). https://doi.org/10.1007/978-3-642-13541-5_30

Kraemer, K., Dedrick, J., Melville, N., Zhu, K.: Global e-commerce: Impacts of National Environment and Policy, p. 444 (2006). https://doi.org/10.1017/CBO9780511488603

Kshetri, N.:1 Blockchain's roles in meeting key supply chain management objectives. Int. J. Inf. Manag. **39**, 80–89 (2018). https://doi.org/10.1016/j.ijinfomgt.2017.12.005

T-H Liao C-J Keng 2013 Online shopping delivery delay: finding a psychological recovery strategy by online consumer experiences Comput. Human Behav. 29 4 1849 1861 https://doi.org/10.1016/j.chb.2013.03.004

Liu, S., Li, Y., Huang, J., Zhao, X.: Understanding the Consumer Satisfaction of the "Last-Mile" Delivery of E-Business Services. In: Li, D., Zhao C., (Eds.), Computer and Computing Technologies in Agriculture XI, pp. 411–418. Springer, Cham (2019). https://doi.org/10.1007/978-3-030-06179-1_41

I Meidutė-Kavaliauskienė A Aranskis M Litvinenko 2014 Consumer satisfaction with the quality of logistics services Procedia – Soc. Behav. Sci. 110 330 340 https://doi.org/10.1016/j.sbspro.2013.12.877

WA Mohammad Y Nazih Diab A Elomri C Triki 2023 Innovative solutions in last mile delivery: Concepts, practices, challenges, and future directions Supply Chain Forum: Int. J. 24 2 151 169 https://doi.org/10.1080/16258312.2023.2173488

J Olsson D Hellström Y Vakulenko 2022 Customer experience dimensions in last-mile delivery: an empirical study on unattended home delivery Int. J. Phys. Distrib. & Logis. Manag. 53 2 184 205 https://doi.org/10.1108/IJPDLM-12-2021-0517

A Otto N Boysen A Scholl R Walter 2017 Ergonomic workplace design in the fast pick area OR Spectrum 39 945 975 https://doi.org/10.1007/s00291-017-0479-x

Patel, R., Parmar, T.: Capstone Project-Ivery case study Amazon Logistics (2020). https://doi.org/10.13140/RG.2.2.15385.03687

DH Prayogo R Domanski P Golinska-Dawson 2024 The key factors for improving returns management in e-commerce in Indonesia from customers' perspectives—an analytic hierarchy process approach Sustainability 16 17 7303

S Rajendran S Wahab Y Ling L Yun 2018 The impact of logistics services on the e-shoppers' satisfaction Int. J. Supply Chain Manag. 7 461 469

R Sann P Pimpohnsakun P Booncharoen 2024 Exploring the impact of logistics service quality on customer satisfaction, trust and loyalty in bus transport Int. J. Qual. Ser. Sci. 16 4 519 541 https://doi.org/10.1108/IJQSS-07-2023-0110

MD Sarder 2020 Logistics Transportation Systems Elsevier

Sorted. How last-mile delivery tracking improves customer experience | Sorted (2024). https://sorted.com/blog/last-mile-delivery-tracking-customer-experience/

M Suguna B Shah SK Raj M Suresh 2022 A study on the influential factors of the last mile delivery projects during Covid-19 era Oper. Manag. Res. 15 1–2 399 412 https://doi.org/10.1007/s12063-021-00214-y

Y Vakulenko P Shams D Hellström K Hjort 2019 Online retail experience and customer satisfaction: the mediating role of last mile delivery Int. Rev. Retail, Distrib. Consum. Res. 29 3 306 320 https://doi.org/10.1080/09593969.2019.1598466

J Visser T Nemoto M Browne 2014 Home delivery and the impacts on urban freight transport: a review Procedia – Soc. Behav. Sci. 125 15 27 https://doi.org/10.1016/j.sbspro.2014.01.1452

M Viu-Roig EJ Alvarez-Palau 2020 The impact of e-commerce-related last-mile logistics on cities: a systematic literature review Sustainability 12 16 6492 https://doi.org/10.3390/su12166492

V Vrhovac S Vasić S Milisavljević B Dudić P Štarchoň M Žižakov 2023 Measuring e-commerce user experience in the last-mile delivery Mathematics 11 6 1482 https://doi.org/10.3390/math11061482

Wijaya, I. W. K., Rai, A. A. G., Hariguna, T.: The impact of customer experience on customer behavior intention use in social media commerce, an extended expectation confirmation model: An empirical study. Management Science Letters, 2009–2020 (2019). https://doi.org/10.5267/j.msl.2019.7.005

Z Xiao J Wang J Lenzer Y Sun 2017 Understanding the diversity of final delivery solutions for online retailing: a case of Shenzhen, China Transp. Res. Procedia 25 985 998 https://doi.org/10.1016/j.trpro.2017.05.473

Y Yu X Wang RY Zhong GQ Huang 2016 E-commerce logistics in supply chain management: practice perspective Procedia CIRP 52 179 185 https://doi.org/10.1016/j.procir.2016.08.002

D Zhang P Zhu Y Ye 2016 The effects of E-commerce on the demand for commercial real estate Cities 51 106 120 https://doi.org/10.1016/j.cities.2015.11.012

Zhang, P., Li, T.: Understanding consumer preferences for logistics services within online retailing of fresh products. Jönköping University (2018)

M Zhou 2020 Understanding consumers' behavior to adopt self-service parcel services for last-mile delivery J. Retail. Consum. Ser. 52 101911https://doi.org/10.1016/j.jretconser.2019.101911

Y Zou T Meng P Zhang W Zhang H Li 2020 Focus on blockchain: a comprehensive survey on academic and application IEEE Access 8 187182 187201 https://doi.org/10.1109/ACCESS.2020.3030491

Y Zuoliang C Li Y Zhenhua L Dai 2011 Third-party logistics service quality and its impact on customer satisfaction of C2C Sci. Res. Manag. 32 8 119 126

Digital Twin-Enabled Production-Logistics Synchronisation for Enhancing Efficiency and Sustainability in Pharmaceutical Manufacturing

Daqiang Guo[1,2(✉)], Jagjit Singh Srai[1], and Ettore Settanni[1]

[1] Centre for International Manufacturing (CIM), Institute for Manufacturing (IfM), University of Cambridge, Cambridge, UK
guodaqiang@hotmail.com

[2] Smart Manufacturing Thrust, Systems Hub, The Hong Kong University of Science and Technology (Guangzhou), Guangzhou, China

Abstract. Despite the pharmaceutical industry's recognition of Industry 4.0, its full integration remains impeded by intricate technical, institutional, and regulatory challenges. To accelerate this transition, this work pioneers a concept of smart production-logistics synchronisation, leveraging the digital twin and innovative operations management strategy, for enhancing efficiency and sustainability in pharmaceutical manufacturing. A digital twin-enabled framework for transforming smart and sustainable pharmaceutical manufacturing is proposed. Following the framework, this paper presents an intelligent decision-making strategy by leveraging digital twin-enabled real-time information sharing and informed decision-making for synchronising production and logistics operations. A case study from a pharmaceutical manufacturer illustrates the potential benefits, with an average cutting of 18.60% in the production lead time, 67.31% in the logistics lead time, and 33.75% in the total energy consumption, respectively. Furthermore, the study demonstrates the resilience of the proposed strategy to logistics uncertainties, showcasing its effectiveness in mitigating delays and improving efficiency. These findings highlight the transformative potential of innovative operations management strategies enabled by industrial digital technologies in pharmaceutical manufacturing.

Keywords: Industry 4.0 · smart medicines manufacturing · digital twin · production-logistics synchronisation · lead time · energy consumption

1 Introduction

By adopting emerging technologies, the pharmaceutical industry is exploring the transformative potential of Industry 4.0, giving rise to the concept of Pharma 4.0 or Pharma Industry 4.0, with the goal of creating a more agile, smart, and personalized pharmaceutical sector [1, 2]. The transformation will require a corresponding shift in pharmaceutical

M. Li et al. (Eds.): ICLS 2025, *Proceeding of the 19th International Congress on Logistics and Supply Chain Management Systems*, pp. 136–149, 2026.
https://doi.org/10.1007/978-981-95-7700-2_11

manufacturing towards small-scale, adaptive and coordinated production processes, thus bolstering efficiency, enhancing quality, promoting sustainability and reducing waste [3, 4].

Despite the potential benefits, the pharmaceutical industry lags behind in embracing the new industrial revolution, largely due to extensive technical, institutional and regulatory complexities [5, 6]. To accelerate the use of industrial digital technologies (IDTs) in the pharmaceutical industry, the British government has established the Digital Medicines Manufacturing (DM2) Research Centre. This initiative is part of the Made Smarter Innovation program's £53 million investment in smart manufacturing and connected supply chain research, aiming to enhance productivity in medicine development and manufacturing while fostering a patient-focused supply system. This paper will discuss the advancement of the concept of smart synchronisation of production and logistics in pharmaceutical manufacturing, leveraging digital twins to boost efficiency and sustainability, as a part of the recently launched DM2 project in the UK.

The rest of this paper is organized as follows. Section 2 provides a brief overview of the current state-of-the-art and a digital twin-enabled smart pharmaceutical manufacturing framework. Section 3 presents the coordinated decision-making model of production and logistics under the digital twin-enabled smart pharmaceutical manufacturing environment. Section 4 presents a case study to demonstrate the effectiveness of the proposed approach. Section 5 concludes the paper by summarizing the key contributions and suggesting future research directions.

2 Related Work

This section will begin with a brief overview of the state-of-the-art in digital twins for pharmaceutical manufacturing, and then present a framework for transforming smart pharmaceutical manufacturing through the use of digital twins.

2.1 Digital Twins in Pharmaceutical Manufacturing

The term of digital twin, was first introduced by Grieves at a Society of Manufacturing Engineering conference in Michigan in October 2002, generally consists of three key elements: a physical part, a digital counterpart, and their connections [7]. While the term has been in circulation for some time, it is recent years being actively considered in the manufacturing context with the advancement of IDTs in Industry 4.0, particularly the convergence of the Internet of Things (IoT) sensing and networking, 3D modelling and reconstruction, cyber-physical systems (CPS) integration and interaction, data analytics and artificial intelligence (AI). By building a digital representation of a manufacturing asset, a manufacturing process, or a manufacturing system that dynamically updated as its physical counterpart changes, manufacturers could gain real-time insights of their manufacturing assets, production processes, and manufacturing systems, this allows real-time monitoring energy consumption of the equipment, improving operational efficiency, and making optimal and predict decisions to quickly adapt to changes [8, 9].

With such great potential benefits, in recent years, researchers and practitioners are beginning to explore the application of digital twins in pharmaceutical manufacturing. For example, during the design phase, the authors discussed the potential benefits of drug development and clinical trials with the support of digital twins and the generative artificial intelligence [10]. During the production phase, the work presents an under-development digital twin for modelling and optimizing the active pharmaceutical ingredient (API) process to improve techno-economically optimal performance [11]. In addition to significant efforts devoted to logistics and production, some work has also explored the use of digital twins to enhance pharmaceutical quality control within this highly regulated industry [12, 13]. Along with the growing integration of data analytics, cloud computing and artificial intelligence, new business models and paradigms like supply chain digital twins [14], human digital twins [15], and digital patient twins [16], could be developed to enhance personalized healthcare services and autonomous production processes. While attention has been given to the application of digital twins in pharmaceutical manufacturing, the field is still in its infancy. To realize the full potential of the digital twin in the pharmaceutical sector, a generic framework that guides the digital transformation of pharmaceutical manufacturing is necessary. With this in mind, the next section will present a digital twin-enabled framework for transforming smart and sustainable pharmaceutical manufacturing.Subsequent paragraphs, however, are indented.

2.2 A Digital Twin-Enabled Framework for Smart and Sustainable Pharmaceutical Manufacturing

Figure 1 shows a digital twin-enabled framework for transforming smart and sustainable pharmaceutical manufacturing adapted from our previous work [17, 18]. As illustrated in Fig. 1, the overall framework consists of the perception, interaction, cognition, and services layers. This framework aims to digitally transform pharmaceutical physical life-cycle activities, i.e., research and discovery, production, logistics, consumption, and waste management, in a cost-efficient and scalable manner with modularity, interoperability, and synchronisation principles.

The perception layer serves as the foundational technical structure within the framework, emphasizing the real-time perception and mapping physical entities (e.g., raw materials, production processes, service systems) into digital twins through IoT sensing and networking, communication interfaces, cloud/edge computing, and lightweight visualizations. The interaction layer facilitates real-time engagement between the physical and digital twins through online dashboards, industrial wearables, human-machine interfaces, and augmented/virtual/mixed reality environments. The cognition layer functions as the central intelligence hub, extracting valuable insights from data through prescriptive and predictive analytics, leveraging techniques such as big data, AI, mathematical optimization, and real-time simulation. Finally, the application layer delivers tailored value-added services on demand, including modeling, monitoring, and optimizing aspects such as customer service, quality, cost, time efficiency, well-being, and sustainability, to address the varied needs of all stakeholders involved.

In summary, through its comprehensive provision of perception, interaction, cognition, and application functionalities for modelling, interacting with, analysing and utilizing digital twins, the framework presents a cost-effective and scalable solution for revolutionizing pharmaceutical lifecycle activities spanning design, manufacturing, and

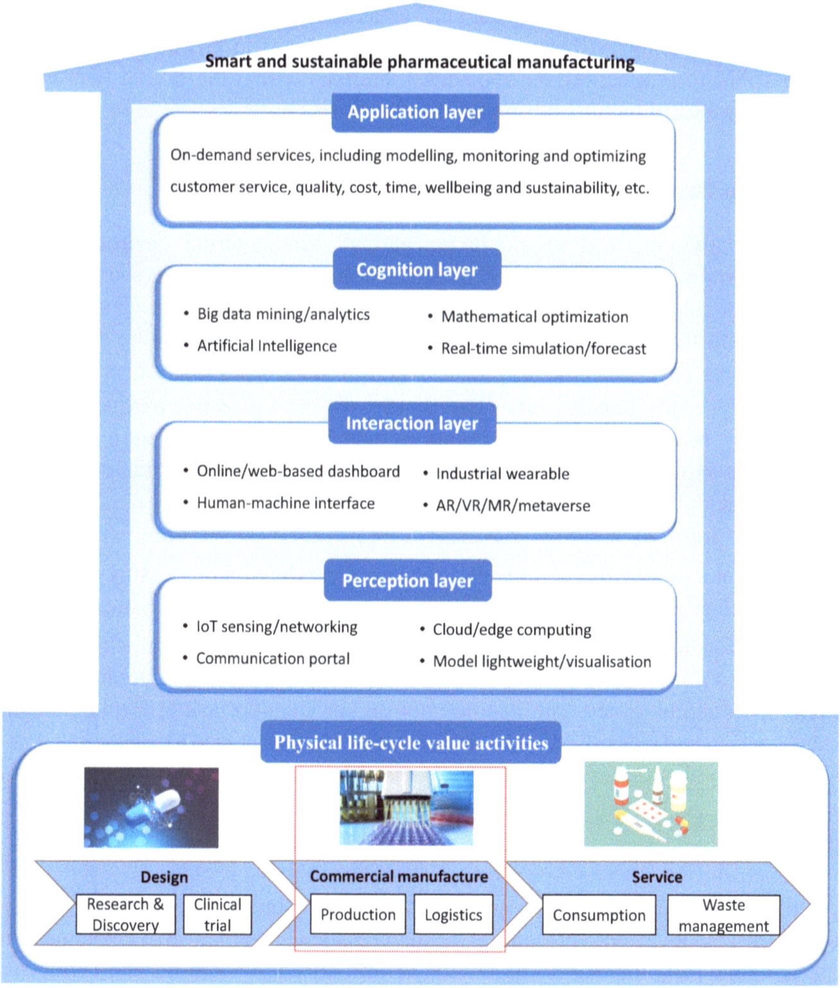

Fig. 1. A digital twin-enabled framework for transforming smart and sustainable pharmaceutical manufacturing (adapted from [17] and [18])

service. This transformation paves the way for smarter and more sustainable practices in pharmaceutical manufacturing.

3 Intelligent Decision-Making of Production-Logistics Synchronisation Under Digital Twin-Enabled Smart Pharmaceutical Manufacturing Environment

In a digital twin-enabled smart pharmaceutical manufacturing environment, multiple manufacturing resources, processes, and capabilities can be perceived in real-time. This visibility establishes a foundation for intelligent decision-making, facilitated by instantaneous information feedback and coordination. Following the framework of digital twin-enabled transformation for smart and sustainable pharmaceutical manufacturing, the focus of this section will introduce an intelligent decision-making model designed for synchronising production and logistics operations within the digital twin-enabled smart pharmaceutical manufacturing environment.

3.1 Problem Description

In the digital twin-enabled smart pharmaceutical manufacturing environment, real-time data pertaining to all involved manufacturing resources, processes, and capabilities is meticulously recorded and shared throughout the system. Formally, consider a finite customer demands $\{O^t_1, O^t_2, ..., O^t_c, ..., O^t_n\}$ within a rolling horizon t are accepted, where each order O^t_c includes several product types from a product family $\{F_1, F_2, ..., F_f, ..., F_F\}$ and specifies the quantity required U from a product family F_f. Each order O^t_c has an arrival date T^c_a marking when it is accepted, and a due date T^c_d indicating the expected completion time. Within the time horizon t, the company has the capacity with a finite set of production systems $\{PS_1, PS_2, ..., PS_m, ..., PS_{m_t}\}$ and a finite set of logistics systems $\{LS_1, LS_2, ..., LS_n, ..., LS_{n_t}\}$. Assume, without losing generality, that a production system PS_m requires a production processing time of PS^f_m for a batch of product F_f, and a logistics system LS_n requires a logistics processing time of LS^f_n for that batch of product F_f. In a production system, switching from F_f to $F_{f'}$ involves a setup task with a setup time $S_{ff'}$. The tasks are non-preemptive; each available production system can handle only one production task at a time, and each logistics system can process only one logistics task at a time. Once a task begins, it must be completed without interruption.

3.2 Mathematical Formulation

Given the problem description, it can be formulated as a mixed-integer linear programming (MILP) model. Before presenting the mathematical formulation of the model, Prior to outlining the mathematical formulation, we introduce the notations and variables, as summarized in Table 1.

The model aims to minimize the overall lead time, combining the lead time for production tasks (C^t_P) and the lead time for logistics task (C^t_L) across all customer orders within the designated time horizon t, which can be formulated as follows.

$$\text{Minimize } (C^t_P + C^t_L) \tag{1}$$

Subject to:

$$C^t_P = \text{Max}(PS^e_m(F^u_{fc})) \tag{2}$$

$$C^t_L = \text{Max}(LS^e_n(F^u_{fc})) \tag{3}$$

$$\sum_{m=1}^{m_t} x^{PS_m}(F^u_{fc}) = 1, \forall u, f, c \tag{4}$$

Table 1. Notations and variables for the mathematical formulation

Notations	Description
$\{O_1^t, O_2^t, ..., O_c^t, ..., O_C^t\}$	Finite set of customer orders
$\{F_1, F_2, ..., F_f, ..., F_F\}$	Finite set of product families
$\{PS_1, PS_2, ..., PS_m, ..., PS_{m_t}\}$	Finite set of production systems
$\{LS_1, LS_2, ..., LS_n, ..., LS_{n_t}\}$	Finite set of production systems
$\left\{F_{fc}^1, F_{fc}^2, ..., F_{fc}^u, ..., F_{fc}^U\right\}$	Finite set of production tasks for producing required uth batch product F_{fc}^u from F_f in O_c^t, $u = 1, 2, ..., U$
T_a^c	Arrival date of customer order O_c^t
T_d^c	Due date of customer order O_c^t
PS_m^f	Production processing time of PS_m for a batch of product F_f
$E(PS_m^f)$	Energy consumption for per production processing time of PS_m
LS_n^f	Logistics processing time of LS_n for a batch of product F_f
$E(LS_n^f)$	Energy consumption for per logistics processing time of LS_n
$S_{ff'}$	Setup time for switching production from F_f to $F_{f'}$ in a production system
S_f	Initial setup time for starting the production for F_f in a production system
$E(S_{ff'})$	Energy consumption for per setup time of $S_{ff'}$
E_{PS_m}	Energy consumption for per idle time of production system PS_m
E_{LS_n}	Energy consumption for per idle time of production system LS_n
t	Planning rolling time horizon
M	Arbitrary large number
Variables	Description
$PS_m^s(F_{fc}^u)$	Start time of production task for F_{fc}^u in PS_m
$PS_m^e(F_{fc}^u)$	End time of production task for F_{fc}^u in PS_m
$LS_n^s(F_{fc}^u)$	Start time of logistics task for F_{fc}^u in LS_n
$LS_n^e(F_{fc}^u)$	End time of logistics task for F_{fc}^u in LS_n
$x^{PS_m}(F_{fc}^u)$	Boolean variable, 1 if the production task for F_{fc}^u is performed with PS_m, 0 otherwise

(continued)

Table 1. *(continued)*

Notations	Description
$y^{LS_n}(F^u_{fc})$	Boolean variable, 1 if the logistics task for F^u_{fc} is performed with LS_n, 0 otherwise
$xx^{PS_m}(F^u_{fc}, (F^u_{fc})')$	Boolean variable, 1 if the production task for F^u_{fc} precedes the production task for F^u_{fc} within PS_m, 0 otherwise
$yy^{LS_n}(F^u_{fc}, (F^u_{fc})')$	Boolean variable, 1 if the logistics task for F^u_{fc} precedes the logistics task for F^u_{fc} within LS_n, 0 otherwise

$$PS^e_m(F^u_{fc}) - PS^s_m(F^u_{fc}) \geq PS^f_m + M\left[x^{PS_m}(F^u_{fc}) - 1\right], \forall m, u, f, c \tag{5}$$

$$\sum_{n=1}^{n_t} x^{LS_n}(F^u_{fc}) = 1, \forall u, f, c \tag{6}$$

$$LS^e_n(F^u_{fc}) - LS^s_n(F^u_{fc}) \geq LS^f_n + M\left[y^{LS_n}(F^u_{fc}) - 1\right], \forall n, u, f, c \tag{7}$$

$$PS^s_m(F^u_{fc}) \geq t + S_f, \forall m, u, f, c \tag{8}$$

$$PS^e_m(F^u_{fc}) \leq T^c_d, \forall m, u, f, c \tag{9}$$

$$M\left[xx^{PS_m}(F^u_{fc}, (F^u_{fc})') + x^{PS_m}(F^u_{fc}) + x^{PS_m}((F^u_{fc})') - 3\right] \leq PS^s_m((F^u_{fc})') - PS^e_m(F^u_{fc}) - S_{ff'}, \forall m, u, f, c \tag{10}$$

$$M\left[x^{PS_m}(F^u_{fc}) + x^{PS_m}((F^u_{fc})') - xx^{PS_m}(F^u_{fc}, (F^u_{fc})') - 2\right] \leq PS^s_m(F^u_{fc}) - PS^e_m((F^u_{fc})'), \forall m, u, f, c \tag{11}$$

$$M\left[yy^{LS_n}(F^u_{fc}, (F^u_{fc})') + y^{LS_n}(F^u_{fc}) + y^{LS_n}((F^u_{fc})') - 3\right] \leq LS^s_n((F^u_{fc})') - LS^e_n(F^u_{fc}), \forall n, u, f, c \tag{12}$$

$$M\left[y^{LS_n}(F^u_{fc}) + y^{LS_n}((F^u_{fc})') - yy^{LS_n}(F^u_{fc}, (F^u_{fc})') - 2\right] \leq LS^s_n(F^u_{fc}) - LS^e_n((F^u_{fc})'), \forall n, u, f, c \tag{13}$$

$$PS^s_m(F^u_{fc}) - LS^e_n(F^u_{fc}) \geq 0, \forall m, n, u, f, c \tag{14}$$

$$x^{PS_m}(F^u_{fc}) \in \{0, 1\}, \forall m, u, f, c \tag{15}$$

$$y^{LS_n}(F^u_{fc}) \in \{0, 1\}, \forall n, u, f, c \tag{16}$$

$$xx^{PS_m}(F^u_{fc}, (F^u_{fc})') \in \{0, 1\}, \forall m, u, f, c \tag{17}$$

$$yy^{LS_n}(F^u_{fc}, (F^u_{fc})') \in \{0, 1\}, \forall n, u, f, c \tag{18}$$

Equation (2) defines the lead time for production tasks, while Eq. (3) defines the lead time for logistics tasks. Equations (4) and (5) ensure that each production task is assigned to exactly one available production system with the appropriate processing time, and once initiated, it must be completed within the capacity of that system to meet the demand. Equations (6) and (7) similarly ensure that each logistics task is assigned to a single available logistics system with its corresponding processing time, and once started, it must be completed within the system's capacity. Equation (8)specifies that the first job task requires an initial setup. Equation (9) ensures that the completion time for each production task does not exceed the order's due date. Equations (10) and (11) state that production tasks are non-preemptive, and a setup is needed when transitioning between different product families. Equations (12) and (13) indicate that logistics tasks are also non-preemptive. Equation (14) requires that a production task can only commence once the corresponding logistics task has been completed. Equations (15) through (18) define the allowable ranges for the decision variables.

4 Case Study

To evaluate the effectiveness of the proposed approach, in this section, a case study from a pharmaceutical manufacturer will be carried out. The partner company manufactures both sterile and non-sterile medicines on-site, utilizing batch and bespoke production methods. To maintain competitiveness, the company is eager to embrace the new industrial revolution through the implementation of digital technology interventions. To assess the performance of the manufacturing system both before (referred to as the current state scenario) and after (termed as a future state scenario) digital technology interventions with digital twin-enabled smart manufacturing environment, the case study focuses on comparisons between the two scenarios.

Table 2 list a dataset generated from the historical data from the company with a nondimensionalized unit. As shown in Table 2, in this case, the dataset includes three customer orders associated with acceptance dates and due dates, comprising a total of thirty-nine products from five product families. The columns of production processing time and logistics time illustrates the processing time of each product family in the current production system and logistics system, drawn from corresponding uniform distributions. In addition, Formula (19) presents a setup matrix that delineates the setup time required when transitioning production between distinct product families. For instance, S_{12} denotes the setup time when switching production from product family PROD_1 to PROD_2, which is 3 units.

$$S_{ff'} = \begin{bmatrix} 0 & 3 & 5 & 8 & 10 \\ 6 & 0 & 5 & 8 & 10 \\ 6 & 3 & 0 & 8 & 10 \\ 6 & 3 & 5 & 0 & 10 \\ 6 & 3 & 5 & 8 & 0 \end{bmatrix} \tag{19}$$

Table 2. The dataset for the case study

Customer order	Product family	Quantity	Production processing time	Logistics processing time	Order accept date	Order due date
1	PROD_1	10	$U(10,15)$	$U(4,7)$	2022/01/03	2022/03/02
	PROD_2	5	$U(8,10)$	$U(3,5)$		
	PROD_3	3	$U(10,13)$	$U(8,10)$		
2	PROD_2	6	$U(8,10)$	$U(3,5)$	2022/01/05	2022/02/19
	PROD_4	3	$U(2,5)$	$U(2,5)$		
3	PROD_1	5	$U(10,15)$	$U(4,7)$	2022/01/07	2022/02/17
	PROD_3	2	$U(10,13)$	$U(8,10)$		
	PROD_4	2	$U(2,5)$	$U(2,5)$		
	PROD_5	3	$U(12,16)$	$U(6,10)$		

In the current state scenario, the company adopts first in first out (FIFO) rule for dispatching customer orders, allocating jobs to a production system and a logistics system. Relatively, the production-logistics synchronisation strategy is employed in the future state. To compare the performance of the two scenarios, in addition to measures of the lead time of the production tasks C_P^t (as defined in Formula (1)) and the lead time of the logistics tasks C_L^t (as defined in Formula (2)), the measure of total energy consumption E_T^t is introduced as the follows.

$$E_T^t = E_P * W_P^t + E_L * W_L^t + E_I * I^t \tag{20}$$

where E_P, E_L, E_I, denotes the energy consumption coefficient of per production processing time unit, per logistics processing time unit, and per idle time unit, respectively. W_P^t presents the total processing time of production tasks, W_L^t presents the total processing time of logistics tasks, and I^t presents the total idle time. $W_P^t = 2W_L^t = 4I^t$ is used in this case.

The mathematical model is coded using the optimization programming language embedded in the IBM ILOG CPLEX version 12.10.0, and solved using the default branch-and-cut method, which combines cutting planes and branch-and-bound techniques. The computations were performed on a 64-bit machine with an Intel Core i7-1265U CPU running at 1800 MHz and 16 GB of RAM.

Figure 2 illustrates the overall performance of both the current state and the future state. As shown in Fig. 2, compared to the current state, the future state results in an average cutting of 18.60% in the production lead time, 67.31% in the logistics lead time, and 33.75% in the total energy consumption, respectively. With digital twin-enabled real-time information sharing and informed decision-making, synchronised organization and operations between production and logistics tasks are enhanced, thus reducing waiting and waste, and improving overall efficiency and sustainability in the medicines manufacturing.

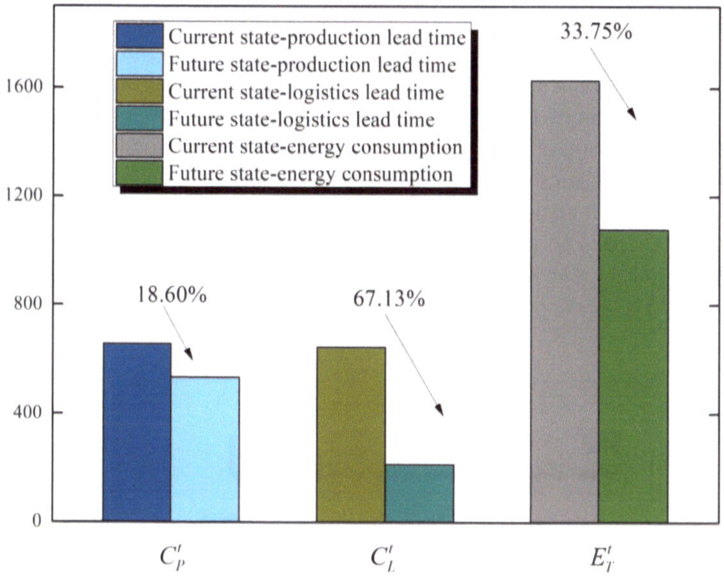

Fig. 2. The overall performance of both the current state and the future state

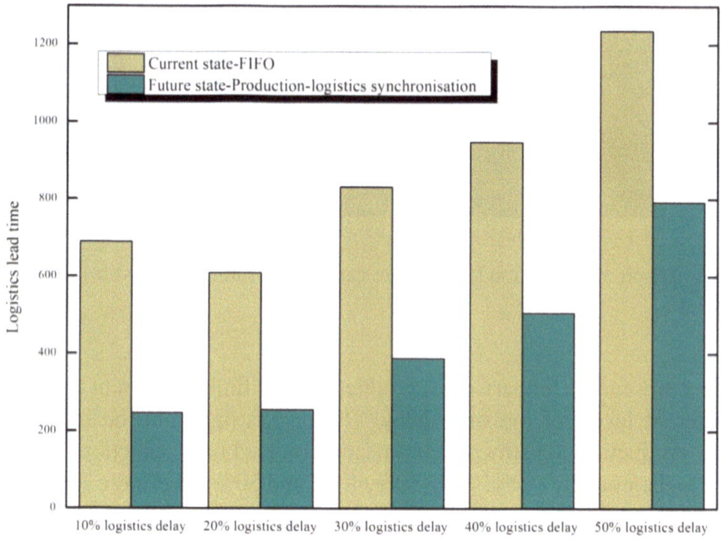

Fig. 3. Comparison of logistics lead time in current and future states with varying degrees of logistics delay

To further investigate the performance of the proposed smart production-logistics synchronisation approach, comparisons are conducted between the current and future states, considering the uncertainties in logistics. The degree of uncertainty in logistics is defined as the percentage of delays in logistics tasks, with delays being randomly drawn from a corresponding uniform distribution of processing times. For instance, a 10% logistics delay indicates that 10% of the total logistics delay stems from randomly delayed processing times drawn from a uniform distribution between 0 and 10. Figure 3 illustrates a comparison of logistics lead times between current and future states across various levels of logistics delay. It's evident that logistics delay adversely affects the performance of the logistics system. Notably, as the delay in logistics increases from 10% to 50%, there is an observed reduction in logistics lead time in the future state compared to the current state. Specifically, reductions of 64.20%, 57.96%, 53.31%, 46.73%, and 35.87% are noted, respectively.

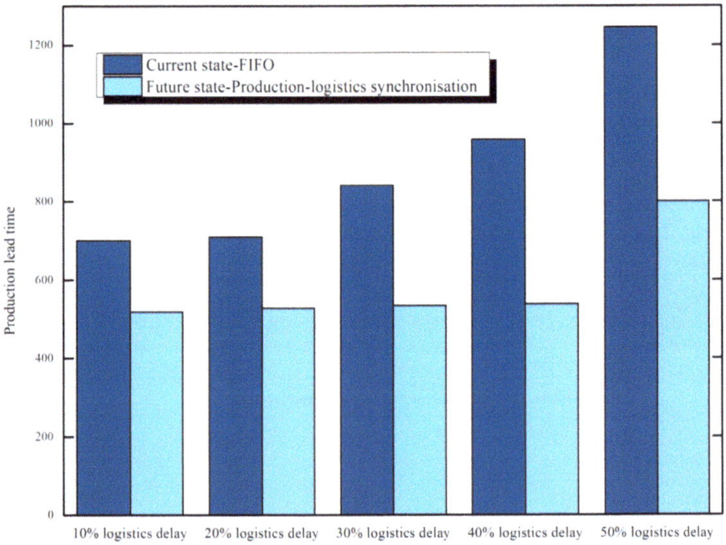

Fig. 4. Comparison of production lead time in current and future states with varying degrees of logistics delay

Figure 4 presents a comparison of production lead times in current and future states across different levels of logistics delay. The results highlight the impact of future state-smart production-logistics synchronisation on lead time reduction. Under varying degrees of logistics delay (10%, 20%, 30%, 40%, and 50%), the future state consistently demonstrates significant reductions in production lead time compared to the current state. Specifically, reductions of approximately 25.96%, 25.49%, 36.46%, 43.80%, and 35.79% are observed, respectively. The results indicate that as logistics delays worsen, the benefits offered by the envisioned future state regarding production lead time become increasingly evident.

Figure 5 illustrates the comparison of energy consumption between current and future states across varying degrees of logistics delay. It's evident that logistics delay contributes to an increase in total energy consumption. However, the implementation of smart production-logistics synchronisation in the future state results in notable reductions. On average, reductions of approximately 32.89%, 31.57%, 33.65%, 33.78%, and 40.81% are observed compared to the current state across different levels of logistics delay (10%, 20%, 30%, 40%, and 50%). This reduction is attributed to the avoidance of unnecessary waiting and waste, facilitated by the smart production-logistics synchronisation strategy.

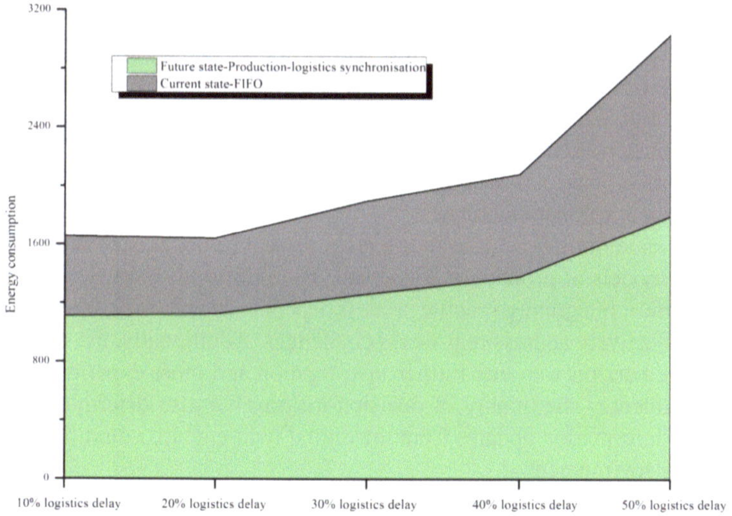

Fig. 5. Comparison of energy consumption in current and future states with varying degrees of logistics delay

The findings from the study have significant managerial implications for optimizing operations in medicines manufacturing. The comparison between current and future states reveals substantial improvements in production lead time, logistics lead time, and total energy consumption with the implementation of smart production-logistics synchronisation. By leveraging digital twin-enabled real-time information sharing and informed decision-making, organizations can synchronise production and logistics tasks more effectively, reducing waiting times and waste. This leads to enhanced overall efficiency and sustainability in manufacturing processes. Moreover, the study demonstrates that as logistics delay increases, the benefits of the smart production-logistics synchronisation strategy become more pronounced, particularly in terms of lead time reduction and energy consumption. These insights underscore the potential of innovative operations management strategies enabled by IDTs for enhancing efficiency and sustainability in pharmaceutical manufacturing operations.

5 Conclusion

The pharmaceutical industry is moving towards Pharma Industry 4.0 to create a smarter, more personalized sector, using IDTs. Despite facing significant challenges, initiatives like the DM2 Research Centre in the UK are poised to accelerate this transition. By leveraging the digital twin and innovative operations management strategy, this paper this work pioneers a concept of smart production-logistics synchronisation for enhancing efficiency and sustainability, as a part of the recently launched DM2 project.

The contribution of this work is summarized as follows: Firstly, a digital twin-based framework comprising perception, interaction, cognition, and service layers is proposed for digitally transforming pharmaceutical lifecycle activities in a cost-efficient and scalable manner. Secondly, an intelligent decision-making model, enabled by real-time information sharing and coordination, is designed for synchronising production and logistics operations within the digital twin-enabled smart pharmaceutical manufacturing environment. Finally, the effectiveness of the proposed smart production-logistics synchronisation approach is verified through improvements in production lead time, logistics lead time, and total energy consumption, demonstrated through a case study from a pharmaceutical manufacturer.

There are some limitations, and future research will be conducted. For instance, the mathematical models of production-logistics synchronization simplify production and logistics activities. Integrating specific process dependency and precedence information is crucial to effectively address real-world challenges. Additionally, the selection of an optimal rolling horizon warrants further investigation and more experimental tests, as it not only influences the quality of decision-making but also determines the uncertainty level of information updates from the digital twin-enabled smart pharmaceutical manufacturing environment.

Acknowledgment. We gratefully acknowledge the funding provided by the Digital Medicines Manufacturing (DM2) Research Centre (Grant Ref: EP/V062077/1) and Guangzhou-HKUST(GZ) Joint Funding Program (2025A03J3658 & 2024A03J0680).

References

1. Ding, B.: Pharma industry 4.0: literature review and research opportunities in sustainable pharmaceutical supply chains. Process. Saf. Environ. Prot. **119**, 115–130 (2018)
2. Saha, E., Rathore, P., Parida, R., Rana, N.P.: The interplay of emerging technologies in pharmaceutical supply chain performance: an empirical investigation for the rise of Pharma 4.0. Technol. Forecast. Soc. Change, **181**, 121768 (2022)
3. Barenji, R.V., Akdag, Y., Yet, B., Oner, L.: Cyber-physical-based PAT (CPbPAT) framework for Pharma 4.0. Int. J. Pharmaceut. **567**, 118445 (2019)
4. Arden, N.S., Fisher, A.C., Tyner, K., Lawrence, X. Y., Lee, S.L., Kopcha, M.: Industry 4.0 for pharmaceutical manufacturing: Preparing for the smart factories of the future. Int. J. Pharmaceut. **602**, 120554 (2021)
5. Sharma, M., Sehrawat, R., Luthra, S., Daim, T., Bakry, D.: Moving towards industry 5.0 in the pharmaceutical manufacturing sector: challenges and solutions for Germany. IEEE Trans. Eng, Manag. (2022)
6. Dal Mas, F., Massaro, M., Rippa, P., Secundo, G.: The challenges of digital transformation in healthcare: An interdisciplinary literature review, framework, and future research agenda. Technovation **123**, 102716 (2023)
7. Grieves, M.W.: Digital twins: past, present, and future. In: The Digital Twin, pp. 97–121. Springer International Publishing, Cham (2023)

8. Guo, D., Zhong, R.Y., Lin, P., Lyu, Z., Rong, Y., Huang, G.Q.: Digital twin-enabled Graduation Intelligent Manufacturing System for fixed-position assembly islands. Robot. Comput.-Integr. Manuf. **63**, 101917 (2020)
9. Kamble, S.S., Gunasekaran, A., Parekh, H., Mani, V., Belhadi, A., Sharma, R.: Digital twin for sustainable manufacturing supply chains: Current trends, future perspectives, and an implementation framework. Technol. Forecast. Soc. Chang. **176**, 121448 (2022)
10. Bordukova, M., Makarov, N., Rodriguez-Esteban, R., Schmich, F., Menden, M.P.: Generative artificial intelligence empowers digital twins in drug discovery and clinical trials. Expert Opin. Drug Discov. **19**(1), 33–42 (2024)
11. Gerogiorgis, D.I., Castro-Rodriguez, D.: A digital twin for process optimisation in pharmaceutical manufacturing. In: Computer Aided Chemical Engineering , Vol. 50, pp. 253–258. Elsevier (2021)
12. Lopes, M.R., Costigliola, A., Pinto, R., Vieira, S., Sousa, J.M.: Pharmaceutical quality control laboratory digital twin–a novel governance model for resource planning and scheduling. Int. J. Prod. Res. **58**(21), 6553–6567 (2020)
13. Coito, T., Martins, M.S., Firme, B., Figueiredo, J., Vieira, S.M., Sousa, J.M.: Assessing the impact of automation in pharmaceutical quality control labs using a digital twin. J. Manuf. Syst. **62**, 270–285 (2022)
14. Srai, J., Settanni, E.: Supply chain digital twins: Opportunities and challenges beyond the hype (2019)
15. Okegbile, S.D., Cai, J., Niyato, D., Yi, C.: Human digital twin for personalized healthcare: Vision, architecture and future directions. IEEE Netw. **37**(2), 262–269 (2022)
16. Fischer, R.P., Volpert, A., Antonino, P., Ahrens, T.D.: Digital patient twins for personalized therapeutics and pharmaceutical manufacturing. Front. Digital Health **5**, 1302338 (2024)
17. Guo, D., Zhang, T., Rong, Y., Huang, G.Q., Srai, J.S.: Lightweight digital twin as a service (LDTaaS): a cost-efficient digital transformation approach for manufacturing SMEs. In: Low-Cost Digital Solutions for Industrial Automation (LoDiSA 2023), Vol. 2023, pp. 28–33. IET (2023)
18. Guo, D., Mantravadi, S.: The role of digital twins in lean supply chain management: review and research directions. Int. J. Prod. Res. **63**(5), 1851–1872 (2025)

Author Index

M. Li et al. (Eds.): ICLS 2025, *Proceeding of the 19th International Congress on Logistics and Supply Chain Management Systems*, p. 151, 2026.
https://doi.org/10.1007/978-981-95-7700-2

MIX
Papier aus verantwortungsvollen Quellen
Paper from responsible sources
FSC® C105338
FSC
www.fsc.org

If you have any concerns about our products,
you can contact us on
ProductSafety@springernature.com

In case Publisher is established outside the EU,
the EU authorized representative is:
Springer Nature Customer Service Center GmbH
Europaplatz 3, 69115 Heidelberg, Germany

Printed by Libri Plureos GmbH
in Hamburg, Germany